MW01273774

Japan and Enlarged Europe

Partners in Global Governance

P.I.E.-Peter Lang

Bruxelles · Bern · Berlin · Frankfurt am Main · New York · Oxford · Wien

Takako UETA & Éric REMACLE (eds.)

Japan and Enlarged Europe

Partners in Global Governance

« International Insights »
No.4

This volume is the result of a joint research project between the International Christian University (the 21ˢᵗ Century Center of Excellence Program – CoE), the Study Group on European Policies (SEP-GEPE) and the Université libre de Bruxelles (Institut d'études européennes – IEE).

© P.I.E.-Peter Lang S.A.
PRESSES INTERUNIVERSITAIRES EUROPÉENNES
Brussels, 2005
1 avenue Maurice, 1050 Brussels, Belgium
info@peterlang.com; www.peterlang.net

ISSN 1780-5414
ISBN 90-5201-259-8
US ISBN 0-8204-6643-3
D/2005/5678/14
Printed in Germany

Bibliographic information published by "Die Deutsche Bibliothek"

"Die Deutsche Bibliothek" lists this publication in the "Deutsche Nationalbibliografie"; detailed bibliographic data is available in the Internet at <http://dnb.ddb.de>.

CIP available from the British Library, GB and the Library of Congress, USA.

Contents

List of Abbreviations

ACP	African, Caribbean and Pacific (Country)
AEC	ASEAN Economic Community
APEC	Asia-Pacific Economic Cooperation
ASEAN	Association of South East Asian Nations
ASEM	Asia-Europe Meeting
ASPAC	Asia Pacific Conference
CAP	Common Agricultural Policy
CBDR	(Principle of) Common But Differentiated Responsability
CDM	Clean Development Mechanism (in the UNFCCC)
CEEC	Central and Eastern European Country
CFC	Chlorofluorocarbon
CFE	Treaty on Conventional Forces in Europe
CFSP	Common Foreign and Security Policy (of the European Union)
CH_4	Methane
CIS	Commonwealth of Independent States
CO_2	Carbon Dioxide
COP	Conference of the Parties (to the UNFCCC)
CSCE	Conference on Security and Cooperation in Europe
CSO	Committee of Senior Officials (of the CSCE)
CU	Customs Union
DAAD	Deutscher Akademischer Austausch Dienst
DAC	Development Assistance Committee (of the OECD)
DDA	Doha Development Agenda (of the WTO)
DDR	Disarmament, Demobilisation and Reintegration (of Soldiers)
DPRK	Democratic People's Republic of Korea
EC	European Community
ECCP	European Climate Change Programme

ECJ	European Court of Justice
ECOWAS	Economic Community of West African States
ECSC	European Coal and Steel Community
EEOL	Equal Employment Opportunity Law
EES	European Employment Strategy
EFTA	European Free Trade Association
EIAS	European Institute for Asian Studies
EPA	Economic Partnership Agreement
ESDP	European Security and Defence Policy (of the European Union)
ESS	European Security Strategy
ET	Emissions Trading (in the UNFCCC)
ETUC	European Trade Union Confederation
EU	European Union
EUIJ	European Union Institute in Japan
FDI	Foreign Direct Investment
FTA	Free Trade Area
FTAA	Free Trade Area of the Americas
FY	Fiscal Year
FYRoM	Former Yugoslav Republic of Macedonia
G7/8	Group of the Seven/Eight Most Industrialised Countries
GATS	General Agreement on Trade in Services
GATT	General Agreement on Tariffs and Trade
GDP	Gross Domestic Product
GEF	Global Environmental Facility
GHG	Greenhouse Gas
GNP	Gross National Product
HCOC	The Hague Code of Conduct (Against Ballistic Missile Proliferation)
HFC	Hydrofluorocarbon
HIPC	Highly Indebted Poor Country
IAEA	International Atomic Energy Agency
ICC	International Criminal Court
IEA	International Energy Agency (of the OECD)
IMF	International Monetary Fund

ITTO	International Tropical Timber Organisation
IUCN	The World Conservation Union
JI	Joint Implementation (in the UNFCCC)
JICA	Japan International Cooperation Agency
JTUC	Japan Trade Union Confederation
KEDO	Korean Peninsula Energy Development Organisation
LDC	Least Developed Country
MERCOSUR	Common Market of the Southern Cone (of Latin America)
METI	Ministry of Economy, Trade and Industry (of Japan)
MFN	Most Favoured Nation (clause of the GATT)
MoE	Ministry of Environment (of Japan)
MRA	Mutual Recognition Agreement
MW	Megawatt
N_2O	Nitrous Oxide
NAFTA	North American Free Trade Agreement
NATO	North Atlantic Treaty Organisation
NEPAD	New Partnership for Africa's Development
NGO	Non Governmental Organisation
NIS	New Independent States
OAU	Organisation of African Unity
ODA	Official Development Assistance
OECD	Organisation for Economic Cooperation and Development
OECF	Overseas Economic Cooperation Fund
OMC	Open Method of Coordination
OSCE	Organisation for Security and Cooperation in Europe
PCA	Partnership and Cooperation Agreement
PFC	Perfluorocarbon
PKF	Peace-keeping Force (in Transdniestria)
PKO	Peace-keeping Operation
PRT	Provincial Reconstruction Team (in Afghanistan)
PSI	Proliferation Security Initiative
R&D	Research & Development
RA	Revisionist Approach

RTA	Regional Trade Area
SAARC	South Asian Association for Regional Cooperation
SADC	Southern African Development Community
SF6	Sulfur Hexafluoride
TICAD	Tokyo International Conference on African Development
UK	United Kingdom
UN	United Nations
UNCED	United Nations Conference on Environment and Development (= the Rio Earth Summit)
UNDP	United Nations Development Programme
UNEP	United Nations Environment Programme
UNFCCC	United Nations Framework Convention on Climate Change
UNHCR	United Nations High Commissioner for Refugees
UNMIK	United Nations Mission in Kosovo
UNMISET	United Nations Mission of Support in East Timor
UNTAC	United Nations Transition Authority in Cambodia
UNTAET	United Nations Transitional Administration in East Timor
USA	United States of America
USAID	United States Agency for International Development
USD	United States Dollar
WB	World Bank
WC	Washington Consensus
WCED	World Conference on Environment and Development
WMD	Weapons of Mass Destruction
WNIS	Western New Independent States
WTO	World Trade Organisation

Introduction

Takako UETA and Éric REMACLE

Professors at the International Christian University
and Université libre de Bruxelles, respectively

In 2001, Japan and the European Union celebrated the tenth anniversary of their joint Hague Declaration and Joint Action Plan. During the 1990s, these two "civilian powers" have learned from each other how to contribute to world peace and stability as well as to economic, trade and financial governance. Their bilateral cooperation has been intensified as well as their combined contributions to the G8 and multilateral organisations like the United Nations and the World Trade Organisation.

I. Past, Present and Future

The decade of cooperation which started in 2001 has been characterised by important changes in the world environment.

'World governance' has become a motto for both Japan and Europe. The signing of the Kyoto Protocol on Climate Change represents, for example, a remarkable effort of international regulation mainly due to the combined efforts of Japan and the European Union. The G8 has been enlarged to include the Russian Federation and a likely enlargement of the United Nations Security Council will probably be decided in 2005 and could have an influence on Japan and Europe.

In the security field, the terrorist attacks on New York and Madrid, and the wars in Afghanistan and Iraq have transformed perceptions of world security, both in Europe and Japan. The stabilisation of the Balkans has not yet been secured but, due to the efforts of all G8 powers, there is peace in this area neighbouring the EU's territory.

In the economic sphere, the increase of the American deficit, the financial crises in several parts of the world, the acceleration of the processes of globalisation and regionalism in trade along with the accession of the People's Republic of China to the World Trade Organisation, have been key features of a new world order.

The European Union has implemented four major internal changes which have had a deep impact on the world stage: the introduction of the single currency, the creation of EU military capabilities, the enlargement from fifteen to twenty-five member states and the signing of the Treaty Establishing a Constitution for Europe.

Japan and the enlarged European Union have now become actors and partners in the process of global governance. What can they do together in the future for a more secure world, sustainable development and global governance? These are the questions addressed in this book.

Part One of this work analyses the security dimension of Japan-EU relations. It discusses the impact of the enlargement of the European Union, the neighbourhood policy and the European security strategy. Will these developments contribute to reinforce the Union's external policies and will Japan become a stronger partner for Europe in the light of Japan's contribution to the stability of Europe and the emphasis on the human security agenda?

The second part overviews the major joint agenda for sustainable development within the context of the implementation of the Millennium Development Goals adopted by the United Nations in 2000. Global climate change, the Doha Development Agenda, norms of international development and assistance policies are widely discussed. To what extent do these initiatives contribute to long-term sustainable development and the fulfilment of the Millennium Goals? Have Japan's and Europe's views converged on these issues and can they build new joint initiatives?

The third and last part of this volume addresses the question of global governance from an economic and institutional perspective. Economic bilateral and multilateral trade relations are discussed, as well as the impact of the enlargement and the debate about the European social model (the so-called "Lisbon agenda"), but also the emergence of regional groupings and trends towards regionalism, the G8 and UN agenda's and the articulation between Japan, Europe and their key third partner in the triangle of world governance: the United States of America. Can these three actors be complementary rather than competitors in these fields? What is the relationship between multilateralism, bilateralism and regionalism? Is the global agenda manageable by common institutions and how can they articulate their functions and priorities?

Even as they raise and analyse many problems, the conclusions of most of the authors tend towards optimism regarding the evolution of Europe-Japan relations. Since there is little academic literature about the question of relationships between Japan and the European Union, we expect this volume to fulfil the dual functions of filling a notable gap in the published literature while giving food for thought to those interested in the field.

II. Acknowledgements

The editors of this volume have built a network of scholars and decision-makers interested in the study of Japan-Europe relationships and have organised a series of annual seminars in Brussels since 1998, under the aegis of the Study Group on European Policies (SEP-GEPE, Belgian branch of the Trans-European Policy Studies Association – TEPSA), the International Christian University (The 21st Century Center of Excellence Program – CoE) and Université libre de Bruxelles (The Institut d'études européennes – IEE/Jean Monnet Centre of Excellence). Their combined efforts and various contributions are readily and gratefully acknowledged.

We especially thank the Japan Foundation and the Japanese Mission to the EU for their on-going support to this series of seminars.

This book is a selection of updated contributions to the 2001, 2002 and 2003 seminars.[1] Where appropriate, these have been revised during 2004 to take account of recent developments. The editors would like to thank all those who participated in these workshops, including those who did not have the opportunity to contribute to this volume. We bear, of course, full responsibility for the selection and editing of the chapters, including titles and sub-headings.

As 2005 has been declared the EU-Japan Year of People-to-People Exchanges, we feel that the publication of this volume is particularly timely. This book is itself a record of, and testimony to, the many contacts and close working relationships established through our seminars. It is in this light that we hope our work will contribute to the strengthening of Japan-Europe contacts, particularly between faculty and students.

---

[1] Some contributions to the 1998, 1999, 2000 seminars have been published in Ueta, T., Remacle, É. (eds.), *Japan-EU Cooperation: Ten Years after the Hague Declaration, Studia Diplomatica*, LIV(1-2), Brussels, 2002.

PART ONE

WORLD STABILITY
AS A COMMON CHALLENGE

CHAPTER 1

Evolution of Japan-Europe Relations since the End of the Cold War

Takako UETA

Professor, International Christian University

I. The Year 2004

The year 2004 was an eventful year in Japan-European relations. Firstly, the Foreign Ministry of Japan reorganised its European Affairs Bureau thoroughly in order to correspond to the reality of Europe in view of EU enlargement. Secondly, the European Commission created the EU Institute in Japan (EUIJ) which is a centre of excellence of academic exchange, education and information with the EU. Thirdly, the Foreign Ministry of Japan organised the Ministerial Conference on Peace Consolidation and Economic Development of the Western Balkans in April in Tokyo. Geographically, far from the Balkans, it shows Japan's commitment to the stabilisation of the Balkans. In her opening speech, Foreign Minister, Mrs Yoriko Kawaguchi explained as follows:

> The process for EU and NATO membership for the countries of this region is a powerful measure for further stabilizing the region. Japan supports the region's integration into the Euro-Atlantic structures. We intend to play a complementary role for the stabilization of the region while coordinating efforts with the EU as a global partner.[1]

Finally, the Foreign Ministry of Japan organised a conference, "Enlargement of the European Union and Security Policies of Visegrad-4" in March 2004. The senior officials of the Foreign Ministry of these countries were invited to exchange views which included those of

---

[1] Opening Speech by Yoriko Kawaguchi, Minister for Foreign Affairs at the Ministerial Conference on Peace Consolidation and Economic Development of the Western Balkans in Tokyo, 5 April 2004.

19

academic experts. For the first time, an exchange of views on security questions with Central and East European countries took place. Ten years ago, it was unimaginable that Japan would organise security talks with the CEE countries.

This chapter traces the evolution of Japan-EU political relations after the end of the Cold War in Europe.[2]

II. Reorganisation of the European Affairs Bureau of the Foreign Ministry

In summer 2004, the Foreign Ministry of Japan established the European Policy Division which is responsible for general coordination of the European Affairs Bureau, comprehensive foreign policy toward Europe and policy toward the EU. It deals with the political dimension of the EU, and European countries as well. The European Division comprises the European and transatlantic organisations including NATO, OSCE (Organisation for Security and Cooperation in Europe), and the Council of Europe. In comparison to its bilateral relations with European countries, it shows that the Japanese Foreign Ministry started to attach more importance to its policy toward European institutions. In particular, it came to recognise the significance of the EU as an actor in the international political arena. The counterparts of this Division are the EU Division and the Security Policy Division of the Foreign Ministry of European countries.

Traditionally, the European Affairs Bureau comprised the First West Europe Division which included the original member countries of the ECSC (European Coal and Steel Community) and the Second West Europe Division comprised former EFTA (European Free Trade Association) countries including the UK and Northern European countries.

In addition to the newly created European Policy Division, the Western Europe Division comprises France, Monaco, Andorra, Belgium, the Netherlands, Italy, Luxemburg, the Holy See, San Marino, Malta, the UK, Ireland, Iceland, Sweden, Norway, Finland, Denmark, Spain, Portugal, Estonia, Latvia and Lithuania.

The Central and South Eastern Europe Division comprises Germany, Austria, Switzerland, Lichtenstein, Poland, Hungary, Czech Republic, Slovakia, Bulgaria, Romania, Albania, FYROM (Former Yugoslav Republic of Macedonia), Slovenia, Croatia, Bosnia and Herzegovina,

---

[2] This chapter is in part a revised version of the author's article: T. Ueta, "Japan and the European Security Institutions," in T. Ueta and É. Remacle (eds.), *Japan-EU Cooperation: Ten Years after the Hague Declaration, Studia Diplomatica*, Vol. LIV: 2001, Nos. 1-2, Institut Royal des Relations Internationales, 2003, pp. 131-148.

Greece, Cyprus, Serbia and Montenegro, Ukraine, Belarus and Moldova.

Besides these Divisions, the European Affairs Bureau comprises the Russian Division, the Central Asia and Caucasus Division, the Russia Assistance Division and the Japan-Russia Exchange Programs Division. Generally speaking, the counterparts of these geographical Divisions are the Asian Affairs Bureau of the Foreign Ministry of European Countries. In the Economic Affairs Bureau, the Economic Integration Division was created. It is responsible for foreign policy toward regional organisations including the EU.

III. Evolution of Japan-Europe Relations

Japan's foreign policy toward Europe was governed by a bilateral approach until recently. During the Cold War period, the only country with which Japan had security and political exchanges was the US, which was based on alliance relations. There were no political and security talks with European countries although Japan and Europe belonged to the Western camp.

An influential high-ranking senior diplomat, Deputy Minister for Foreign Affairs, Mr Hisashi Owada was the key person for the enhanced policy toward Europe after the end of the Cold War in Europe. He pursued the establishment of political and security dialogues and consultations with Europe, which led to having bilateral structured relations as well as institutionalised relations with European organisations. He explained his policy as follows:

> The idea was to transform the shape of the relationship built almost exclusively on the trade in goods to the one built on a much broader basis, comprising not only a broader economic agenda like investment and industrial cooperation, but also political and social agendas like cooperation in the fields of environment, social welfare and security. The Japanese initiative was motivated by the desire on the part of Japan to strengthen the trilateral partnership between three regions of the world – East Asia, Europe and North America – and especially between Japan and Europe... The other factor to be considered was the impact of the integration of the world economy as a result of globalization in the economic field... A central problem then is whether the trilateral countries are able and willing to gather together in overcoming these constraints and to engage in the process of adjustment and coordination necessary to maintain the stability of the system and to overcome common difficulties.[3]

---

[3] H. Owada, "The Japan-EU Joint Declaration and its Significance toward the Future," in T. Ueta and É. Remacle (eds.), *Japan-EU Cooperation...*, *op. cit.*, pp. 17-18.

A. Bilateral Relations

The first country in Europe to have bilateral political-military con-sultations with Japan was the UK in November 1990. Japan started the same talks with Germany and with France in June 1994. Japan has a bilateral cooperation and consultation framework with the UK, France and Germany, which are based on the following diplomatic documents: "UK/Japan Action Agenda: Special Partnership around the World" issued in September 1996; "France-Japan 20 actions for the Year 2000" November 1996; "Action Agenda for Japanese German Partnership" May 1996. These framework documents have been implemented and officials from concerned countries have used them as a guideline for their day-to-day work. In the field of political cooperation, these action plans identified almost the same agendas which cover international security, regional cooperation, and regional security organisations. The international security dimension covers non-proliferation, disarmament and UN-related issues.

Based on this document, in October 2000, foreign ministers, Mr Kono and Mr Fischer, launched seven pillars for cooperation: con-tributions to international peace and stability; strengthening interna-tional economic and trade relations; contributions to the global and social issues; contributions to stability in various regions (the Korean Peninsula, China, Former Yugoslavia, Russia, South Asia, New Inde-pendent States, etc.); further development of Japan-German political relations; promoting bilateral economic relations; promoting mutual understanding and cultural relations.

Japan and Germany are cooperating in the reconstruction of security structure of Afghanistan. Japan is the lead nation of the disarmament, demobilisation and reintegration of ex-combatants (DDR). In the Indian Ocean, the Japanese Naval Self-Defence Forces supports Operation Enduring Freedom. Their missions are refueling coalition ships and transportation.

Germany is the lead country of police reconstruction and is contrib-uting to the ISAF (International Security Assistance Force) and is de-ploying Provincial Reconstruction Teams (PRTs). The two countries are coordinating their efforts in the DDR process and police reconstruction process closely.[4]

In assistance for reconstruction in Iraq, the two countries are cooper-ating and coordinating their efforts in the training of Iraqi police offi-

---

[4]   Fact sheet, Japanese-German Cooperation and Coordination in the Assistance for Reconstruction of Afghanistan, 9 December 2004, Ministry of Foreign Affairs.

cers; the preservation of cultural remains; the training of experts in electric power engineering; and the training of Iraqi diplomats.[5]

In February 2004, Japan, Germany and France agreed to establish a Coordination Committee on humanitarian and reconstruction projects for Iraq. Japan and France decided to cooperate on the support in the cultural area, especially for rebuilding cultural facilities and safeguarding heritage. Besides that, the two countries agreed to support Iraqi athletes, to cooperate in the medical and health field, and continue their assistance to the NGO's working in Iraq.[6]

The UK Labour Government keeps the bilateral "Action Agenda" which was agreed under John Major's Government, and released the "UK-Japan Common Vision for the 21st Century" in January 1998. This document consists of three pillars: reform and investment in the future; enhancing Asia-Europe relations; towards a better community. The two Prime Ministers, Mr Hashimoto and Mr Blair, attached importance to encouraging "people-to-people links" between the two countries. In September 1999, Foreign Ministers Koumura and Cook launched "Action Agenda 21: The UK and Japan in the 21st Century." Based on a "Common Vision" document, the two countries defined wide-ranging cooperation in 21 areas: education; culture and sport; UK-Japan 21st Century Group; parliamentary exchanges; exchange of government personnel; regional links; non-governmental organisations; trade and investment; finance; world trade and international finance; science and technology; health and social security; employment, reform of government; diplomacy, national security, conflict prevention and peace-keeping; reform of the United Nations; humanitarian and development assistance; environment; disarmament and non-proliferation; human rights; counter-terrorism, international crime and drugs.

In the field of conflict prevention, in October 2001, the Government of Japan and UK dispatched a joint fact finding mission to Sierra Leone to identify possible conflict prevention projects for joint implementation. This mission was followed by the decision in December 2002. Japan decided to contribute 300 Million Yen (*ca* 1.5 Million UK Pounds) to Sierra Leone in order to assist the "Community Reinte-

---

[5] Fact sheet, Japanese-German Cooperation and Coordination in the Assistance for Reconstruction in Iraq, 9 December 2004, Ministry of Foreign Affairs.

[6] Cooperation for Reconstruction of Iraq-Partnership of Japan and France, 2 March 2004, Ministry of Foreign Affairs.

gration Programme: Phase 2," which was initiated by the UK. The UK committed 8.7 Million Pounds.[7]

As for Iraq, the Japanese Self-Defence Forces are dispatched for humanitarian and reconstruction assistance. Their safety is protected by Dutch forces. After withdrawal of the Dutch forces in March 2005, the UK agreed to cooperate in the safety of Japanese forces.

In June 1997, the first-ever Japan-Nordic summit meeting at the highest level was held in Bergen, Norway. Prime Minister Hashimoto joined the five Nordic countries' regular meeting. They exchanged views on the situation in Russia, the Baltic States, the Korean Peninsula, China, Hong Kong and Myanmar. Reform of the UN, peace-keeping operations and the environment were other subjects of common interest. The second summit meeting between Japan and the Nordic countries took place in Iceland in June 1999.

When Prime Minister, Mr Koizumi visited Warsaw and Prague, the "Joint Statement towards Strategic Partnership" was launched in August 2003. The document of Japan and Poland consists of four points: "Overview of the relations and prospects for Strategic Partnership," "Political dimension and international issues of mutual interest," "Economic dimension," and "Cultural dimension and People-to-People exchange." "Political dimension and international issues of mutual interest" covers Iraqi reconstruction, North Korean nuclear issue, the threat of international terrorism, the UN reforms, human security, the Proliferation Security Initiative (PSI), the G8 Global Partnership against the Spread of Weapons and Materials of Mass Destruction, the Missile Technology Control Regime (MTCR), and the Kyoto Protocol.

The Japan-Czech Joint Statement consists of "Overview of the relations," "Political dimension and international issues of mutual interest," "Economic dimension" and "Cultural dimensions and People-to-People exchange." The political dimension comprises the reconstruction of Iraq, the situation on the Korean Peninsula including the nuclear issue, the UN reforms, the MTCR and The Hague Code of Conduct against Ballistic Missile Proliferation (HCOC), and the Kyoto Protocol.

---

[7]   Joint Press Release by the Governments of Japan and UK, Japan-UK Cooperation in the field of Conflict Prevention-Joint Funding of the Community Reintegration Programme in Sierra Leone, 13 December 2002, Ministry of Foreign Affairs.

B. *Japan and the European Security Institutions*

1. OSCE

Since Japan is situated in the region adjacent to OSCE countries, it has direct security interest in the OSCE area. The OSCE is the only forum in which Japan has direct access and can give some input on issues of European security.[8]

Japan has had a special participating status since the Helsinki Summit in July 1992. The first part of the summit document, the "Helsinki Summit Declaration," includes the following paragraph on non-participating states: "We have expanded dialogue with non-participating States, inviting them to take part in our activities on a selective basis when they can make a contribution." The second part of the document, "Helsinki Decisions," defined the relations between the CSCE and Japan as follows:

> In accordance with paragraph 45 of the Prague Document, the participating States intend to deepen their cooperation and develop substantial relationship with non-participating States, such as Japan, which display an interest in the CSCE, share its principles and objectives, and are actively engaged in European cooperation through relevant organizations. To this end, Japan will be invited to attend CSCE meetings including those of Heads of State and Government, the CSCE Council, and the Committee of Senior Officials and other appropriate CSCE bodies which consider specific topics of expanded consultation and cooperation. Representatives of Japan may contribute to such meetings, without participating in the preparation and adoption of decisions, on subjects in which Japan has a direct interest and/or wishes to cooperate actively with the CSCE.[9]

Japan has had better access to various OSCE meetings than any other non-member country because Japan shares OSCE principles as revealed by Japan's significant and unique contributions to the stability in the OSCE area, and by Japan's legitimate security interests there. Japan is able to participate in the Permanent Council, which is a day-to-

---

[8]   For further details of Japan's relations with the CSCE/OSCE, see T. Ueta, "Japan and the CSCE," in M. Lucas (ed.), *The CSCE in the 1990s*, Nomos, Baden-Baden, 1993, pp. 207-222; T. Ueta, "Japan and the OSCE," in D. Warner (ed.), *Preventive Diplomacy: The United Nations and the OSCE*, The Graduate Institute of International Studies, Geneva, 1996, pp. 37-44; T. Ueta, "Japan and the OSCE Security Model," OSCE Seminar: Regional Security and Cooperation, 2-4 June 1997, Vienna, REF.PC/463/97, 2 June 1997; T. Ueta, "Japan and the OSCE," in Institute for Peace Research and Security Policy at the University of Hamburg (ed.), *OSCE Yearbook 1997*, Nomos, Baden-Baden, 1998, pp. 415-425.

[9]   CSCE Helsinki Document 1992: The Challenge of Change, Helsinki, 10 July 1992.

day decision-making body,[10] and the plenary of the Forum for Security Cooperation,[11] which is a body for negotiation, consultation, and cooperation of arms control and military contacts, including confidence- and security-building measures. In the early days of the conflict in Yugoslavia, on 26 August 1993, the Vienna Group of the Committee of Senior Officials, which became the Permanent Council in 1995, agreed that "Japan would be invited to be present at future meeting of the *ad hoc* informal open-ended Group in Vienna for regular consultations among the participating States on how to pursue CSCE missions to Kosovo, Sandjak and Vojvodina."[12]

The negotiations and discussion in the OSCE fora are a "mirror of European Security situations. Japan can understand the priorities of urgent agendas, and can get first-hand information which enables Japan to have a balanced view. This helps Japan to set the order of its contri- bution to regional conflicts in the OSCE area, not only in the framework of the OSCE but also the other fora or on a bilateral basis. Japan main- tains day-to-day contacts with the Secretariat and the delegations in Vienna. The successive CSCE/OSCE Secretary-Generals, the Directors of the Conflict Prevention Centre, and the High Commissioner for National Minorities have visited Japan and exchanged views there. In addition, Japan has sent experts on various CSCE/OSCE missions and has made financial contributions. Japan has also supported seminar activities of the OSCE.

Japan hosted two OSCE-Japan conferences, one in December 2000: "Comprehensive Security in Central Asia-Sharing OSCE and Asian Experiences"[13] and the other one in March 2004: "2004 OSCE-Japan Conference on the Search for Conflict Prevention in the New Century Circumstances-European Security Mechanisms and Security in Asia."[14]

---

[10] From the first meeting of the Committee of Senior Officials (CSO), Japan was invited to attend. When the Permanent Committee was established, Japan requested to be invited. On 13 January 1994, Japan attended for the first time a meeting of the 4th Plenary of the Permanent Committee (former body of the Permanent Council). CSCE Permanent Committee, *Journal* No. 4, 13 Jan. 1994. See Permanent Committee, *Journal* No. 3, 21 December 1993, decision (b).

[11] When the Forum for Security Cooperation was established, Japan asked to be invited to attend. On 28 October, 1992, Japan attended 6th Plenary meeting of its Special Committee for the first time. CSCE Forum for Security Cooperation, *Journal* No. 6, 28 October 1992. See Forum for Security Cooperation, *Journal* No. 5, Annex, Chairman's Statement, 21 October, 1992.

[12] CSCE The CSO Vienna Group, *Journal* No. 26, 26 August 1993.

[13] OSCE, SEC.GAL/6/01, 25 January 2001.

[14] OSCE, SEC.GAL/88/04, 16 April 2004.

2. EU

On the occasion of the official visit of Prime Minister Kaifu to The Hague, during the Dutch presidency of the EC in July 1991, "the Joint Declaration on Relations between Japan and the European Community and its Member States" (the Hague Declaration) was launched. Based on Mr Owada's belief that Japan needed to strengthen relations with Europe, and inspired by the Transatlantic Declaration in 1990, he took the initiative to negotiate the Hague Declaration. This declaration enhanced on-going political dialogue and set up an annual summit meeting. It set a broad agenda for cooperation and dialogues including international security, cultural exchange, and other topics. The prominent product was the Japan-EC joint-proposal of the UN register system of conventional arms' transfer, which was adopted and implemented.

There has been an increasing number of exchanges and contacts between Japan and the EU. Japan has had consultations with several working groups of the Council Secretariat of the EU. Also in Tokyo, various consultations and exchanges of views with the EU member countries have been upgraded.

These consultations produced a concrete result. The EU took the situation in North Korea into account. The EU proposed a resolution on the "Situation of human rights in the Democratic People's Republic of Korea" to the Commission on Human Rights. This resolution referred to the abduction issue as follows: "*The Commission on Human Rights,* […] 2. *Note with regrets* that the authorities of the Democratic People's Republic of Korea have not created the necessary conditions to permit the international community to verify these reports in an independent manner and calls upon the Government to respond to these reports and these concerns urgently. including [...] (f) By resolving, clearly and transparently, all the unresolved questions relating to the abduction of foreigners."[15] This resolution was adopted in April 2003.

In his policy speech on 13 January 2000, at the IFRI (Institut français des relations internationales) in Paris, Japanese Foreign Minister, Mr Kono explained that Japan would like to strengthen its political relationship with Europe. The reasons given were that both regions share common values and face the same challenges. Security issues link them as global partners, whereas globalisation was deepening the economic interdependence between them. Mr Kono proposed three pillars of cooperation between Japan and Europe: "Realizing shared

---

[15]   Situation of human rights in the Democratic People's Republic of Korea, Commission on Human Rights Resolution 2003/10, 51st meeting, 16 April 2003.

values while respecting diversity;" "Strengthening of Japan-Europe political cooperation;" and "Sharing the benefits of globalization."[16]

In terms of the aim of political dialogues, he suggested the following: "In response to such development in the EU as the rapid unification of foreign and security policies, I believe that Japan, in addition to enhancing its existing exchanges with member countries, should advance cooperation with the EU in the political realm through improved contacts between us." In particular, the following three areas were singled out for political cooperation; conflict prevention; disarmament/non-proliferation; and the reform of the UN. Lastly, he designated the next ten years starting from the year 2001, the "Decade of Japan-Europe Cooperation."[17] On the occasion of the Japan-EU annual summit meeting on 19 July 2000, both agreed to launch a decade of Japan-EU cooperation and to adopt a "new political document" based on the Hague Declaration.

In December 2001, the Japan-EU summit meeting in Brussels launched a new document, "Shaping our Common Future. An Action Plan for EU-Japan Cooperation." The year 2001 was the tenth anniversary of the Hague Declaration. This Action Plan deals with four major aims: (1) Promoting Peace and Security; (2) Strengthening the Economic and Trade Partnership Utilising the Dynamism of Globalisation for the Benefit of All; (3) Coping with Global and Societal Challenges, and "Bringing Together People and Cultures." It sets a wide range of concrete actions including dealing with "Aging Society and Employment," "Education," and "Developing Civil Society Links and Encouraging Inter-Regional Exchange."

For the purpose of deepening the existing political dialogue in the foreign policy area, the EU and Japan decided to intensify contacts as follows: "On behalf of the EU Council, the High Representative for Common Foreign and Security Policy (CFSP) will keep the Foreign Minister of Japan informed of important development in the CFSP, including the European Security and Defence Policy. The Japanese Minister will, in turn, inform the EU of key developments in Japanese foreign policy." There were telephone conversations between Mr Solana and Japanese Foreign Minister.

In the Action Plan, the section on "Promoting Peace and Security" includes the United Nations Reform; Arms Control, Disarmament and

---

[16] "Seeking a Millennium Partnership: New Dimensions in Japan-Europe Cooperation," Policy speech on Japan-Europe relations by Foreign Minister Yohei Kono at the French Institute of International Relations (IFRI) in Paris, on Thursday 13 January 2000.

[17] *Ibid.*

Non-Proliferation; Human Rights, Democracy and Stability; Conflict Prevention and Peace-building; and the Specific Regional Issues (Korean Peninsula, the Balkans, Russia, China, Middle East Peace Process, African regional organisations, East Timor and Cyprus).

The Action Plans are a living document. On the occasion of the Japan-EU annual summit meeting, implementation of the Action Plan was reviewed and has set actions to be targeted by the next Japan-EU summit. In June 2004, the 13th Japan-EU summit meeting was held immediately after the European Council which adopted the Treaty establishing a Constitution for Europe. This summit meeting issued a "Joint Press Statement," and four documents which ensure effective cooperation: "Japan-EU Joint Declaration on Disarmament and Non-proliferation," "Joint Statement on Cooperation on Information and Communication Technology," "Japan-EU Joint Initiative for the Enhancement of Intellectual Property Rights in Asia," and "Cooperation Framework of Promoting of Japan-EU Two-Way Investment."

In the Joint Press Statement, in the part "For the peace and stability of the international community," Japan and the EU paid special attention to cooperation on Iraq, the DPRK (Democratic People's Republic of Korea), the Middle East, Afghanistan, the Western Balkans, the proliferation of weapons of mass destruction and their means of delivery, and terrorism. They reaffirmed the importance of human security and "reiterated their commitment to an effective multilateralism and a fair and just rules-based international order, with the United Nations at its heart, which is essential in meeting the challenges in international security."[18]

As for "actions to be targeted by the next summit, in the field of "Promoting Peace and Security," there are five items:

- Consult each other regularly in the appropriate framework on policy which might have an influence on respective regional security.

- Strengthen cooperation on reconstruction in post-conflict areas such as Iraq and Afghanistan.

- Further cooperate on disarmament and non-proliferation on the basis of the Joint Declaration issued at this Summit.

- Cooperate closely for peace consolidation and economic development in the Western Balkans, especially strengthening policy coordination on Kosovo.

- Make joint efforts to promote the peace process in Sri Lanka based on the principles of the Tokyo Declaration and in close cooperation with the US and Norway, as recently expressed in the strong

---

[18]   13th Japan-EU Summit, Tokyo, 22 June 2004, Joint Press Statement.

messages conveyed by the co-chairs following their meeting in Brussels on 1 June.[19]

3. Council of Europe and NATO

Since 1996, Japan has had the status of observer in the Committee of Ministers of the Council of Europe. The Consul General of Japan in Strasbourg is the permanent observer. Japan has been invited to partici-pate in a number of ministerial meetings. Since 1974, the Parliament of Japan has participated in the discussion on the activities of the OECD by the Parliamentary Assembly of the Council of Europe. This has enabled Japan to participate in various meetings at expert level in a comprehensive way. Japan needs to be involved in law-making activi-ties since the Council of Europe produces influential treaties in a global-ised world, including clone technology, cyber crime, anti-terrorism, money laundering and anti-fraud. This body has acted as a standard setter.

In the framework of the Council of Europe, Japan has sent experts to various seminars as well as offered financial assistance to seminars. In November 2001, Japanese personnel joined the election observers of the Council of Europe on the occasion of the election in Kosovo.

As for NATO, there are two frameworks for exchange of views be-tween Japan and NATO: seminar activities among governmental offi-cials and academics on a regular basis, and senior officials' talks. The first seminar took place in June 1990 in Belgium.[20] In September 1991, NATO Secretary-General Mr Manfred Wörner paid the first official NATO visit to Japan. In October 1997, Dr. Solana as the Secretary-General of NATO visited Tokyo. The Japanese governmental officials and parliamentarians have had opportunities to exchange views at NATO when necessary.

IV. The EU Institute in Japan

On 1 April 2004, the first centre for academic excellence in studies of the EU opened in Tokyo. As a result of a tender, the EU Institute in Japan (EUIJ) will be managed by a consortium of universities, including Hitotsubashi University, International Christian University (ICU), Tokyo University of Foreign Studies (TAFS) and Tsuda College. The second EUIJ will open in the western part of Japan. The EUIJ is similar to the EU Centres in the US, Canada, Australia and New Zealand. The European Commission contributes 75% of the budget of the 1.3 million

---

[19]   *Ibid.*, Annex: Actions to be targeted by the next Japan-EU Summit.

[20]   E. Grove (ed.), *Global Security: North American, European and Japanese Interde-pendence in 1990s*, Brassey's, London, 1991.

euro for 42 months and the four universities contribute the rest of the budget.

The Japan-EU summit document of 22 June 2004, the Joint Statement referred to the EUIJ as follows: "They welcomed the formal opening on the day of the Summit of the first EU Institute in Japan. The institute represents a significant new resource to inform Japan about the EU and will act as a common meeting place where people from their countries may share ideas."[21] The annex of this document, "Actions to be targeted by the next Japan-EU Summit" says "Welcoming the establishment of the first EU Institute in Japan and plans for a second EU Institute to open in 2005, encourage intellectual exchanges between Japan and the EU, in particular between the EU Institutes and other institutions in Europe and Japan, to promote mutual understanding" in the part of "Objective 4: Bringing Together People and Culture."[22]

President Prodi gave a speech on the occasion of the opening ceremony on 22 June 2004. He explained that "Mutual awareness must be raised and knowledge increased. We want to foster education, research and outreach activities that focus on matters relating to the European Union. And we think these objectives can be better achieved and will have more impact if things are *done by Japanese for Japanese*."[23]

From the academic year 2005 (April 2005 to March 2006), the EUIJ in Tokyo will offer a number of EU-related courses to students in Japan and will invite professors and experts from Europe for a few courses. Those students who take the required units of the EU courses will be awarded the Certificate of EU Studies. From April 2006, the EUIJ in Tokyo will offer a graduate course of EU Studies of the University of Air (Broadcasting University) which will encompass EU economics, EU law, EU external relations, EU Science and Technology Policy as well as Japan-EU relations. The Ministry of Education and Science authorised the University of Air. It has more than 80,000 students, which includes various generations throughout Japan.

The EUIJ in Tokyo awards grants for graduate students as well as internships. The first student finished her internship at the Secretariat of the European Parliament in 2004. It is offering EU-related information by international conferences, business seminars, courses open to the general public, as well as its website[24] and newsletter.

---

[21] 13th Japan-EU Summit, Tokyo, 22 June 2004, Joint Press Statement.

[22] *Ibid.*, Annex: Actions to be targeted by the next Japan-EU Summit.

[23] Mr Romano Prodi, President of the European Commission, Speech 07/2004, 22 June 2004, Opening the First EU Institute in Japan, Palace Hotel, Tokyo.

[24] http://euij-tc.org.

Hitherto, there have been very few courses on the EU or Modern European Studies taught in Japan. No Japanese university has any European Studies Programme and no university degree in European Studies. There is only one university research institute on Europe. Nanzan University in Nagoya has a European Studies Institute. In all of the Japanese Universities there are many courses on European languages, on classics, philosophy, literature, ancient and medieval history of Europe. However, no single university in Japan has a systematic curriculum which offers courses on the EU.

Because of this situation, in the year 2000, the German academic exchange institution, DAAD (Deutscher Akademischer Austauschdienst) made a donation to the University of Tokyo, Komaba campus and established "DESK (Deutschland-und Europastudien in Komaba, German and European Studies in Komaba) in order to set more courses on Modern Europe as well as to disseminate information by way of open lectures. The EUIJ and the DESK will contribute to improve awareness of the EU in Japan.

V. Future Perspective

On 13 December 2002, a statement on the enlargement of the EU was issued by Ms Kawaguchi, Foreign Minister of Japan, immediately after the European Council as follows:

1. The Government of Japan expresses its congratulations for the decision of the Copenhagen European Council on 13 December (local time) to enlarge the European Union. Japan pays its respects to the efforts made by the EU and the countries newly joining the EU, and hopes that the present enlargement will lead to the stability and prosperity of Europe and the international community as well.

2. Japan and the EU share common values and special responsibilities in the international community. Under the Decade of Japan-Europe Cooperation that started last year, Japan intends to steadily implement the Action Plan for EU-Japan Cooperation on which the leaders of Japan and the EU agreed, with a view to deepening collaboration on the basis of strategic partnership between Japan and the EU.

3. Japan strongly hopes that the enlargement of the EU will be achieved with openness and transparency to the areas outside the region. Japan reiterates its request that the EU and its new member states ensure that Japanese business and Japanese companies operating in Europe, in particular, will not be disadvantaged by the enlargement.[25]

---

[25] Statement by Ms Yoriko Kawagchi, Minister for Foreign Affairs, on the Enlargement of the European Union, 13 December 2002.

On 1 May 2004, she congratulated the enlargement of Europe and reiterated the 2nd and 3rd points again. There was a lot of press coverage of this enlargement in Japan. The EU became more visible than ever in Japan.[26]

The Hague Declaration is the watershed of Japan-EU relations. After this Declaration, political and security cooperation between Japan and the EU turned out to be more important. In the "European Security Strategy (A Secure Europe in a Better World)," Japan is classified as a country with which the EU "should look to develop strategic partnerships."[27]

The end of the Cold War in Europe has opened a way to closer cooperation between Japan and Europe. The year 2005 is designated as "EU-Japan Year of People to People Exchanges." Throughout the year, numerous events and activities will take place in Japan and in the EU countries, which will surely enhance awareness and understandings among them.

When the Common Foreign and Security Policy of the EU is more consolidated, it will be easier for Japan to develop political and security cooperation. The future of Europe will guide the course of Japan-Europe relations.

---

[26] Statement by Ms Yoriko Kawaguchi, Minister for Foreign Affairs, on the Enlarged European Union, 1 May 2004.

[27] *A Secure Europe in a Better World, European Security Strategy*, Brussels, 12 December 2003.

CHAPTER 2

The European Security Strategy and Its Impact on Europe-Japan Relations

Éric REMACLE

*Professor of Political Science,
Université libre de Bruxelles*

I. From Civilian Powers to Global Military Actors

During the Cold War, both the European Community and Japan kept a low profile as far as security policy was concerned. This has led some authors to consider them as two "civilian powers" who have in common the use of non-military means for addressing security interests.[1] As a defeated power in 1945, Japan, like Germany, agreed to adopt an article in its Constitution prescribing military self-restraint and has therefore used civilian means as key foreign and security policy instruments.[2] As far as Europe is concerned, the concept of "civilian power Europe"[3] was

---

[1]   Keukeleire, St., "The European Union and Japan: Partners in Global Crisis Management and Global Stabilisation?," in Ueta, T., Remacle, É. (eds.), *Japan-EU Cooperation: Ten Years after the Hague Declaration, Studia Diplomatica*, LIV(1-2), 2002, pp. 159-184; Maull, H. W., *Europe and Japan. A Relationship in Search of Roles*, Japan Center for International Exchange, Tokyo, 1996.

[2]   Maull, H. W., "Germany and Japan: The New Civilian Powers," in R. K. Betts (ed.), *Conflict after the Cold War: Arguments on Causes of War and Peace*, Macmillan, New York, 1994, pp. 492-504.

[3]   The concept was quoted for the first time in Duchêne, F., "Europe in World Peace" in R. Mayne (ed.), *Europe Tomorrow*, Fontana/Collins, London, 1972, pp. 32-49 and *id.*, "The EC and the Uncertain Ties of Interdependence," in M. Kohnstamm, W. Hager (eds.), *A Nation Writ Large*, Macmillan, London, 1973, pp. 1-21. For a recent discussion, see Zielonka, J., *Explaining Euro-Paralysis. Why Europe is Unable to Act in International Politics*, Basingstoke, Macmillan, 1998; Whitman, R., *From Civilian Power to Superpower? The International Identity of the European Union*, Macmillan, Basingstoke, 1998; Smith, K., "The End of Civilian Power Europe: A Welcome Demise or Cause for Concern?," *The International Spectator*, Vol. XXXV, No. 2, 2000, pp. 11-28; Stavridis, S., "Militarising the EU: The Concept

---

invented in the 1970s and 1980s in order to reflect the absence of the European Communities in military affairs due to the failure of the EDC in 1954, and to NATO's dominance on the West European security, which reduced the security competence of the European Political Cooperation to its "political and economic aspects" according to Title III of the Single European Act adopted in 1986.

The concept of security was commonly considered identical to military security for much of the early part of the Cold War. With the *détente*, a broader concept of security emerged that included human rights, as well as environmental and economic concerns beyond the traditional military concerns.[4] The 1975 Helsinki Final Act and its association with comprehensive and cooperative security,[5] and the reports from the Palme and Brundtland Commissions, illustrated these trends among policy circles.[6] Academic literature also attempted to formulate new theoretical insights into security questions and played a pioneering role in proposing new approaches to security during the 1990s.[7]

The integration of the concept of comprehensive security has become a notable feature of official documents issued by Western and/or West European organisations since the mid-1990s. In 1995, the twenty-seven countries who were variously member states, observers, associate

---

of Civilian Power Europe Revisited," *The International Spectator*, Vol. XXXVI, No. 4, 2001, pp. 43-50.

[4] See e.g. Ullman, R., "Redefining Security," *International Security*, Vol. 8, No. 1, Summer 1983, pp. 162-177; Nye, J. E., Lynn-Jones, S. M., "International Security Studies: A Report of a Conference on the State of the Field," *International Security*, Vol. 12, No. 4, Spring 1988, pp. 5-27.

[5] For a definition, see e.g. Nolan, J. E., "The Concept of Cooperative Security," in J.E. Nolan (ed.), *Global Engagement. Cooperation and Security in the 21ˢᵗ Century*, The Brookings Institution, Washington DC, 1994; Cohen, R., Mihalka, M., *Cooperative Security: New Horizons for International Order*, The Marshall Center Papers No. 3, George C. Marshall European Center for Security Studies, Garmisch, 2001.

[6] Independent Commission on Security and Disarmament (Palme Commission), *Common Security: A Blueprint for Survival*, Simon & Schuster, New York, 1982; World Commission on Environment and Development (Brundtland Commission), *Our Common Future*, OUP, Oxford, 1987.

[7] Buzan, B., Kelstrup, M., Lemaitre, P., Waever, O., *The European Security Order Recast: Scenarios for the Post-Cold War Era*, Pinter, London, 1990; Buzan, B., *People, States and Fear: An Agenda for International Security Studies in the Post-Cold War Era*, Harvester Wheatsheaf, London, 1991, 2ⁿᵈ edition; Booth, K. (ed.), *New Thinking about Strategy and International Security*, Harper Collins, London, 1991; Klare, M., Thomas, D.C. (eds.), *World Security: Trends and Challenges at Century's End*, St. Martin's Press, New York, 1991; Clarke, M (ed.), *New Perspectives on Security*, Brassey's, London, 1993; Lipshutz, R. D. (ed.), *On Security*, Columbia University Press, New York, 1995.

members or associate partners of the Western European Union (WEU) adopted a Common Concept about European security paving the way towards defining European security interests.[8] NATO's key documents of the 1990s, especially the successive versions of the Alliance's Strategic Concept adopted in Rome in 1991 and Washington in 1999, also reflected a similar evolution.

Reference has been made to a cooperative and comprehensive approach to security in key treaty articles and declarations of the European Union within the framework of its Common Foreign and Security Policy (CFSP) since 1992. Article III-292 of the EU's draft Constitution states that the Union's external policies have to be conducted in order to:

(a) safeguard its values, fundamental interests, security, independence and integrity;

(b) consolidate and support democracy, the rule of law, human rights and the principles of international law;

(c) preserve peace, prevent conflicts and strengthen international security, in accordance with the purposes and principles of the United Nations Charter, with the principles of the Helsinki Final Act and with the aims of the Charter of Paris, including those relating to external borders;

(d) foster the sustainable economic, social and environmental development of developing countries, with the primary aim of eradicating poverty;

(e) encourage the integration of all countries into the world economy, including through the progressive abolition of restrictions on international trade;

(f) help develop international measures to preserve and improve the quality of the environment and the sustainable management of global natural resources, in order to ensure sustainable development;

(g) assist populations, countries and regions confronting natural or man-made disasters; and

(h) promote an international system based on stronger multilateral cooperation and good global governance.[9]

In parallel, Japan has also extensively reformulated its approach to security during the 1990s in order to take into account the impact of the end of the Cold War and of its rapidly changing environment (financial crisis in Asia, China's rising power, North Korea's nuclear ambitions, US war on terror). The Japanese Minister of Foreign Affairs (1996-1998), and subsequently, Prime Minister (1998-2000) Obuchi Keizo,

---

[8]   Western European Union (WEU), *European Security: A Common Concept of the 27 WEU countries*, WEU Council of Ministers, Madrid, 14 November 1995.

[9]   *Treaty Establishing a Constitution for Europe, Official Journal of the European Union*, series C 310, Vol. 47, Brussels, 16 December 2004 (http://europa.eu.int/eur-lex/lex/JOHtml.do?uri=OJ:C:2004:310:SOM:EN:HTML).

has been a key actor in this process and promoted the concept of "human security" in order to open up a more assertive and independent international role for Japan without undermining its alliance with the United States.[10]

Echoing the first use of the human security concept in the 1994 Human Development Report of the United Nations Development Programme (UNDP), the Japanese government has supported the framing of a holistic definition of security by the Commission on Human Security co-chaired by the former UN High Commissioner for Refugees Sadako Ogata and Nobel Peace laureate, Amartya Sen. According to the final report of this commission, "the aim of human security is to protect the vital core of all human lives in ways that enhance human freedoms and human fulfilment. Human security means protecting fundamental freedoms – freedoms that are the essence of life [...]. It means creating political, social, environmental, economic, military and cultural systems that together give people the building blocks of survival, livelihood and dignity."[11] The commission also proposed a list of policy recommendations aiming at:

1. Protecting people in violent conflict.
2. Protecting people from the proliferation of arms.
3. Supporting the security of people on the move.
4. Establishing human security transition funds for post-conflict situations.
5. Encouraging fair trade and markets to benefit the extreme poor.
6. Working to provide minimum living standards everywhere.
7. According higher priority to ensuring universal access to basic health care.
8. Developing an efficient and equitable global system for patent rights.
9. Empowering all people with universal basic education.
10. Clarifying the need for a global human identity while respecting the freedom of individuals to have diverse identities and affiliations.[12]

Though based on wider principles and conceptual approach, the Japanese approach to human security has developed convergences with the Canada/Norway-led Human Security Network established in 1999 which now brings together thirteen member states.[13] These two ap-

---

[10] Evans, P. E., "Human Security and East Asia," *Journal of East Asian Studies*, Vol. 4, No. 2, May-August 2004, pp. 263-284.
[11] Commission on Human Security, *The Final Report*, 2003, p. 4 (see http://www.humansecurity-chs.org/finalreport/).
[12] *Ibid.*, pp. 133-142.
[13] See http://www.humansecuritynetwork.org/network-e.php.

proaches were decisive in inspiring the agenda and decisions of the 2000 United Nations Millennium Summit. Furthermore, the financial crisis in South East Asia at the end of the 1990s has increased the interest of Asian countries in the concept of human security.[14] The trauma of the December 2004 tsunami catastrophe is likely to reinforce such an interest.

Both Europe and Japan have also faced since the early 2000s a very new agenda related to military power since the early 2000s. In 1999, the Helsinki European Council launched the process leading to the creation of the European Security and Defence Policy, while Japan took an active part in the US so-called "war on terror" after September 11, 2001, sending non-combat troops to Iraq since 2003. The prospect of a permanent seat for Japan on the United Nations Security Council is also part of this changing agenda.

It is therefore useful to study what impact these developments, and especially the adoption of the European Security Strategy, will have on their mutual relationships.[15]

II. The EU Security Strategy

A. *Origin and Philosophy of the Strategy*

The incentive for the adoption of a Security Strategy by the European Union was the American attack on Iraq in 2003. Facing internal divisions on such a key security question, EU Foreign Affairs Ministers, meeting in Corfu in May 2003 asked the High Representative for CFSP, Javier Solana, to draft a document equivalent to the National Security Strategy of the United States of America, adopted by President Bush in September 2002 and written by his National Security Advisor, Condoleeza Rice.[16] A first draft was proposed by Javier Solana to the Thessaloniki European Council in June 2003. The final text was adopted by the Brussels European Council on December 12, 2003 under the title *A Secure Europe in a Better World – European Security Strategy*.[17]

As mentioned previously, the security interests of the European Union had already been partly defined in previous CFSP documents and

---

[14]   Evans, P. E., "Human Security and East Asia," *op. cit.*

[15]   I am grateful to Sven Biscop, Barbara Delcourt, Paul M. Evans, Gerrard Quille and Takako Ueta who have provided me with background information and comments which have contributed to this paper, and to Taichi Nakamura for research assistance.

[16]   See http://www.state.gov/documents/organization/15538.pdf.

[17]   See http://ue.eu.int/uedocs/cmsUpload/78367.pdf. All further quotations come from this version.

the WEU 1995 "Common Concept" may also be seen as an attempt to unite European states around a security concept. Not surprisingly, the European Security Strategy (ESS) follows the same lead and defines European security interests along classical geographical lines, as well as in the values associated with the Union's origins and summarised in Article III-292 of the EU Constitution. These security interests are both regional and global, as implied by Biscop and Coolsaet's succinct and apt choice of title: "The World Is the Stage".[18]

The strategy articulates therefore a framework based upon a comprehensive or holistic approach to security. The underlying comprehensive security concept leads to a clear statement that the EU and its member states will cooperate to tackle their security priorities in a framework that emphasises multilateral institutions (specifically the UN and regional organisations) and the rule of law (upholding the principle of the use of force as a last resort). This means that even security 'threats' (weapons of mass destruction, regional conflicts, state failure, terrorism and organised crime) should be addressed through 'effective multilateralism'. In other words, by supporting the UN system, strengthening national responses through EU synergies and by addressing root causes such as poverty and weak governance through community instruments and regional dialogue.[19]

The Brussels version, adopted in December, differed from the Thessaloniki (June) version in emphasis rather than content. It was drawn up to emphasise the social 'concerns' in European security rather than the military 'threats'. In this respect, it emphasised 'global challenges' and 'key threats', unlike the first draft, which focused solely on the threats. According to some analysts, this was the result of amendments inspired by a "civilian power" approach, especially from Germany and the neutral states, in order to 'soften' the more offensive and military-oriented style of the initial version which had been written by the British diplomat, Robert Cooper, who has since been appointed in the EU Secretariat-General.[20] But the changes made were mostly confined to shifting paragraphs around within the document and adding new sub-headings rather than changing text and substance. The two key changes that were made were the removal of the term 'pre-emption'

---

[18] Biscop, S., Coolsaet, R., *The World Is the Stage – A Global Security Strategy for the European Union*, Notre Europe, Paris, 2003.

[19] Quille, G., "The European Security Strategy: A Framework for EU Security Interests?," *International Peacekeeping*, Vol. 11, No. 3, Autumn 2004, pp. 1-16.

[20] Remacle, É., "La stratégie européenne de sécurité: plus occidentale qu'européenne," in B. Delcourt, D. Duez, É. Remacle (dir.), *La guerre d'Irak. Prélude d'un nouvel ordre international ?*, P.I.E.-Peter Lang, Brussels, 2004, pp. 47-59.

considered too "American" and some new language about WMD.[21] These changes and the new balance between the emphasis on challenges and threats were sufficient to appeal to diverse member state interests and might be one more case of constructive ambiguity as well as the seed of future disputes of interpretation between member-states. It might especially seem very paradoxical that the paragraphs which shape an EU international identity and differentiate it from the USA are those referring to the global challenges and civilian means, while the threat assessment in the "hard security" sphere is very similar to the American one. Does this mean that, on becoming a military power, the EU will be unable to differentiate itself from the US?

B. The Three European Specific Approaches according to Javier Solana

Javier Solana's answer to this question is 'no' for three reasons: the holistic character of the European approach; its cooperative methodology based on an 'effective multilateralism' and its ambition to build security communities.

The Secretary-General/High Representative considers the holistic approach illustrated by the document to be original and a consequence of the differences with Washington. He argues, with reference to a comprehensive notion of security, that active engagement is in Europe's security interests since these are affected by poor governance, insecurity, poverty and conflict far beyond its borders. Europe must therefore meet these challenges, and is well-placed to do so with a range of diplomatic, development, economic, humanitarian and military instruments.[22]

This comprehensive approach to understanding security moves beyond a traditional military threat assessment to identify what Solana describes as the 'new environment' where diffuse challenges must be addressed by the Union. These challenges, such as poverty, energy dependence, climate change and bad governance must be considered as key security challenges for the Union because of their role in contributing to regional instability which, in turn, affects European interests directly and indirectly, as does open violence like the Middle Eastern conflict.

---

[21] In the June draft, it was "the single most important threat" to European security and became in the final version "potentially greatest threat to our security," especially if combined with international terrorism and state failure.

[22] Solana, J., *Speech on the State of the Union,* European Union Institute for Security Studies, Paris, 30 June 2003.

In addition to the 'old threat' represented by these regional conflicts, the strategy identifies 'new threats' which are a combination of traditional concerns related to the proliferation of WMD and new forms of terrorism, failed states and organised crime. It states that their novelty lies in their combination: "Taking these different elements together – terrorism committed to maximum violence, the availability of weapons of mass destruction and the failure of state systems – we could be confronted with a very radical threat". But the ESS insists that the answer to such problems involves the use of a full range of instruments, a 'comprehensive security toolbox', not only the use of force: "In contrast to the massive visible threat in the Cold War, none of the new threats is purely military; nor can any be tackled by purely military means. Each requires a mixture of instruments. Proliferation may be contained through export controls and attacked through political, economic and other pressures while the underlying political causes are also tackled. Dealing with terrorism may require a mixture of intelligence, political, military and other means. In failed states, military instruments may be needed to restore order, humanitarian to tackle the immediate crisis. Economic instruments serve reconstruction, and civilian crisis management helps restore civil government. The European Union is particularly well-equipped to respond to such multi-faceted situations." According to Javier Solana, the same multi-faceted approach is needed for tackling disarmament and threat prevention and from his point of view, this is what differentiates the European concept from the preemptive concept of the Bush Administration.[23]

A second innovation in the European approach is the emphasis on international cooperation and multilateralism: "no single country is able to tackle today's complex problems entirely on its own". The ESS therefore emphasises the depth and primacy of the transatlantic link and collaboration, even with an uncharacteristically messianic discourse: "Acting together, the European Union and the United States can be a formidable force for good in the world". It quotes as other strategic partners the other members of the G8 and the United Nations Security Council: Russia first, then Canada, China, Japan, and also India. The methodology of this cooperative approach is defined as an 'effective multilateralism' which aims at three strategic objectives: extending the zone of security around Europe; strengthening the international order; and thirdly, countering the threats.

The first of these strategic objectives reflects the existing role of the EU, mostly through the enlargement process, but now in its wider

---

[23]   Quille, G., Pullinger, P., "The EU Seeking Common Ground for Tackling the Threat from WMD," *Disarmament Diplomacy*, No. 7, December 2003.

neighbourhood. It has been recognised that the very powerful carrot of enlargement has had an important impact on stabilising the EU's periphery, but considering that there will be some time for adjustment after the next round of enlargement, that process needs to be invigorated in both consolidating security within the EU's enlarged borders and in extending stability beyond. The second strategic objective provides the means by which a regional multilateral actor, the EU, can extend its influence and support international responses to security challenges through "the development of a stronger international society, well-functioning international institutions and a rule-based international order". This objective places the importance of the UN system centre-stage, along with the transatlantic relationship. In this vein, Javier Solana states: "The fundamental framework for international relations is the United Nations Charter. Strengthening the United Nations, equipping it to fulfil its responsibilities and to act effectively, must be a European priority. If we want international organisations, regimes and treaties to be effective in confronting threats to international peace and security we should be ready to act when their rules are broken".[24] The third objective responds to the 'new threats' and emphasises the EU's strengths based upon its response to September 11 with "a package that included the creation of a European arrest warrant, measures to attack terrorist financing and an agreement on mutual legal assistance with the US".[25]

Likewise, it refers to existing approaches to support non-proliferation such as with its new Strategy on WMD and an Action Plan which includes a commitment to the universalisation of non-proliferation and disarmament norms and regimes, along with a commitment to make those regimes effective by dealing with compliance and enforcement issues. The case of the negotiations about the Iranian nuclear programmes between the Iranian government and the representatives of the three major European states (France, Germany and the UK), in parallel to the talks with, and pressure from, the International Atomic Energy Agency (IAEA), has been quoted as an example of the European methodology in this field.[26]

The reference to effective multilateralism allows two interpretations. One is that multilateralism matters: as a matter of principle, the EU sticks strongly to the multilateral frameworks at the universal level

---

[24] Solana, J., *Speech on the State of the Union, op. cit.*

[25] Quille, G., Pullinger, S., *op. cit.*

[26] This methodology has inspired pleas for a new American attitude towards Iran, see Brzezinski, Z., Gates, R. M., Maloney, S., *Iran: Time for a New Approach*, Report of an Independent Task Force sponsored by the Council on Foreign Relations, Washington DC, 2004.

(United Nations, World Trade Organisation), but also at the regional level (NATO and the ESDP-NATO relations are quoted among the key policy implications of the ESS, and OSCE, Council of Europe, MERCOSUR, ASEAN, the African Union, as well as other key regional organisations). The other interpretation is that effectiveness matters: multilateralism is nothing when there is no determination and readiness to use force to implement its decisions. This implies, according to some analysts, to develop a 'robust' approach to Petersberg tasks and a strategic culture, whereby "the institutional confidence and processes to manage and deploy military force as part of the accepted range of legitimate and effective policy instruments, together with general recognition of the EU's legitimacy as an international actor with military capabilities (albeit limited)".[27] Of these two focuses on 'effective multilateralism', the latter makes the EU very similar to the United States while the former contributes to shaping Europe's identity in opposition to a simplistically unilateral America. But this oversimplification does not help in understanding the actual motivations of states opting for multilateralism.[28] And again, these two interpretations and their different rationales are part of the constructive ambiguity of the document and of future divergences when discussing the scope of Petersberg tasks and military capabilities.[29] Interestingly, the ESS also keeps the balance between the call for 'increasing' capabilities (*via* a rise of military expenditure) and calling for their 'improvement' (*via* pooling, rationalisation, specialisation and other qualitative approaches).

A last point regarding the peculiarity of the European approach to regionalism and its impact on security might be made here. Javier Solana considers the Union's security interests as coming from its ability to build a security community:[30] "The creation of the European Union has been central to this development. It has transformed the relations between our states, and the lives of our citizens. European countries are committed to dealing peacefully with disputes and cooperating through common institutions".[31] The success of the Union, the enlargement and the member sates' commitment to its institutions is

---

[27] Cornish, P., Edwards, G., "Beyond the EU/NATO Dichotomy: The Beginnings of a European Strategic Culture," *International Affairs*, Vol. 77, No. 3, July 2001, pp. 587-603.

[28] Pollack, M. A., "Unilateral America, multilateral Europe?," in J. Peterson, M. A. Pollack (eds.), *Europe, America, Bush. Transatlantic Relations in the Twenty-first Century*, Routledge, London-New York, 2003, pp. 115-127.

[29] Quille, G., "The European...," *op. cit.*, pp. 10-12.

[30] About security communities, see Adler, E., Barnett, M., *Security Communities*, Cambridge, Cambridge University Press, 1998.

[31] Solana, J., *Speech on the State of the Union, op. cit.*

underlined in recognition of the role of the EU in contributing to security in Europe. This regionalist/institutionalist dimension of the EU security strategy is another way of defining multilateralism. It also implies the development of the enlargement of the Union and its neighbourhood policies as key security instruments.[32] Extending its own security community, stabilising its environment and promoting deep regional integration on other continents are considered to be inter-related institutionalist policies, all dedicated to the Union's security interests in a way which is not only original, but finally also inspired by the 'civilian power' approach.[33]

III. Japan-EU Security Relationships after the ESS

When establishing permanent bilateral relationships through the Hague Declaration in 1991, both Japan and the European Union had one eye on their probable evolution from civilian powers into another kind of international actor.

Both had an interest also in developing new security agendas to help them build an international identity without undermining their close respective relationships with the United States of America.[34]

Therefore, during the 1990s, they have mainly emphasised their role in conflict prevention, civilian crisis management, post-conflict stabilisation, nation-building, development assistance, i.e., an extended civilian-power agenda. This agenda has helped both of them to achieve a stronger international profile, despite criticism about their absence of participation in major peace-keeping military activities. The promotion by Japan of the concept of "human security" and the overlap between this concept and the EU's holistic approach to security even hold the possibility of building a joint conceptual agenda.[35]

The European Security Strategy and the recent Japanese security initiatives continue to be inspired chiefly by these types of "soft security" concepts and agendas. As we have seen, they provide much visibility,

---

[32]   See also hereafter Pal Dunay's and Shigeo Mutsushika's contributions about the neighbourhood policy.

[33]   Telò, M., *European Union and New Regionalism*, Aldershot, Ashgate, 2001; *id.*, *L'Europa potenza civile*, Rome, GLF Editori Laterza, 2004.

[34]   See also hereafter Fraser Cameron's contribution about the USA-EU-Japan triangle.

[35]   Within Europe, a group of scholars, led by Mary Kaldor from the London School of Economics, has promoted the adoption of the "human security" concept by the European institutions, see *A Human Security Doctrine for Europe. The Barcelona Report of the Study Group on Europe's Security Capabilities*, Barcelona, 15 September 2004 (http://www.lse.ac.uk/Depts/global/Human%20Security%20Report%20Full.pdf).

credibility and identity to both actors and allow them to define easily a common security agenda.

But, on the other hand, each for its own diverse reasons has opted for taking a "hard security" approach, parallel to its soft-security stance. Following the attacks of September 11, the fight against terrorism and proliferation of weapons of mass destruction have been considered key security questions by both Europe and Japan. Europe has decided to build its own military capabilities in order to upgrade its power and influence *vis-à-vis* the American ally in crisis management, following the Kosovo crisis. Japan, for its part, feels the need to prove its readiness to act as a credible permanent member of the United Nations Security Council and has an interest in deploying robust military means in its geographic neighbourhood with Washington's support. The paradox of this parallel move is that, though reinforcing the two actors' international military positions, it could damage their ability to build a discourse and an identity different from that of the United States. It could also make it more difficult to build bridges between their security concepts and hinder the establishment of joint initiatives.

The European Security strategy has already identified Japan as a 'strategic partner' but the post-September 11 and post-Iraqi situation reduces the number of opportunities for framing a wider joint EU-Japan security agenda. These difficulties could even increase if, in 2005, Japan gets a permanent seat in the United Nations Security Council while the European Union remains unrepresented and has to rely mainly on the good will of the '*directoire*' of major European powers. In such a scenario, much imagination and political initiative will be needed from both actors in order to strengthen their security relationships and cooperation.

Joint action in implementing the recommendations of the report of the United Nations Secretary-General's High-Level Panel on Threats, Challenges and Change,[36] as well as the cooperation in the field of peace-keeping operations which both actors have started to experience since 2003, could pave the way for just such a new joint Action Plan in security matters.

---

[36] *A More Secure World. Our Shared Responsibility, Report of the Secretary-General's High-Level Panel on Threats, Challenges and Change*, United Nations, New York, December 2004 (www.un.org/secureworld/).

CHAPTER 3

The Concept of 'Civilian Power' in the Light of the Constitutional Evolution of the European Union

Mario TELÒ

Université libre de Bruxelles

In Europe, the roots of the notion of 'civilian power' are to be found not only in the Enlightenment, Liberalism, Christianity and Democratic Socialism, but also in the tragic legacy of the first half of the 20th century. This had a direct impact on the post-war Constitutions of the defeated powers such as Germany, Japan and the new Italian Republic. Thus, Article 11 of the 1948 Italian Constitution (similarly to the Japan Constitution art. 9) refers to the 'repudiation of war' as a 'means for settling international disputes', the willingness to accept 'limitations of sovereignty where they are necessary for a legal system of peace and justice', and the promotion of 'international organisations furthering such ends'. The concept of civilian power refers to the memory of the tragedies of the last century, the Holocaust and the self-critical historical memory developed by the peoples of Europe after 1945.

However, the political potential of the EC and its member states was not limited to that of the 'downsized' defeated and postcolonial powers. This radically innovative political culture pervaded the epistemic community of the founding fathers at the heart of European integration. The first open debate on civilian power Europe occurred within the historical and geo-political context of the second half of the 20th century, characterised by the bipolar world and the Cold War.[1] In fact,

---

[1] See F. Duchêne, "The European Community and the Uncertainties of Interdependence," in M. Kohnstamm and W. Hager (eds.), *A Nation Writ Large? Foreign Policy Problems before the European Community*, Macmillan, London 1973, pp. 1-21) and H. Bull ("Civilian Power Europe: A Contradiction in Terms," in L. Tsoukalis (ed.), *The European Community: Past, Present and Future*, Blackwell, Oxford, 1983, pp. 150-57).

most commentators acknowledge that the EC emerged and prospered in part due to the external federating element provided by the tensions of the bipolar world, even if this did mean that all member states, more or less, relied on the powerful American ally for nuclear security and political leadership, and renounced a political role for Europe.[2]

The post-1989 period, the end of the bipolar world, the demise of the Soviet nuclear threat and the collapse of the socialist system have certainly not provided the idyllic conditions for the 'end of history'. They have, however, furnished Europe with a new window of opportunity and created the geopolitical space for a world accommodating new economic and political actors in what has been redefined 'global governance'.[3] In this new scenario, the important decisions of the Maastricht Treaty to institutionalise the first parts of a common foreign and security policy and construct federal monetary union (in other words, touching on the 'sovereign competence' of member states) have led to the revival of the theoretical issue of 'another power'. This has stimulated a new debate on the variety of international actors, realism and legitimacy of a European path to international actorness and power, as shown also by catch-phrases referring to the EU such as 'the ironies of sovereignty', a 'gentle power', an 'ambiguous power'.[4]

In François Duchêne's pioneering work, it is not methodologically clear to what extent the concept of civilian power is normative or analytical: the 'European Community could have the opportunity to show the influence that can be exercised through wide political cooperation that has emerged mainly to implement new forms of power'.[5] The basis of such potential influence is provided by the values declared and practised at both internal and external levels. These include human rights, democracy, peace and the non-violent settlement of conflicts, justice and tolerance, combined with the non-military instruments used by the EU to conduct external relations and international actions and, above all, the possible dissemination of elements of the regional integration experience to other continents, as a way of achieving democracy and lasting peace. Even if Headley Bull's realist criticism of EC Civilian power as a 'contradiction in terms' was appropriate during the

---

[2] H. Wallace and W. Wallace, *Policy Making in the European Union*, Oxford University Press, Oxford 1996.

[3] J. N. Rosenau and E. O. Czempiel (eds.), *Governance without Government: Order and Change in World Politics*, Cambridge University Press, Cambridge – New York 1992.

[4] See the texts cited by Keohane in "Ironies of Sovereignty: The European Union and World Order," *Journal of Common Market Studies*, Vol. 40, No. 4, 2002.

[5] Duchêne, "The European Community and the Uncertainties of Interdependence," in *op. cit.*, p. 19.

nuclear confrontation stage between the two superpowers, the issue now is whether it is completely obsolete against a background of the conflicts in the Balkans in the 1990s, Europe's continuing military subordination to the US and the EU's difficulties in facing the challenges of the post-September 11 period. The disappearance of the traits typical of the half century defined by the nuclear threat and the balance of power between the US and the USSR offers Europe new choices and opportunities. The question is whether the conditions have matured in Europe for a notion of civilian power that can overcome the objections of realism. We shall begin by discussing the concept of political power, which is central to the redefinition of the concept of civilian power.

Referring to Robert Dahl, we may say that the framework of the traditional notion of power is that of a negative-sum game ('A's power implies B's lack of freedom') and that, in the case of conflict between political power and economic or cultural power, the political always prevails.[6] This classic notion of power, which dates back to Machiavelli and Bodin, was adjusted to fit the modern state by Max Weber, who defined it as the capacity to impose one's will even when faced with opposition. It was on this basis that European political theory influenced the realist and neo-realist school of international relations, particularly in terms of the version that dominated American political science after the Second World War.[7] In Europe, Hinsley and others focussed on the basic right of sovereign power and the right to declare war in the context of the inter-state system.[8] The internal sovereignty of the supreme power of the state is the prerequisite for the affirmation of its external sovereignty amidst an inter-state system which, although to some degree organised by international law, lacks a central authority. The German political scientist Carl Schmitt emphasises this distinctiveness of true sovereign power by its notion of capacity of cope with "state of exception".

This classical notion of sovereign power is notoriously subject to criticism both in Europe and the USA. Its alternative is provided by the two main versions of constitutionalism as 'shared sovereignty' which has deep roots in the history of political thought and institutions: the federalist tradition (especially its American version), on the one hand,[9] and 'mixed government', on the other. This latter version was expertly presented by Norberto Bobbio as a theoretical (and also historical if we

---

[6]   N. Bobbio, *Stato, governo e società. Per una teoria generale della politica*, Einaudi, Torino, 1986.

[7]   K. Waltz, *Theory of International Politics*, Addison-Wesley, Reading (Mass.), 1979.

[8]   E. H. Hinsley, *Sovereignty*, Cambridge University Press, Cambridge, 1986.

[9]   Keohane, "Ironies of Sovereignty," quoted.

think of examples such as the Republic of Venice) notion of power, far from the classic modern realist tradition, defined by a compromising balance between different procedures, principles, social forces and institutions.[10] The two versions of 'shared sovereignty' should not be confused: for example, Hegel underestimated the American federal form and defined it as a pre-state – 'neither a true state, nor a true government'.[11] However, he defends the "mixed constitution" of constitutional monarchies as a complementary combination of different principles. The mix of the monarchic, aristocratic and democratic principles constitutes the maximum degree of wisdom, since it is only this Ciceronian 'aequatum et temperatum' system (mixed constitutions in the modern world) that ensures stable governments and guarantees a balance between different forces and principles.

The theoretical question that has long been posed is whether such institutions inevitably turn out to be fragile because they are intrinsically 'monstrous' (in chapter 29 of *Leviathan*, Hobbes uses the image of the man 'that had another man growing out of his side') or because, in exceptional historical situations, the real sovereign eventually emerges (as claimed by Carl Schmitt, for example). Or, on the contrary, it could be the increasing internal polyarchic pluralism and the multiple external interdependence that inevitably defuses the unitary concept of sovereign political power, to the benefit of various forms of 'shared sovereignty'. The very existence of a complex political system like the EU stimulates a new line of theoretical research on sovereignty. Of course, its political development during the decades of the bipolar world avoided encroaching significantly on issues not only of peace or war, but also of political union and this aspect clearly prevented it from being considered a sovereign power. It is no coincidence that its political constitution has been compared to the two forms of divided sovereignty. However, it is its original post-realist nature that poses an unavoidable conceptual challenge. To what degree is this specifically intrinsic aspect of the EU compatible with its growth as a global political power?

We have not space enough to referring to the rich and variegated renewal process which has taken place within international relations theory over the last twenty years or so, and to the questioning of the theoretical premises of the classic meaning of political power and international power beyond the neo-realist school: the theory of regimes, the 'theory of complex interdependence', neo-institutionalism and constructivist theory. However, we will put forward further argu-

[10] N. Bobbio, "Governo misto," in N. Bobbio (ed.), *Matteucci and Pasquino, Dizionario di politica, op. cit.*

[11] G. W. F. Hegel, *Vorlesungen über die Philosophie der Geschichte (1832-45)*, Suhrkamp, Frankfurt a. M., 1986.

ments by summarising some results which complement research conducted on the history of political philosophy and comparative institutionalist studies.

1) The *longue durée* tendency as regards the decline of classic state sovereignty due to the complex interdependencies of the market, trade, socio-cultural processes, the mass-media and the technological revolution. In this context, we refer to the decline of the primacy of military and security questions (not only the nuclear deterrent) on the international agenda and the growth in the political importance of trade, cultural, economic and technological links etc. This has had inevitable consequences on the hierarchy of international relations and carries implications for the growing significance of civilian (aid, trade, sanctions and diplomacy) as compared to military means in terms of international influence.[12]

2) The variety and plurality of international public and private actors, national and international actors, multinational companies, transnational networks, as well as the emergence of functional approaches aimed at reorganising authority within the context of globalisation and overcoming the absolute centrality of the state as the organising factor of political space.

3) The questioning of the unitary nature of international action by the state, due to the internal complexity of the decision-making process, the participation of civil society groups and the growing importance of transnational interest networks and coalitions.[13]

4) The overcoming (harking back to Kant), of the classic realist distinction between two spheres, i.e. domestic and international, anchoring peace to the internal democratic constitution of each of the units of the system.

5) The clear insufficiency of the state when faced with the major emergencies of global governance, peace, the environment, economic and financial instability, hunger, poverty, infectious and endemic diseases, humanitarian disasters etc. This inevitably encourages cooperation among states and the functional strengthening of multilateral institutions, both regional (such as the EU) and global. This can lead to an enhanced role for international organisations and regimes and the strengthening of their capacity not only to manipulate and bind, but also to guide the autonomous preferences of member states.

---

[12] R. O. Keohane and J. S. Nye, *Power and Interdependence*, Harper Collins, New York, 1989.

[13] M. Castells, *La société en réseaux. L'ère de l'information*, Fayard, Paris, 1997.

6) The growing international influence of 'structural' power (based on knowledge, know-how, and technology) as compared to military or economic power.[14]

7) The importance of multilateralism and the relevance of its broad non-utilitarian interpretations. These not only anchor it to the typical values of historically changing hegemonic power,[15] but also pave the way for its renewal: from a constructivist viewpoint, there is a need for a re-thinking of the notion of international power, given the presence of a non-military power (like the EU) which wants to be a global power in the name of its interests and values and is intersubjectively recognised as a relevant multilateral actor by many external partners.

8) The European Community and European Union understood as salient case studies and workshops for all these innovative traits. The EU is also the most advanced example of a difficult and contradictory development that has gradually led the various European states to accept shared and civilised sovereignty: the progressive limitation of the *ius ad bellum* during the 20th century, from the 'Kellog-Briand' Pact on the UN Charter to the political role of the Security Council, from the emergence of international law and increasingly binding multilateral organisations to the voluntary and progressive limitations of national sovereignty introduced by the 'Schuman Plan' (1950) and every European treaty since then, up to and including the Treaty of Nice (December 2000) and the text of the European Convention (2003).

9) Finally, comparative research on politics and institutions shows that the transformation of sovereign power involves both the Union and each member state as object and subject within a growing 'Europeanisation' process, in the sense of a civilian power. Germany, in particular, which, represents the challenging heart of the European construction, has paradoxically recovered – and at the same time limited – its international sovereignty since 1990 (see the Maastricht Treaty, 1992) and between the two Iraqi crises to the point where it has attracted criticism for its timidity (and worse). For decades, Italy has made use of the far-sighted Article 11 of its Constitution as a lever for the internal integration of European Treaties which are increasingly aimed at reinforcing supranationality. There is a clear similarity in the paths taken by Italy and Germany, the two defeated WWII-powers, at least until 2001.[16]

---

[14] S. Strange, *States and Markets*, Pinter, London 1988; id., *The Retreat of the State: The Diffusion of Power in the World Economy*, Cambridge University Press, New York, 1996.

[15] J. G. Ruggie (ed.), *Multilateralism Matters. The Theory and Praxis of an Institutional Form*, Columbia University Press, New York, 1993.

[16] This parallelism was rightly emphasised by G. E. Rusconi, *Germania, Italia, Europa. Dallo stato di potenza alla potenza civile*, Einaudi, Torino, 2003, particularly in

France has learned to reconcile its republican national identity with the political strengthening of the European Union better than in the past.[17] The Franco-German engine, the symbol of the overcoming of classic power politics, seems to now reconcile the German struggle for peace and the French attachment to republican political power better than in the past, and clearly goes beyond both respective illusions, i.e. those of 'Great Switzerland' and Gaullist *grandeur*. Finally, thanks to the stimulus provided by the inclusion of the Petersberg (peace-keeping) civilian and military tasks in the Amsterdam Treaty, states with traditions of neutrality (such as Austria and the Scandinavian countries) have proved they are not an obstacle to political union. Indeed, they are helping to mould its most innovative features. Of course, this 'Europeanisation' of national policies encounters resistance amongst those states and groups who conceive of Europe as a large market overshadowed by NATO. Today a modest conception of civilian power, subordinating the idea of Europe to that of the West, can be found in post-communist countries, amongst the Mediterranean Right and in Britain, where it is based on a deep-rooted bipartisan sovereign state culture. Despite the more markedly pro-European stances taken by the Blair government from 1997 to 2001 (Amsterdam Treaty, Saint-Malo understanding on European defence with France, early support for the "Lisbon Strategy") the constant priority given by the United Kingdom to its 'special relationship' with the US is potentially detrimental to the political role of the EU. Nevertheless, even in Britain a section of public opinion realises that greater commitment to both monetary union and the political constitution might be in the national interest. If the British government could overcome its old idea of Europe as a subset of its 'western' global policy, it would be able to increase its influence over the EU and shape its role as a world civilian power. It would be helped in this respect by its past as a great multilateral trading power at a time when Britain dominated the seas, but was weak militarily. If this does not occur, however, the most likely development will be the emergence of two concentric circles or a 'variable geometry' Europe: a common market and law area, separate from a group of core nations more committed to international political autonomy.

Chapters 10-14. See also W. Heydrich, J. Krause, U. Nerlich, J. Nötzold and R. Rummel (eds.), *Sicherheitspolitik Deutschlands: neue Konstellation, Risiken, Instrumente*, Nomos, Baden-Baden, 1992, in particular the article by H. W. Maull, "Zivilmacht: die Konzeption und ihre sicherheitspolitische Relevanz," pp. 771-886. Twenty years after Duchêne, this German perspective, although excessively anchored to a normative conception, is important because it is connected to the national development of the main European power.

[17] M. G. Cowles, J. Caporaso, and T. Risse, *Transforming Europe*, Cornell University Press, Ithaca (NY), 2001.

In brief, the development of a new theory of sovereign power as 'shared sovereignty' is interwoven with the (albeit difficult) 'Europeanisation' of large European states, which has been taking place for decades. The heart of this lies in the transformation of member states (and not just the EU itself) into civilian powers not only 'by defect', as evidence of the limited sovereignty typical of defeated countries, but also as a choice which has been renewed fifty years after the end of the war by the losers, the winners and neutral states. As regards the future, fundamental variables include the willingness of member states to take the step of equipping both themselves and the EU with those elements that can make the civilian power option credible in the 21st century: a) appropriate resources and means (including military ones) to support and implement the 'international policing' actions required by the peace policy of a credible civilian power: b) stronger common institutions and a shared strategic vision. Of course, the different conceptions of the EU's global role and the relationship between Europe and the West constitute formidable factors of uncertainty.

Thus, the EU finds itself at a crucial historical crossroads. The continuity of Europe as a peaceful civilian power is deeply rooted in history, both in terms of ideals and practices. These roots are both modern (from Humanism to the Enlightenment. In royal history, the balance achieved by the European Concert can be interpreted as multilateral, as is also obviously the case for British commercial multilateralism) and pre-modern (the concepts of open Europe and supranationality are rooted in classic Greek, Roman and Christian philosophies). From the federalism at the origins of the New Deal, up to the Marshall Plan and the 'liberal' decades, American culture and 'soft power' have also played an important role in the political revival of the values of multilateralism, shared sovereignty and the limits this implies for state sovereignty. Nevertheless, the new challenge which emerged in the 1990s centres on the relationship between this legacy, enriched by decades of European integration, and *political* Union: i.e. the constitutionalisation of the Union is occurring in a new international context that is linked to new historical events and changes: from the fall of the Berlin wall to the securisation of the global agenda, is becoming clear that the Union's (albeit important) adjustment to the challenges of global governance in the 1990s is still not sufficient. The achieved revision of realist political theory is again being challenged and, in part, this is because the normative theories on the cosmopolitan world order even if important, are not exhaustive for defining a new regional civilian power able to cope with the challenges of the 21st century.

References

Allen, D., Smith, M., "Western Europe's Presence in the Contemporary International Arena," in *Review of International Affairs*, 1990, No. 16, pp. 19-37.

Archibugi, D., Held, D., Koehler, M. (eds.), *Re-imagining Political Community. Studies in Cosmopolitan Democracy*, Polity Press, London, 1998.

Bull, H., "Civilian Power Europe: A Contradiction in Terms," in L. Tsoukalis (ed.), *The European Community, Past, Present and Future*, Blackwell, Oxford, 1983, pp. 150-70.

Carlsnaes, W., Smith, S. (ed.), *European Foreign Policy: the EC and Changing Perspectives*, Sage, London, 1994.

Cowles, M. G., Caporaso, J., Risse, Th., *Transforming Europe*, Cornell University Press, Ithaca NY, 2001.

Eliassen, K. A. (ed.), *Foreign and Security Policy in the E.U.*, Sage, London, 1998.

Fawcett, L., Hurrel, A. (ed.), *Regionalism in World Politics. Regional Organisations and International Order*, Oxford University Press, New York, 1995.

Galtung, J., *The EC: A Superpower in the Making*, Allen & Unwin, Londra, 1973.

Ginsberg, R., "Conceptualizing the European Union as an International Actor: Narrowing the theoretical Capability-Expectation Gap," *Journal of Common Market Studies*, Vol. 37, No. 3, pp. 429-54.

Gnesotto, N., *La puissance et l'Europe*, Presses de la Fondation nationale des Sciences politiques, Paris, 1998.

Habermas, J., "Why Europe Needs a Constitution," *New Left Review*, No.11, September-October 2001.

Hettne, B., "The Double Movement: Global Market versus Regionalism," in R. W. Cox (ed.), *The New Realism. Perspectives on Multilateralism and World Order*, United Nations University Press, Tokyo/New York/Paris, 1997.

Hettne, B., Inotai, A., Sunkel, O. (eds.), *Globalism and the New Regionalism*, Macmillan/St. Martin's Press, Basingstoke/New York, 1999.

Coleman, W., Underhill, G. (eds.), *Regionalism and Global Economic Integration: Europe Asia and the Americas*, Routledge, London, 1998, pp. 42-67.

Hill, C. (ed.), *The Actors in Europe's Foreign Policy*, Routledge, London/New York, 1996.

Hill, C., "Closing the Capabilities-Expectations Gap?," in J. Peterson and H. Sjursen (ed.), *A Common Foreign Policy for Europe?*, Routledge, London and New York, 1998, pp. 18-38.

Holland, M. (ed.), *Common Foreign and Security Policy. The Record and Reforms*, Pinder, London, 1997.

Keohane, R. O., "Ironies of Sovereignty: The European Union and World Order," *Journal of Common Market Studies*, Vol. 40, No. 4, 2002.

Keukeleire, S., *Het buitenlands beleid van de Europese Unie*, Kluwer, Deventer, 1998.

Kupchan, Ch., *The End of the American Era. US Foreign Policy and the Geopolitics of the XXI Century*, A. Knopf, New York, 2002

Lamy, P., Pisani, J., Ferry, L., *L'Europe de nos volontés*, Fondation Jean-Jaurès, Paris, Cahier No. 27, 2002.

Laursen, F., "The EC in the World Context: Civilian Power or Superpower," in *Futures*, September 1991, pp. 747-759.

Laursen, F. (ed.), *Comparative Regional Integration. Theoretical Perspectives*, Ashgate, Aldershot, 2003.

Manners, I., Whitman, R. G., "Towards Identifying the International Identity of the European Union: A Framework for Analysis of the EU's Network of Relations," *Journal of European Integration*, Vol. 21, pp. 231-249.

Mansfield, E. D., Milner, H. V. (eds.), *The Political Economy of Regionalism*, Columbia University Press, New York, 1997.

Mattli, W. , *The Logic of Regional Integration. Europe and Beyond*, Cambridge University Press, Cambridge, 1999.

Maull, H. W., "Die 'Zivilmacht Europa' bleibt Projekt," *Blätter für Deutsche und internationale Politik*, 12, 2002, pp. 1467-78.

Piening, C. , *Global Europe. The EU in World Affairs*, Rienner, London, 1997.

Remacle, É., Seidelmann, R., *Pan-European Security Redefined*, Nomos, Baden-Baden, 1998.

Rhodes, C., *The European Union in the World Community*, Lynne Rienner, Boulder, 1998.

Sapir, A., "The Political Economy of EC Regionalism," in *European Economic Review*, No. 42, 1998, pp. 717-32.

Seidelmann, R. (ed.), *Crises Policies in Eastern Europe*, Nomos, Baden-Baden, 1996.

Smith, K., "The End of Civilian Power Europe: A Welcome Demise or a Cause for Concern?," *International Spectator*, Vol. 35, No. 2, pp. 11-28.

Stavridis, S., *Why the Militarizing of the EU is Strengthening the Concept of Civilian Power Europe*, EUI Working papers series, Fiesole, No. 2001/17, 2001.

Telò, M. (ed.), *Europe, New Regionalism. Regional Actors and Global Governance in a Post-hegemonic Era*, Ashgate, Aldershot, 2001.

Therborn, G., *European Modernity and Beyond. The Trajectory of European Societies 1945-2000*, Sage, London, 1995.

Thurow, L., *Head to Head: the Coming Economic Battle among Japan, Europe and America*, Brealey, London, 1992.

Whitman, R. G., *From Civilian Power to Superpower? The International Identity of the European Union*, Macmillan, London, 1998.

CHAPTER 4

The New Neighbourhood Policy of the Enlarged European Union

A Sceptical Preliminary Assessment

Pál DUNAY

Stockholm International Peace Research Institute

I. Introduction

The external relations of the European Union were dominated during the last decade of the 20th and in the beginning of the 21st century by considerations related to the biggest enlargement in its history. It was somewhat less visible that during the same time period the EU became a genuine and *sui generis* actor in international politics. This subtle, lasting change makes it indispensable for the Union to take a position on developments in the world at large, including its periphery. The fact the EU is enlarging and thus getting closer to eastern and south-eastern Europe while intensifying its foreign political activity makes it necessary to pursue an active and conceptually solid policy *vis-à-vis* what we might call its 'new neighbourhood'.

The EU – beyond its global role – has a set of external relations in Europe, which looks like a multi-layer cake. It consists of the following elements:

1. The Accession States, which have already finished their accession talks and became members of the Union on 1 May 2004. This group includes eight East-Central European countries and two Mediterranean states.

2. States negotiating Accession which are involved in ongoing accession negotiations with the promise of membership in 2007. Only two countries, Bulgaria and Romania, belong to this group at the moment.

3. Membership Applicant States, which have not yet started their accession talks. Currently this group consists of two countries, Croatia and Turkey.

4. Countries which have concluded Stabilization and Association Agreements with the Union. This group includes five countries of South-eastern Europe, and includes Albania, Bosnia and Herzegovina, Croatia and Macedonia, as well as Serbia and Montenegro.[1]

5. Those countries, which have concluded Partnership and Cooperation Agreements with the EU. These are all successor states of the former Soviet Union, with the exception of Belarus,[2] Tajikistan[3] and Turkmenistan.

6. The "Wider Europe" States: The EU Commission launched the "Wider Europe" initiative in March 2003, which extends to countries of the Southern Mediterranean and the Western Newly Independent States (NIS). The former group includes Algeria, Egypt, Israel, Jordan, Lebanon, Libya, Morocco, the Palestinian Authority, Syria, Tunisia, whereas the latter includes Belarus, Moldova and Ukraine. Russia, which also belongs to the "new neighbourhood" was mentioned separately in the Commission Communication.[4]

One might feel tempted to include several other instruments in the discussion which put the countries of the Union's periphery in further categories *vis-à-vis* the EU. The various assistance programmes and the largely moribund Barcelona Process, or Euro-Mediterranean Partnership are examples of just such instruments. However, to my mind the above list, gives a fair indication of the complex relationship which the EU has developed with its periphery.

This chapter analyses the "wider Europe" concept as part of the development of EU policy towards its broader periphery. I also examine the assumptions associated with its launch and its prospects against the backdrop of scarce financial resources. I attempt to give a preliminary

---

[1] Moldova was admitted to the framework of the Stability Pact for South-eastern Europe. This opens the prospect of Moldova's eligibility to sign a Stabilisation and Association Agreement as well. For the prospects of Moldova in its association with the EU see A. Zagorski, "Policies towards Russia, Ukraine, Moldova and Belarus," in R. Dannreuther (ed.), *European Union Foreign and Security Policy: Towards a Neighbourhood Strategy*, London, Routledge, 2004, pp. 89-91.

[2] The EU Council of Ministers decided in September 1997 not to conclude a Partnership and Cooperation Agreement with Belarus.

[3] The Commission was entitled on 13 October 2003 to negotiate a Partnership and Cooperation Agreement with Tajikistan.

[4] See Communication from the Commission to the Council and the European Parliament: Wider Europe – Neighbourhood: A New Framework for Relations with Our Eastern and Southern Neighbours. Brussels, 11.3.2003 COM (2003) 104 final.

answer to the question of whether the EU can gain sufficient influence without offering the prospect of membership to countries on its periphery.

II. Preventing Exclusion without Inclusion

Western institutions since the end of the East-West conflict have pursued similar policies towards their eastern neighbourhood. First, they went through a phase of familiarisation, in order to compensate for their lack of knowledge and to get to know the smaller countries of Eastern and Central Europe and latterly, the less known successor states of the former Soviet Union. Early political dialogue with east-central Europe and the Phare programme formed part of this initiative. The next major step, partly overlapping with the first, was to establish ties of cooperation with the countries of the region to the east. These did not extend to a commitment to offer membership to the countries involved. The EU used association agreements for this purpose. A sharp divide opened up, however, as soon as the institutions or some of their members expressed their readiness to accept some of these countries as members. In the case of the EU, this happened at the Copenhagen Council in 1993 and in the case of NATO, between January and July 1994. At first, the commitment was theoretical but candidates, in some cases excessively optimistic about the success of their transformation and the prospects of membership, knew that they were the addressees of the conditions of accession in question. Supporting the transformation of Eastern and Central Europe entailed a relatively early commitment by the respective institutions to membership for the countries involved. The prospective members also passed through a phase when it was far from clear that they would advance to a point where membership would be within their reach. It can be concluded from this that it was the prospect of membership on the side of the institution and its anticipation on the side of the candidates which contributed significantly to motivating the candidate-countries to take resolute steps in carrying further their transformation.

This same pattern was followed for several countries. Some have recently gained membership while others have seen EU accession come progressively closer. It was in the interest of the EU to create and maintain a situation in which successful transformations would be rewarded by membership. The policy of the EU thus carried the ambiguous (and latterly, not so ambiguous) promise of accession. The whole idea focussed upon avoiding sharp divides between those who were in line for membership and those who were not. Sharp differences could have taken away a major factor of external motivation for transformation. Beyond the prevailing practical reasons there has been some "political correctness" about the process, to avoid discriminating against countries which were less promising candidate-members.

The EU has been gradually absorbing its periphery and will continue to do so in the coming decades. It has been a question for quite some time what to do about states, which are in the vicinity of the enlarged 25 (27[5]) members EU. This is particularly the case for those countries which are geographically close to the EU but are very far from the standards the EU has set for membership. This is the fundamental dichotomy which the EU will have to address. The concept of a wider Europe is an attempt to deal with this problem.

When the EU considered this matter for the first time, giving rise to a General Affairs Council decision of November 2002, the main aim was to "set up a framework for relations with Ukraine, Moldova and Belarus".[6] Thus the EU wanted to address its new eastern neighbours, of which two had expressed their interest in gaining membership in the EU. The inclusion of Belarus could be interpreted as a powerful message. Where the appropriate domestic political conditions prevail, the EU is prepared to offer the prospect of more intensive cooperation to Minsk as well. Russia was mentioned separately in all related documents although she also belongs to the eastern neighbourhood of the EU. This concept was extended to the southern Mediterranean upon the insistence of Italy.[7] The southern Mediterranean has been interpreted very broadly, extending to the ten countries mentioned above.

If one takes a closer look to the wider Europe initiative as announced by the Commission in March 2003, it can be concluded that there is one connecting element in the concept i.e. to make an offer to a large group of countries, which had previously no prospect of EU membership. Their situations are, of course, very different in many respects, ranging from geography to their political situation and their status *vis-à-vis* the EU. The weak consistency of the group of countries undermines the cohesion of the document, however. Hence, the only way to legitimise a document, which brings so many different actors under the same roof, is to regard it as a lasting framework for cooperation. It requires that specific documents provide for the details of each bilateral (EU – partner country) relationship. There are such documents in existence in most cases (the exceptions being Belarus and Libya). As the framework

---

[5] The accession of Bulgaria and Romania expected by 2007-8 will increase the number of EU members to 27.

[6] A. Ortega, "A New EU Policy on the Mediterranean," in J. Batt *et al.*, *Partners and neighbours: A CFSP for a Wider Europe*, Chaillot Papers No. 64, Paris, Institute for Security Studies, September 2003, p. 89.

[7] H. Timmermann, "Die EU und die 'Neuen Nachbarn' Ukraine und Belarus," *Stiftung Wissenschaft und Politik – Studie*, Berlin, SWP, October 2003, p. 7.

document contains such a broad array of measures, it is necessary to identify those primarily applicable to each relationship. The Commission document put forward the idea of an "Action Plan" to be agreed upon for this purpose.[8]

It is worth taking a look at the level of consistency of the Commission document at this juncture. *Geographically* there are countries which are separated from the 25 members of the EU by sea whereas others are on the same continent. The countries of the southern Mediterranean belong to the former category, whereas those of Eastern Europe belong to the latter. The geographical position of the Eastern European is far from identical, however. Belarus and Ukraine are "new neighbours" in the sense that they have become neighbours of the EU due to the 1 May 2004 enlargement. Russia is not a new neighbour at all as it has a border of more than twelve hundred kilometres with Finland, a country, which has been an EU member since 1995. After 2004, the only difference is that Russia now shares borders with four more EU member countries: Estonia, Latvia, Lithuania and Poland. Moldova was not a neighbour of any member state in the past and will not be in the future, as long as Romania is outside the Union.

The political course of the countries in this group is as varied as their geography although they have one common element: none of them is a full-fledged democracy. Israel may be regarded an exception. The extent of non-democratic, or in some cases, dictatorial tendencies, varies, however. Hence, differentiation is possible but not particularly easy. Many eastern European countries have been going through economic difficulties. Russia has been exempt from this lately due to its rich natural resource base while Belarus has been economically insulated by its umbilical cord relationship with Moscow.

There is no consistency as regards the prospect of the relationship between the individual countries and the EU. The countries of the southern Mediterranean are not entitled to membership according to the EU legal regulation in force. Article 49 of the Amsterdam Treaty on European Union stipulated that any "European State which respects the principles set out in Article F (1) may apply to become a member of the European Union".[9] The draft Constitutional Treaty released by the European Convention stipulates that the "Union shall be open to all European States which respect the values referred to in Article 2, and are committed to promoting them together".[10] One entity of the southern

---

[8] See Communication...: Wider Europe – Neighbourhood, pp. 17-18.

[9] *Ibid.*, p. 3.

[10] Draft Constitutional Treaty as released by the European Convention. Art. I-57, Conditions of eligibility and procedure for accession to the Union.

Mediterranean, the Palestinian Authority has no statehood and bearing in mind the turbulence in the region, it is uncertain when or whether it will become a state. Unless conditions are revised, there is thus a severe constraint on the future relationship with the southern Mediterranean. In the case of the countries of the western NIS the potential for future EU membership exists, as those countries are undoubtedly European, is present, but such a prospect is undeniably distant. There is an important distinction to be seen between Moldova and Ukraine, which have indicated their interest in gaining membership, and Belarus and Russia, which have not.

Beyond the differences between those countries which form part of "wider Europe" the concept gives the impression of another element of inconsistency, i.e. there are two sub-regions of Europe, which are apparently missing from the concept. The first one is the Balkans. It has been excluded from the concept as the EU has declared that the region carries the prospect of membership. This is certainly correct, in the sense that the EU has made unspecific promises to grant membership to these countries at some future point. Slovenia has already joined. Croatia is an applicant country, although accession talks have not yet begun. Other successor states of the former Yugoslavia and Albania are further removed from the prospect of membership. Most of them are neighbours of old or new EU member states. As their membership prospects are uncertain and no timetable commitment has been given, there would have been some sense to treating them similarly to countries of the western CIS. This need not necessarily have been interpreted as a step back in their progression towards EU membership. At the other end of neighbourhood policy Caucasus countries are also absent. Although they are not contiguous with any EU member country neither is Moldova. There is only one difference between the situation of Moldova on the one hand and Armenia and Georgia on the other. That is that the former is neighbour of a negotiating candidate (Romania) whereas the other two are neighbours of a non-negotiating candidate (Turkey). Neither can the states of the Caucasus be separated from the western NIS on the basis of the level of their economic development.

In brief, there is reason to conclude that the wider Europe concept lacks elementary consistency. It can be regarded as a political message to those countries with which the Union is willing to engage, without knowing what such an engagement might entail in the long run. It seems clear that the main guiding principle of the concept is to engage without conceding either the prospect, or the promise of EU membership. It is a structure under which bilateral EU – partner relations may, or may not flourish.

III. Influence without the Prospect of Membership

The European Union has been a highly successful actor and a factor of political influence in the era of the post-communist transition of East-central Europe. Although I think that a good part of the transition would have taken place anyway due to the desire of people of the region to change their fate, it is certain that western institutions, most notably the EU, have contributed to the process. The activity of the EU has represented an interesting combination. The EU combined the role of a vehicle for change with providing an end-goal – membership. It was a vehicle for change as it fostered transformation, all of which made membership eventually possible. It is, however, open to question what the role of the EU might be where the two factors of influence i.e. conditionality in the process of transition and the provider of the end result (membership), are separated. This may present a major challenge to the Union.

> The difficulty lies in the fact that the most effective regional policy tool at the disposal of the Union to this end has been conditionality, and conditionality really works only when eventual membership is at stake. When it is not, it proves a much weaker instrument, as the experience of the past decade has shown...[11]

It is generally accepted that the not too distant prospect of membership played a decisive role in East-central Europe. External assessments are not always free of exaggeration, however. As the President of the Commission put it:

> By holding up the goal of membership we enabled these governments to implement the necessary reforms. Only this prospect sustained the reformers in their efforts to overcome nationalist and other resistance and fears of change and modernisation.[12]

It would be better to take a somewhat agnostic view and conclude that it is not known what the relative importance of the various contributing factors was in the transformation process. It is certain that internal and external factors were at work.

If it is the prevailing view that the chance to attain the goal of membership was essential in gaining influence in the transition countries'

---

[11] A. Missiroli, "The EU and Its Changing Neighbourhoods: Stabilisation, Integration and Partnership," in J. Batt *et al., op. cit.*, p. 21. Similarly cf. J. Batt, *The EU's New Borderland*, Centre for European Reform Working Paper, London, October 2003, p. 2.

[12] R. Prodi, "A Wider Europe – A Proximity Policy as the Key to Stability," Brussels, 5-6 December 2002, p. 2. http://europa.eu.int/rapid/start/cgi/guesten.ksh?p_ action. gettxt=gt&doc=SPEECH/02/61...

political and economic transformation, then it may be illusory to assume that a programme, which specifically excludes the prospect of membership can induce a similarly smooth process. Furthermore, membership has become an increasingly difficult goal to achieve as a result of the internal development of the EU. Countries which joined in the 1980s which were less developed than the EC, acceded before the advent of the single market programme and monetary union. "So they were joining a much less integrated and smaller EU market than the new applicants".[13] If one starts out from the assumption that the EU will continue to deepen, its development will not be halted due to internal disagreements and that the current big enlargement will not present insurmountable difficulties to it, then accession will be even more demanding than it is at present.

The "wider Europe" concept is burdened by the fact that it focuses on the process of approximation without membership. It is doubtful whether it could be successful without it. It would represent a different approach, however if a "proximity policy" *"[did] not start with the promise of membership and it [did] not exclude eventual membership. This would do away with the problem of having to say 'yes' or 'no' a country applying for membership at too early a stage."*[14] This approach would open a new avenue and oppose those who see the concept as literally excluding membership. It would mean that proximity policy would become an EU delaying tactic, employed to avoid getting into the enlargement/accession trap again.

IV. Moving Towards a Positive Agenda

It can be argued that the European Union and its member states have to a large extent a negative agenda towards the Southern Mediterranean and the Western CIS. In both cases priority was given to prevent the spill-over of certain sources of instability. In the case of the former these have been illegal migrants and terrorists, whereas in case of the latter they have been migrants and organised criminals. This was complemented by the desire not to export instability in any form from the territory of these countries to the EU. Last but not least, it is the expectation of the EU that the flow of rich natural resources, which are concentrated in some countries of the two regions, will be uninterrupted.[15]

---

[13] H. Grabbe, *Profiting from EU Enlargement.* Centre for European Reform, London, 2001, p. 32.

[14] R. Prodi, "A Wider Europe – A Proximity Policy as the Key to Stability," *op. cit.,* p. 4 (emphasis in the original).

[15] There may be some who are of the view that this presentation is biased and simplistic and it does not give credit to the contribution of the EU. It is suffice to mention the

The operative question is whether the "wider Europe" concept will move away from this and complement it by a substantive positive agenda. It is of course difficult even to attempt to give a final answer to this question before the bilateral accords between the EU and individual countries of the two regions come about. Mutual interest and flexibility in the negotiating the bilateral accords will decide whether they will enrich the programme.

A. Borders

The "wider Europe" concept is based on geographic proximity and, in some cases, contiguity. The issue of borders appears among the considerations of the European Union in several respects. One of them is the question of whether the EU should not address the issue of its borders in general terms. The President of the European Commission, Romano Prodi has raised the issue:

> We need a debate *in Europe* to decide where the limits of Europe lie and prevent these limits being determined by others. We also have to admit that currently we could not convince our citizens of the need to extend the EU's borders still further to the east.[16] (my emphasis)

It would require thorough consideration before such a public debate could be initiated. In particular, if Europe discusses the matter of the borders of a future Europe and decides where to "draw the line," it is effectively erecting a new wall. If we accept that ambiguity regarding the possible future accession of a country to the EU provides Europe with certain leverage, then the conclusion of such a debate would deprive the EU of a desirable political influence. If such a debate must remain inconclusive, then we are entitled to wonder why it had to be conducted in the first place. If the discussion is, in fact, about setting the right priorities, then the question takes on a very different meaning. Hence, which country/group of countries carries better prospect of membership and should be made eligible for more support/assistance from the Communities in order to make it better prepared for member-ship in due course? This would make the debate sensible. Not to men-tion that which ever way the debate goes, it has to be taken into account

---

so-called Barcelona process or the Tacis programme. Neither of them found satisfactory by the regions themselves. It is apparent that the EU offers many things to the southern Mediterranean but it stops short of liberalising free movement of persons further. Free trade will stop short of extending to agricultural produce that would really help some North African countries. In some the support does not offer anything that could be regarded real sacrifice by the EU. Tacis, the main assistance programme to the CIS is run on very limited resources, understandably.

[16] R. Prodi, "A Wider Europe – A Proximity Policy as the Key to Stability," *op. cit.*, p. 3 (emphasis in the original).

that the political reality may change rapidly and the conclusions drawn at one time may be subject to revision not long after. Moreover, declaring that the "boat is full" may result in similarly undesirable consequences. If "Europe" comes to the conclusion that it is not in a position to enlarge for a long period to come, the political elites of aspirant countries may not feel motivated to move in the direction that the EU would prefer.

Innovative thinking will have to extend to this matter in order for the modern concept of borders as separating lines to be revised for this purpose.[17] The fact that borders are heavily affected by current challenges to border regimes must be taken into account. On the one hand, at a time when challenges and threats are often associated with trans-border criminality, terrorism and illegal migration rather than with the potential of traditional military conflicts, the climate may not be favourable to see borders as connecting areas. On the other hand, however, there is reason to assume that the alignment of border management by the new member states of the European Union, in order to become part of the Schengen regime in 2007, will improve their border management capacity, notwithstanding the somewhat worryingly high levels of corrupt practices.[18]

Borders can connect people and separate them. This is the case, in particular, between the EU and three states of the western NIS. The fifteen-member European Union, on the basis of a coordinated policy maintained a normal regime for the free movement of persons between the countries mentioned in the "wider Europe" concept and the Union. Travel was based on the possession of a valid passport and visa.[19] The problem stemmed from the fact that the East-central European accession states benefited from visa-free travel with countries of the western NIS throughout the 1990s. They had to give this up when they aligned their visa regime before EU accession. This has created some problems in their business interests and people-to-people relations with these (NIS) countries. In the end, many countries were ready to accept an asymmet-

---

[17] J. Zielonka, "Introduction: Boundary Making by the European Union," in *idem* (ed.), *Europe Unbound: Enlarging and Reshaping the Boundaries of the European Union*, London and New York, Routledge, 2002, p. 11.

[18] It is recognised in Russia, for instance, that the Finnish-Russian border "is the most secure and best organised border of Russia" in spite of the sharpest contrast between the living conditions on the two sides of the border". For this see Körber Stiftung (ed.), *Russlands europäische Dimension*, Hamburg, Bergedorfer Gesprächskreis, 2003, p. 81, cited by H. Timmermann, "Die EU und die 'Neuen Nachbarn' Ukraine und Belarus," *op. cit.*, p. 9.

[19] Israelis benefit from exceptional visa-free treatment for up to ninety days under the Schengen agreement.

rical solution. To take one example, the accession countries provide Ukrainian citizens with visas free of charge, while Ukraine does not demand a visa from the citizens of countries like Hungary, Poland[20] and Slovakia. In this case, in accordance with the EU *acquis* these accession countries will have to charge visa fees; later it may hinder humanitarian relations with countries further to the East and eliminate the reasonable compromise that has currently been achieved. There are pressing reasons for maintaining the currently established visa regime between the easternmost former Communist members of the EU and the western NIS. A balance has to be struck and maintained between the security and economic interests of the EU as well as its member states and interests in maintaining humanitarian contacts.

Furthermore, if the citizens of wider Europe find that they get no other exposure to the EU "than just by the fact of queuing for a visa,"[21] this may, of itself, create problems in the future.

B. Regional Cooperation

The EU has made efforts to maintain and possibly, extend regional cooperation between border regions encompassing old and new member states. The EU has foreseen the allocation of € 195 million for this purpose in the period of 2001-2006.[22] Less attention has been devoted to cross-border relations between accession countries/new member states and countries involved in the "wider Europe" concept. The Commission has drawn the conclusion that "regional economic cooperation among the WNIS is already quite strong, oriented around traditional flows of trade and investment to and from Russia".[23] Even though the underlying argument is correct, the position outlined in the documents of the Commission gives us some indication of the prospects for the future. Namely, it will be comparatively easy to assemble forces around spending on regional cooperation between "old" and "new" members of the Union (e.g. Austria and the Czech Republic or Slovakia, Germany and Poland, Italy and Slovenia). It will be somewhat more difficult to con-

---

[20] This model was first introduced between Poland and Ukraine. "[T]he Polish government, agreed that Ukraine will not introduce visas for Polish nationals as of 1 July 2003 while Poland will waive fees for visas issued to Ukrainian nationals... "Address by Mr Aleksander Kwasniewski, President of the Republic of Poland," in *European Union Enlargement and Neighbourhood Policy*, Warsaw, Stefan Batory Foundation, 2003, p. 12.

[21] Comment by H. Grabbe, in *European Union Enlargement and Neighbourhood Policy, op. cit.*, p. 59.

[22] For this see Communication on the Impact of Enlargement on Regions Bordering Candidate Countries: Community Action for Border Regions, p. 4.

[23] Communication...: Wider Europe – Neighbourhood, p. 8.

vince the EU to spend more on trans-boundary cooperation between "new" members and countries of the western CIS, partners in the "wider Europe" concept (e.g. Poland and Belarus, Hungary and Ukraine). It may be practically impossible to generate support and financial assistance in order to allow the countries of the wider Europe to cooperate more intensively amongst themselves. Fostering regional cooperation will depend significantly upon the resources allocated to concrete projects. This is where growing doubts may surface, as decisions will be taken at forums where only the member states will be present. They will give preference to their perceived self-interest.

C. Addressing Poverty

Each of the fourteen countries included in the "wider Europe" concept is poorer in *per capita* GDP terms than any of the fifteen member states of the EU. Israel is the only exception in this respect (see chart hereafter).

Chart 1. GDP *per capita* in % of EU

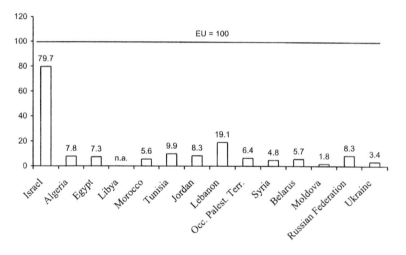

Source: WDI 2002, Worldbank, Commission staff calculation (mentioned in Communication from the Commission to the Council and the European Parliament: Wider Europe – Neighbourhood: A New Framework for Relations with our Eastern and Southern Neighbours, Brussels, 11.3.2003 COM (2003) 104 final, Chart 1, p. 19).

Hence, it is a prominent issue for the two regions, the southern Mediterranean and the western NIS to address poverty and provide for economic vitality. This is the precondition of success of the entire concept. The concept puts forward a set of ideas under the title "A new vision and a new offer".[24] It represents an interesting mix of measures, although most of these aim to boost the macro-economy of the countries concerned. The extension of the internal market and regulatory structures, preferential trading relations and market opening, transport integration, energy and telecommunication networks, promotion and protection of investment, enhanced assistance and new sources of finance are all examples that could be cited in this category. Some other measures provide for the broad political conditions of economic development, like lawful migration and movement of persons, cooperation to prevent and combat common security threats. They involve the EU in conflict prevention and crisis management as well as the promotion of human rights, further cultural cooperation and the enhancement of mutual understanding. This can be summarised as follows: The instruments contain so-called programmatic norms of a fairly general character. They are not sufficiently specific and in some cases simply summarise initiatives presented in other EU documents. Some of the ideas are more advantageous to the EU than to the countries of "wider Europe". Some others would be in the best interests of the population of the Mediterranean and western NIS partners but would be contrary to their powers-that-be. As the idea is to introduce a progressive and benchmarked approach, the situation will be just as asymmetrical as are the power relations between the EU and most of its partners. Again, bearing in mind the general level of future commitments involved, it is extremely difficult to anticipate the real value the set of ideas outlined here will represent.

D. Wider Europe and the EU Budget Crunch

It is clear from the above elements that the Union put forward a framework which addresses some of its genuine concerns. The aim to foster stability in two regions adjacent to the enlarged EU may be in the common interest of both parties. One may have doubts, however when studying the broader ramifications of the concept. These concerns increase further when one considers some of the workings of the newly elaborated plan. The EU will soon draft, and hopefully, agree upon its new financial perspective for the period between 2007 and 2013. This will be the first time that the ten new members will be sitting around the table as equals discussing this matter and it is probably the last time that decisions will have to be taken by consensus on the matter. If one analyses the interests of some major players in the current budget debate, the following conclusion can be drawn: some of the major contributors of the EU budget indicated early on that they intend to

---

[24] Communication...: Wider Europe – Neighbourhood, pp. 9-15.

reduce their contribution in relation to their GDP. More precisely put, the contribution should be reduced to one percent of the total combined GDP of the twenty-five member states (in addition to other budgetary sources). However, the proposal of the Commission is more generous[25] than that of the largest contributors. There is also reason to believe that these are starting positions, rather than the last word on this subject. It is safe to assume that there will not be a major net increase in the budget for the period of the next financial perspective between 2007 and 2013. Some older net beneficiary member states of the EU budget, for their part, do not want to lose the funds that were regularly available to them in the recent past. The new members that joined in 2004 are significantly poorer in *per capita* GDP terms than the EU average. Moreover, the contribution of the ten new member states to the total GDP of the EU is less than five percent while they add approximately twenty percent to the population of the EU. They will be eligible to receive funds as agreed upon during the accession process. Many of the new members have made statements that they find it unacceptable to become net contributors of the EU budget any time soon.[26]

The conclusion that can be drawn from these considerations is that significantly larger budget resources will not be available in the years to come. Bargaining will get tougher than ever. Bearing in mind the consensus rule that had been maintained, on the insistence of Spain, for agreeing upon the financial perspective coupled with the reluctance of the net contributors to pay more, it will be difficult to reach a mutually acceptable agreement. Consensus rule will nearly inescapably lead to the member states being in an extremely strong position to effectively represent their particular interests. This does not fully exclude the possibility that a significant amount of money might be allocated to contribute to the development of countries which are not members of the EU. We must also consider the issue of the setting of priorities when resources are allocated to the EU's external activities. From established practice, one can conclude that priority will be given to those countries and regions, which carry the prospect of membership. This is entirely

---

[25] For this see Commission of the European Communities: Communication from the Commission to the Council and the European Parliament – Building our common Future. Policy Challenges and Budgetary Means of the Enlarged Union 2007-2013, Brussels, 10.02.2004, COM(2004)101, p. 29.

[26] Some of them may actually become net budget-contributors involuntarily. Most importantly, those that do not develop their absorption capacity to attract structural funds and funds under the common agricultural policy fast enough may end up as net recipients soon. Following the 2007 (2008) enlargement of the EU when the average *per capita* GDP of the Union will drop again, countries like the Republic of Cyprus (in case the island is not reunited with the much poorer north) and Slovenia may come close to become net contributors.

understandable. The less developed these countries are upon accession, the more EU resources they will absorb later. Bulgaria and Romania have already been given promises that their preparation will be adequately financed. The EU is also committed to help raise the level of development of countries which may gain membership in the medium-run, such as countries of the Western Balkans. Other external activities may well find themselves consigned to a place further down the list of priorities. The states of "wider Europe" will definitely fall into this category. If one takes a closer look to the political pressure some of the new members have already exerted, even before their accession to the EU, it is also clear that Ukraine and possibly the Russian Federation will have a better chance of preferential treatment from the Union than some other states. This is not only because new members, like Poland, will give preference to the "eastern" versus the "southern" dimension in the wider Europe concept. More importantly, as the largest contributor to the EU budget, Germany continues to share this view. It is open to question whether countries, which have traditionally given preference to the south, like France, Spain and Italy will succeed in compensating for the pressure of the central European continental powers. Therefore, in my opinion, the wider Europe concept will have to be implemented with limited financial resources in the years to come.

V. Conclusion: The Hotchpotch of Ideas

The wider Europe concept is a set of ideas, which may give the impression to the countries of the two regions that they have not been forgotten by an enlarging Europe. On the contrary, they will receive increased attention. Hence it serves an easily understood political purpose in that it demonstrates the engagement of the "Europe of 25" with its adjacent regions. The prospect of membership was an important, if not indispensable, element of the influence of the EU in the successful transformation of east-central Europe. It is thus doubtful whether the concept of a wider Europe can bring EU influence to bear on its two neighbouring regions without offering the prospect of membership. In light of the document of the Commission launching the initiative, it may be premature to draw definitive (or near-definitive) conclusions. The bilateral accords foreseen by the concept may result in healthy differentiation, and may bring some success in certain limited directions.

It must be noted, however, that the shortcomings of the concept are not the only factor in deciding the success (or otherwise) of the policy. It is also due to the fact that none of the countries involved in the process is democratic, with the exception of Israel.[27] Hence the political establishment of thirteen of the fourteen countries mentioned in the concept may not be interested in going beyond a certain point in the process of implementation. Some of those so-called illiberal democracies, ranging from Algeria to Ukraine, authoritarian regimes like Russia, and dictatorships, like Belarus, will not risk their "internal stability" in order to please European democracies for marginal advantages. Wider Europe will have better chance in succeeding in those cases where some major changes take place inside the countries. The EU can foster some liberalisation and democratisation. Democracy cannot be brought about by external forces alone.

The EU has taken so much responsibility with the current and upcoming enlargements, as well as with taking responsibility for the development of some protectorates, such as Bosnia and Herzegovina, that it would be a great surprise if it had sufficient energy left to address effectively the problems of countries which do not carry the prospect of membership in the immediate future. Neither will financial means be sufficient.

It is for these reasons that "wider Europe" is a demonstration of goodwill and political attention, a piece of declaratory policy and not more.

---

[27] Israel's relationship with many EU member states is on the other hand deeply troubled due to the allegation of Tel Aviv that the EU has a pro-Palestinian bias in the Israeli-Palestinian conflict.

CHAPTER 5

The Impact of EU Policy
on Its New Neighbours

The Case
of the Republic of Moldova

Shigeo MUTSUSHIKA

*Professor, The Graduate School of International Relations,
University of Shizuoka Prefecture*

EU enlargement has brought about three phenomena. Firstly, it has produced, together with NATO conditionality, conditionality effects which have kept Central and Eastern Europe relatively stable in comparison with their inter-war situations. Secondly, it made reform of the EU's internal structure inevitable, and the EU has moved towards the adoption of an EU Constitution. Thirdly, it has caused a great geopolitical transformation. Owing to the fifth EU enlargement, the Union's membership will increase to 25 states from the current 15, making the EU an economic, social and political entity with a population of more than 450 million and a GDP of almost € 10,000 billion. As a result of this expansion, it will have common borders with WNIS (Western New Independent States) in addition to the current Mediterranean states. It will face new neighbours with a total population of 385 million.

As far as this third result of EU enlargement – the "Wider Europe" – is concerned, the European Commission in Brussels in October 2002 adopted the Council conclusions on the "New Neighbours Initiative,"[1] and in March 2003 adopted a Communication setting out a new framework for relations over the coming decade with these new neighbours.[2] In these documents the EU made clear its position of seeking to develop

---

[1] New Neighbours Initiative – Council conclusions (doc. 14078/02).

[2] Communication from the Commission to the Council and the European Parliament, Wider Europe – Neighbourhood: A New Framework for Relations with our Eastern and Southern Neighbours, COM(2003)104 final, Brussels, 11.3.2003.

a "ring of friends" with these states because there is a serious security concern, from the EU point of view, concerning its new neighbours. As a recent document on EU security policy states frankly: "Neighbours who are engaged in violent conflict, weak states where organised crime flourishes, dysfunctional societies or exploding population growth on its borders all pose problems for Europe."[3] Therefore, in order to assure its security, the documents stipulates as basic EU policy the desire to conclude an "Action Plan" with its new neighbours which includes political and economic benchmarks, and to offer economic benefits differentially to these new neighbours according to their implementation of the benchmarks. This carrot-and-stick method brings to mind the EU conditionality policy, which has been applied to the Central and East European candidates for EU accession, and which has brought fruitful results. However, there is a sharp contrast between EU policy towards the Central and East European states and that towards its new neighbours. Accession to the EU of these new neighbours is not ex-pected at this time, although the EU has promoted relations with the former Yugoslav states through the stabilisation and association process on the premise of their future accession to the EU.

Here the first question that arises is whether the benchmarks stipu-lated in the Action Plan will produce effective results in the new neighbours in the way EU conditionality has done in the Central and East European states, given that the accession of these states to the EU is not guaranteed. If the benchmarks prove ineffective, the EU will hold common borders with fragile and unstable states, and its security de-mands will not be satisfied. This is the first point to be noted about EU policy towards its new neighbours.

The second point to be emphasised is the growing possibility of a clash between the EU's "New Neighbours" policy[4] and Russia's "Near Abroad" policy towards WNIS. On the one hand, the EU has decided to intensify cooperation with its new neighbours to prevent and combat common security threats and to increase its political involvement in conflict prevention and crisis management in the area. On the other hand, both the Russian Empire and latterly, the Soviet Union made efforts to dominate or to strengthen its influence over its borderlands – Central Asia, the Caucasus, the Balkans, Eastern Europe, and the Baltic region – and since the dismemberment of the USSR, Russia has paid special attention to the former republics of the USSR, calling them "Near Abroad". The EU asserts its willingness to resolve conflicts in the

---

[3] A Secure Europe in a Better World: European Security Strategy, Brussels, 12 De-cember 2003.

[4] The New Neighbours policy was renamed the European Neighbourhood Policy (ENP) after the EU enlargement of May 2004.

new neighbours in cooperation with Russia. But how will Russia react to the increasing interest of the EU in the zone traditionally viewed as being within Russia's sphere of influence? If Russia insists on its 'special interests' in its "Near Abroad," will the EU show understanding and give priority to good relations with Russia, thus sacrificing its influence over conflict resolution and stability in new neighbours? Or will the EU still pursue its security interests in its new neighbours, sacrificing its good relations with Russia?

In this article, we shall think about these two points while examining the concrete case of the Republic of Moldova. We will pay more attention to the second issue because the "Action Plan" is at the time of writing still under discussion.[5] It would therefore be premature to attempt detailed analysis of the first issue at this time.

I. The EU's New Neighbour Policy and Its Action Plan

A. *The Principles and Concepts of the EU in Relation to Its New Neighbours*

The European Council in Brussels (24-25 October 2002) adopted the Council conclusions on the "New Neighbours Initiative" and adopted some general principles for promoting relations with new neighbour states.[6] It confirmed its intention to take forward relations with them based on shared political and economic values. The Presidency conclusions of the Copenhagen European Council (12-13 December 2002)[7] reconfirmed that the Union should remain determined to avoid new dividing lines in Europe, and the European Commission on 11 March 2003 adopted a Communication setting out a new framework for relations with Russia, the WNIS and the southern Mediterranean states that do not currently have a prospect of membership, but which will soon find themselves sharing a border with the Union.[8]

The core of the document consists, in a word, of a carrot-and-stick policy composed of both the conditionality to be imposed on the new neighbour states, and the economic benefits that will be available to them. The economic benefits will be offered to them differentially according to the level of accomplishment that they attain in relation to the conditionalities. The "Communication" suggests that, in return for

---

[5]   The Proposed EU/Moldova Action Plan was published on 9 December 2004.

[6]   New Neighbours Initiative, quoted.

[7]   Presidency Conclusions, Copenhagen European Council, 12 and 13 December 2002, SN 400/02.

[8]   Communication, quoted.

concrete progress, demonstrating shared values and effective implementation of political, economic and institutional reforms, all the neighbouring countries should be offered the prospect of a stake in the EU's internal market. It states that this kind of incentive should be accompanied by further integration and liberalisation to promote the free movement of persons, goods, services and capital (the four freedoms). It goes on to say that, moreover, further measures to enhance integration and liberalisation should be implemented gradually and progressively, responding to positive action on the part of the neighbouring countries. These measures include the extension of the internal market and regulatory structures; preferential trading relations and opening of the market; perspectives for the lawful migration and movement of persons; intensified cooperation to prevent and combat common security threats; greater EU political involvement in conflict prevention and crisis management; greater efforts to promote human rights; further cultural cooperation and enhanced mutual understanding; integration of transport, energy and telecommunications networks and the European research area; new instruments for investment promotion and protection; support for integration into the global trading system; enhanced assistance, better tailored to their needs; and new sources of finance.[9]

In order to realise these policies, definitive policy will be adopted *via* Action Plans developed by the Commission in partnership with the neighbouring countries. Action Plans will be established by the Council, based on proposals from the Commission, and wherever possible with prior discussion with the partner countries concerned. Once agreed in this way, the Communication suggests, these Action Plans could supersede common strategies and thus become the Union's main policy document for relations with its neighbouring countries over the medium term. Action Plans will include political and economic benchmarks by which to judge progress, and depending on the extent of progress made, new concessions will (or will not) be offered. This is the essence of the differentiated policy-making approach of the EU. Benchmarks will be used to offer greater predictability and certainty for the partner countries than traditional 'conditionality', and key benchmarks should include the ratification and implementation of international commitments which demonstrate respect for shared values, in particular the values codified in the UN Human Rights Declaration, and the OSCE and Council of Europe standards.

When it comes to reflecting integration and liberalisation in contractual relations, the Communication also opens the prospect of new Neighbourhood Agreements, supplementing, where needed, the existing

---

[9] Communication, quoted.

Partnership and Cooperation Agreements and Association Agreements. The Communication emphasises, however, that when it comes to the institutional and contractual arrangements of the Association Agreements and Partnership and Cooperation Agreements, the full implementation and exploitation of the provisions contained in the existing Agreements remains a necessary precondition for any new development. Thereafter, the EU will examine the scope for new Neighbourhood Agreements to build on existing contractual relations. In addition, the EU states that its new neighbourhood policy should not override the existing framework for EU relations with Russia, the countries of the WNIS, and the Southern Mediterranean, but rather, it should supplement and build on existing policies and arrangements.[10]

B. The EU/Moldova Action Plan

The EU organised a task force composed of both the European Committee of Enlargement and the General External Relations Department in order to prepare the Action Plan, while Moldova created the Reintegration Department in its Ministry of Foreign Affairs to deal with these arrangements. The first consultative meeting on the Action Plan was held when Mr Huge Mingarele visited Chisinau on 29 January 29 2004, and a second meeting was held in Brussels on 24 February 2004, when Prime Minister Vasile Tarlev visited the city for the sixth meeting of the Cooperation Council between the European Union and the Republic of Moldova. The schedule for the Action Plan will be discussed once more in the third consultation, after which the drafting stage will be completed at the beginning of May 2004, and then the Action Plan, together with the Strategic paper and Country report, will be adopted in the European Council in June 2004.[11]

According to Moldovan officials, this consultation includes almost every aspect of the political, economic, social and security fields, and these have been discussed in three groups. Although specific details of its contents have not yet been made public, one of the main points for consultation is the issue of the terms of the Action Plan. Moldova asserts that the time-frame of the implementation of the Action Plan is not more than two years, as Moldova is likely to have a common border with the EU as a result of the expected Romanian accession in 2007. In addition, as the Partnership and Cooperation Agreement with the EU will expire in 2008, Moldova argues that this agreement should not be

---

[10]   Communication, quoted.

[11]   Interview with Mr Gerhard Lohan, Head of Unit, Russia, Ukraine, Moldova, Belarus, External Relations DG, European Commission in March 2004. The Action Plan was not, in fact, adopted in June 2004.

extended, but should be changed. Moldova maintains its intention to accomplish accession to the EU through the Balkan route, that is to say, through the Balkan Stability and Association process – rather than through the WNIS route, and ultimately wishes to conclude an association agreement with the EU. As the foundation of this policy, Moldova emphasises that it has been a member of the Stability Pact since June 2000, and that it is both a European state and a small Balkan state, in contrast to the three large Slavic states – Russia, Ukraine and Belarus. However, the EU has rejected this demand by Moldova for predictable reasons: the Union seems to have its hands full already dealing with its ten new member states; it may also fear a proliferation of expectations for accession to the EU from its other new neighbours if the possibility of accession of Moldova were to be recognised as an exceptional case. Last, but not least, the EU appears concerned that the Moldovan state is in need of reform on several fronts.

To sketch the background to this Moldovan policy, the parliament of Moldova adopted a resolution stating that its accession to the EU was the supreme objective of the state. This occurred despite President Vladimir Voronin's public commitment, made during the 2002 election campaign, to strengthen the state's ties with Russia, and to participate in the Russia-Belarus confederation. In this election the Communist Party won 71 of 101 seats in parliament, as well as the post of President. Despite this backdrop, the Moldovan government decided to pursue stronger relations with the EU. This transformation in fundamental foreign policy by the Communist Party comes from the fact that Russia is no longer the Soviet Union, which gave economic support to its COMECON members in exchange for their political loyalty. Russia has become a rational player, which pursues its economic, as well as political and military interests like most other states. This Russian reality caused the Moldovan communist leadership to follow approximately the same line as its predecessors, former Presidents Mircea Snegur and Petru Lucinschi, maintaining good relations with the Western countries, as well as Russia.

The increased interest of the Moldovan people in accession to the EU also contributed to the change of mind of the Communist Party. The prospect of Romania's accession to the EU has strengthened this tendency. Immediately after the European Council decided to open accession negotiations with Romania in December 1999, people demanding dual citizenship with Romania stood in long lines in front of the Romanian consulate in Chisinau. They evidently feared that a "Wall of Prut" would be built along the River Prut which divides the two countries, imposing restrictions on the movement of Moldovans across the border with Romania. Indeed, Moldovan citizens are obliged to carry their passports with them when crossing the Romanian border, where previously they could cross with only an identity card. This appears to have led to the following results in an opinion poll in Moldova in April 2003: 61 percent of respondents would vote for accession to the EU in a referendum, if one could be organised.[12]

Therefore, in relation to the question which was raised in the introduction to this chapter, we can say that the preconditions for the effects of conditionality (the benchmarks stipulated in the Action Plan) have been having their effect in Moldova as well. The greater the extent of economic benefits from collaboration with the EU can be felt in Moldova, the more Moldovans will come to expect EU accession, and the more the conditionality effects of the EU will be felt. The more benefits the new members of the EU since May 2004 – as well as Romania and Bulgaria, now in the process of preparing for accession – enjoy, the more Moldovans will expect of membership of the EU, and, as a consequence, the more the effects of conditionality will be increased. The problem is whether the leadership in Moldova is receptive to the demands of the people, and whether it has the will to meet the benchmarks at all costs in order to take on board these demands to become a member of the EU.

II. The EU's Active Involvement in Conflict Prevention and Crisis Management in Its New Neighbours and the Transnistrian Issue

A. Why Has the Transnistrian Issue Not Been Resolved, in Contrast to the Ethnic Problems in Estonia and Latvia?

At the beginning of March 1992, a large scale armed conflict broke out between the Moldovan army and Transnistrian armed forces, with the participation of the Russian 14th army which was stationed in the area and of Cossacks, coming through Ukrainian territory. A cease-fire agreement was signed by Russian President Boris Yeltsin and Moldovan President Mircea Snegur in July 1992.[13] However, the Russian army, including its Peace Keeping Force (PKF), has been stationed in Transnistria since then. In addition, a consensus has not been reached over the legal status of Transnistria, and the authority of the Moldovan government in Chisinau has not yet been extended over the Transnistrian territory. This is the essence of the Transnistrian issue.

---

[12] Institutul de Politici Publice, Barometrul de opinie publica: Republica Moldova, IMAS inc., Chisinau, aprilie 2003, p. 60.

[13] Sfatul Tarii, 1992.7.24, p. 2.

Why then did the Transnistrian conflict break out, and why has this conflict not been resolved in Moldova, in contrast to the Baltic cases? First of all, it is because Moldova could not follow the Baltic model of ethnic conflict resolution, which consisted of keeping stability in the state and society by controlling political participation. This situation reminds one of S. P. Huntington's argument that stability is much more significant than democratisation in the Third World, and that this stability can be attained by institutionalisation through controlling mobilisation.[14] However, as control in the Baltic model had been accomplished mainly according to ethnic criteria, this model came to be called an Ethnic Democracy or Control model.[15] It is said that the transition from the Civic model to the Ethnic model was determined just at the moment of the Moscow putsch in August of 1991, and this model was put into practice through a new citizenship law. This law stipulated that citizenship should be given only to those persons, and their descendants, who were of Estonian or Latvian citizenship just prior to the Soviet invasion of the Baltic states in June 1940. The adoption of this law was justified by the argument that the Soviet army illegally violated the sovereignty of these states in June 1940, and that, as a result, the states should return to that moment and rebuild themselves from where they left off. As the Western states had recognised the Baltic states' independence from the Russian Empire after the First World War, this Estonian and Latvian argument could not be denied. Therefore, Estonia and Latvia's introduction of the Baltic resolution model was accepted.

There have been various evaluations of this model. While it is true that this ethnic model excludes people from participation in political life along ethnic lines, at the same time it is also undeniable that this model contributed to relative stability in both Estonia and Latvia, which were in a vulnerable situation just after gaining their independence. As a result, in contrast to Moldova, no military conflict has broken out in these states. This is partly because the OSCE and the EU pressured the governments of Estonia and Latvia to modify the excessive aspects of their citizenship laws and to integrate their national minorities into their societies. This contributed to the easing of dissatisfaction among national minorities. This in turn brought compromise to these two Baltic societies, and as a consequence, into relatively stable situations. It was at this stage that EU conditionality showed its beneficial effects.

Needless to say, many other elements contributed to the success of the Baltic model. International society – the US, the Scandinavian

---

[14] S. P. Huntington, "Political Development and Political Decay," *World Politics*, Vol. 17, 1965, pp. 386-430.

[15] V. Pettai, "Emerging Ethnic Democracy in Estonia and Latvia," in M. Opalski (ed.), *Managing Diversity in Plural Society*, Ottawa, Forum Eastern Europe, 1998.

states, OSCE, and the EU – demanded that Russia withdraw its army from the Baltic states. The democratic forces in Russia influenced Russian minorities in the Baltic states, preventing the organisation of violent protests, and the Russian army stationed there was directly controlled by the Russian state itself. In addition, as far as the identity of the Russian minorities living in Estonia and Latvia is concerned, the majority of them came to feel sympathy with these states, in particular after their independence. Moreover, there have never been small compact areas clearly differentiated from surrounding regions which might be suitable for secession, along the lines of Kosovo, Nagorno-Karabakh, etc.

However, the situation in Moldova was completely different from that in these two Baltic states. The independence and reunification of Moldova with Romania after the First World War was not recognised by international society because Japan, which signed the Bessarabian treaty stipulating the unity of Romania with Bessarabia in 1920, did not ratify it. This was because it took into consideration its relationship with the Soviet Union, in particular the attached secret protocol contained in the state treaty concluded between Japan and the Soviet Union in 1925. Therefore, Moldova could not put forward the same argument that the Baltic states did in 1991.

Secondly, the fact that Moldovan society is divided into three groups – pro-Romanian, Moldovaist (ethnic Moldovans who consider themselves Moldovan, not Romanian), and pro-Russian and CIS – also prevented Moldova from following the Baltic model. While the pro-Russian group demanded the strengthening of relationships with Russia and the CIS, the ethnic Moldovans were divided into two sub-groups, one (pro-Romanian) demanded unity with Romania, and the other (Moldovaist) insisted on maintaining Moldova's neutrality. The latter asserted that their language is not Romanian, but Moldovan, although the author of the present study found that he could communicate without any problems with ethnic Moldovans using the language (Romanian) which he had studied in Bucharest. It is clear that these two ethnic Moldovan sub-cultural societies could not deal with their ethnic minority issues together, due to their different ethnic identities. Therefore, not only was Moldova unable to control mobilisation in the way that the Baltic states had, but it also had to deal with these three groups taking up a fierce political struggle to realise their own ideal outcomes. It is hardly surprising that Moldovan society became destabilised.

Thirdly, there is a small area clearly differentiated from the surrounding regions which might be ripe for secession. This is the Transnistrian region, which covers 4,118 square kilometres alongside the Dnestr, located between the river and the border with Ukraine. This region was called Transnistria in Romanian and Pridnestrovie in the Russian language. The OSCE has come to use the name Transdnestria, a combination of the two names. This region was a part of the territory of the "Moldavian Autonomous Soviet Socialist Republic," created by Stalin in 1924 within the Soviet Socialist Republic of Ukraine, and annexed into the Moldavian Soviet Socialist Republic on 2 August 1944 on the basis of a decision of the Supreme Soviet of the USSR. Stalin created this Autonomous Republic as a base to prepare for the integration of Moldova into the USSR after the failure of negotiations between the USSR and Romania in the spring of the same year. Therefore, this region had been a symbol of Soviet socialism, and had played a significant role as a strategic base in relation to the Balkans. Even after the collapse of the USSR, the leaders of this region repeatedly insisted on the restoration of the USSR and communism, and they acknowledged themselves as a front base guaranteeing the security of Russia from NATO enlargement.[16] It is perhaps characteristic of the unique history of the region that the statue of Vladimir Ilich Lenin still stands in the centre of Tiraspol. Owing to this history, the people of Transnistria have a different mentality from those living west of the Dnestr River. For example, while only 8.8% of the population in this area supported the independence of Moldova, 45.6% supported integration with Russia, and 41.7% supported an independent state within the CIS.[17]

Fourthly, in contrast to the Baltic states, which were influenced by democratic forces in Russia, we can point out the close relationships between the leaders in Transnistria and nationalistic and conservative forces in Russia. During the Soviet era, Lukiyanov, the former president of the Supreme Soviet of the USSR, sent letters to the leading figures in the USSR asking them to do their best in accordance with the demands of Transnistrian leaders to create a Transnistria Republic within Moldovan territory.[18] After the collapse of the Soviet Union, Aleksandr Rutskoi, the former vice-president of the Russian Federation, repeatedly visited Transnistria and appealed for a "Transnistrian state". The Duma in Russia adopted a decision in 1995 suggesting to Russian President Boris Yeltsin that Russia recognise the independence of the Transnistria.[19] On the other hand, Mr Igor Smirnov, who came from Russia at the end of the 1980s, addressed the Duma demanding that Russia recognise the independence of the Transnistria or the accession of

---

[16] Dnestrovskaya Pravda, 1995.8.22, 9.16.
[17] Fundatia Moldova Moderna, Sondaj comandat de Universitatea din Oslo, Departamentul Studii Europei Orientale, 1999.
[18] Interview with public prosecutor Lutenko, Moldova Suverana, Digest in Russian language, 1992.5.25.
[19] Dnestrovskaya Pravda, 1995.9.16; OMRI Daily Digest, 1995.9.12.

Transnistria to the CIS.[20] Furthermore, although Russia concluded an agreement on 22 October 1994 promising the withdrawal of Russian troops, arms, and munitions from Transnistria within three years, it refused to give force to the agreement on the grounds that the Duma had not ratified it. Another reason for the Russian refusal was the agreement signed in October 1994 on the withdrawal of Russian troops from the Republic of Moldova, which stipulated that the conclusion of an agreement on the legal status of Transnistria constituted a prerequisite for the withdrawal of the Russian army from the area. Moreover, Mr Grachev, the former Minister of National Defence in Russia, in 1995 urged his counterpart in Chisinau to build a Russian army base in Moldova.[21] However, when the Government of Moldova refused the proposal in accordance with its constitution, which prohibits the stationing of foreign troops on its territory, Russia transformed its military presence into a reduced-operation army and peace-keeping force to be stationed there permanently. Moreover, Russia had supported the position of Transnistrian leaders on confederation by introducing the concept of a "common state."

Fifthly, there has been no final decision on the legal status of Trans-nistria, although the OSCE, with Russia and Ukraine, has mediated between the government of Moldova in Chisinau and the leaders of Transnistria. This is partly because, in contrast to the position of the Chisinau government, which argued for a unitary state of Moldova, the Transnistrian leaders insisted on a confederation composed of two independent states in order to attain an independent sovereign state of Transnistria. They did so despite the fact that a cease-fire agreement concluded in July 1992 between Russian President Yeltsin and Moldovian President Snegur stipulated a guarantee of secession of Transnistria from the Republic of Moldova if the latter were to be united with Romania.[22] The leaders of Transnistria may have insisted on its independence partly because they feared the unification of Moldova and Romania – as indeed just such a development had actually occurred in 1918 – and partly because they wanted to keep control of their political and economic interests. It is said that an autocratic regime has been maintained in Transnistria through a monopoly of power by several leaders and their families, and that it has monopolised the area's under-ground economy. From an ethnic point of view, this regime has been maintained through the domination of the ethnic majority Moldovans and Ukrainians by minority Russian leaders. It was reported in 1989 that

---

[20]   Moldova Suverana, 1995.11.21.
[21]   Moldova Suverana, 1995.6.27; Dnestrovskaya Pravda, 1995.6.28.
[22]   Sfatul Tarii, 1992.7.24, p. 2.

the ethnic composition of the population in Transnistria was 39.9% Moldovan, 28.3% Ukrainian, and 25.5% Russian.

Finally, we should mention international society's lack of interest in Moldova. Because of this, all of the above-mentioned problems have dragged on for a long time, in contrast to the situations in the Baltic states of Estonia and Latvia, from which Russian troops had withdrawn by 1994.

B. The Involvement of the EU in the Transnistrian Conflict and Moldova's Reaction

In contrast to the scene sketched in the preceding section, recently the Moldovan situation has changed radically. First of all, the international community has begun to pay more attention to the Transnistrian issue. The OSCE Summit in Istanbul in December 1999 adopted a resolution on the withdrawal of Russian troops, armaments, and munitions from Moldova by the end of 2002, and the OSCE prepared the necessary budget for it. Nevertheless, Russia had not fulfilled its part of this commitment by 2002, or even by the end of 2003, although the Russian army had reduced the number of troops to around 1500 and the amount of munitions to 20,000 tons, from a previous level of 40,000 tons. Accordingly, the international community has often criticised the OSCE for its modest result and Russia for its irresponsibility.

Under these circumstances, the EU began to show interest in the Moldovan situation, expressing apprehension with regard to the limited progress in fulfilling the Istanbul commitments.[23] Previously, the EU refrained from involvement in the Transnistrian issue and left it to the OSCE. It has been reported that the EU imposed on Moldovan officials a condition not to include the Transnistrian issue in the framework of south-eastern cooperation when Moldova requested accession to the Stability Pact.[24]

Nevertheless, the EU embarked on an attempt to resolve the Transnistrian issue. In March 2003, Chris Patten initiated negotiations with Moldova and Ukraine for the creation of mixed Moldovan and Ukrainian customs posts, an issue which had not been resolved through the mediation of the OSCE and Russia. Ukraine signed an agreement in which it promised not to recognise goods other than those exported to Ukraine with the stamps of the Moldovan customs authority in Chisinau. In addition, the EU decided to send an observer to the Commission

---

[23] EN 15272/02, Press 387, p. 181.

[24] V. Gheorghe, "European Strategy of Moldova," Institutul de Politici Publice, 2004.1, p. 1, www.ipp. md/publications/EurStratMold.doc.p.1.

on the Constitution of Moldova in March 2003.[25] Furthermore, the EU, together with the United States, issued a joint statement on 27 February 2003 declaring that, as the leadership of the secessionist Transnistrian region had continually impeded meaningful negotiations through its obstructionism and unwillingness to change the *status quo*, targeted sanctions would be adopted in the form of travel restrictions on members of the Transnistrian leadership considered to be primarily responsible for the lack of cooperation in promoting a political settlement of the conflict. What is more, the EU expressed its concern at illegal activities linked to the conflict in Transnistria.

In addition, debate began both on EU participation in negotiations on the legal status of Transnistria and on the reorganisation of the PKF in Transnistria. As regarding the former issue, the EU discussed whether it would participate in the current negotiation framework, consisting of the OSCE, Russia, Ukraine, Moldova and the representatives of Transnistria, or whether a new framework including EU participation should be created. The latter involved plans for the creation of an EU PKF, as had been proposed by the Dutch Foreign Minister and Chairman-in-Office of the OSCE in July 2003. He suggested the transformation of the current PKF in Transnistria into a multinational force. According to later unofficial discussions regarding this plan, the PKF would be composed of 500 soldiers, including Russians. The formulation of this plan can be seen as related to the dispatch by the EU of police to Macedonia and troops to Bosnia-Herzegovina. In the Moldova-EU Council of Cooperation, held on 18 March 2003, these precedents were discussed in the search for a conflict resolution model for the Transnistrian case. Their application to the Transnistrian conflict was also discussed by the EU Political and Security Committee in May 2003. The final declaration of the Moldova-EU Parliamentary Cooperation Committee in June 2003 reaffirmed a commitment to "a more active participation of the EU in the implementation of the agreement (on the Transnistrian problem)".[26]

Under these circumstances, Moldova reacted strongly to these EU initiatives. Although the Communist party of Moldova emphasised the strengthening of its relations with Russia and its participation in the Russia-Belarus Union during the 2001 election campaign, they redefined state policy priorities after their election victory, putting the accent on Moldova's possible future accession to the EU. They created the National Commission for European Integration, as well as an EU de-

---

[25] N. Popescu, "Noile oportunitati de solutionare al problemei transnistrene prin mecanismele Europei moderne," in Euro Journal.org. Institutul de Politici Publice, p. 14, www.ipp.md/publications/NICU%20Popescu%20Popescu%20definitiv%2028.09. 2003.doc.

[26] N. Popescu, *op. cit.*, pp. 20-21.

partment in the Ministry of Foreign Affairs. The Ministry of Foreign Affairs in Moldova has made very clear that its accession to the EU will be sought through the Balkan Stabilisation and Association process, rather than through the Slavic union with the WNIS. In addition, the visits of the top echelon of Moldovan government to Brussels continued – Foreign Minister Nikolae Dudau in February 2003, Prime Minister Vasile Tarlev in March 2003, and President Vladimir Voronin in June 2003. President Voronin made a request to Mr Javier Solana for the opening of an EU mission to Chisinau and for the direct and active involvement of the US and the EU in conflict resolution in Transnistria.[27]

At the same time, however, the communist government has tried to steer another course in the domestic realm: the Russification of Moldova and Moldovanisation (as opposed to Romanisation) of ethnic Moldovans in the cultural, historical, educational and spiritual spheres. This domestic policy has recently been accentuated, partly because the Moldovan leadership might be obliged to strengthen Moldovan ethnicity and Moldovan and Russian culture should Romaniania accede to the EU in the near future. The leadership of the Communist Party in Moldova may be feeling anxious that the Moldovan ethnicity might otherwise be absorbed into the Romanian nation. This apprehension is understandable when it is remembered that 400,000 to 1,000,000 Moldovans are said to be working abroad. Many of them live in Romance language-speaking states such as Italy and Spain. The Moldovan language is, like Romanian, a Romance language. Thus there might be a possibility that the Moldovan people will be able to participate in the EU together with Romanian people by obtaining Romanian citizenship. In contrast to the people of Moldova, the state of Moldova has no option, however, than to remain outside the EU. As a result, the Moldovan state will become more fragile and even its existence will be threatened. In order to avoid such a danger, the Moldovan communist leaderships have been adopting the above-mentioned policies of Russification and Moldovanisation.

---

[27] Puncte de reper pentru intrevederea d-lui Vladimir VORONIN, Presedintele Republica Moldova cu d-l Javier SOLANA, Secretar General al Cousiliului UE, Inalt Reprezentant pentru Politica Externa si de Securitate Comuna, Bruxells, 23 iunie 2003 (Reference points regarding the meeting between Mr Vladimir Voronin, President of the Republic of Moldova, and Mr Javier SOLANA, General Secretary of the Council of the EU, High Representative for the CFSP, Brussels, 23 June 2003).

C. The Drafting of the Kozak Memorandum and the Movement Opposed to Its Signing

In reaction to these new tendencies in the EU and Moldova, Russia continued to express its traditional position on the pentagonal negotiation process on the Transnistrian issue when Veceslav Trubnicov, Deputy Minister at the Russian Ministry of Foreign Affairs visited Chisinau, and when Mr Novojirov, Special Envoy of the Russian Ministry of Foreign Affairs, visited Chisinau and Brussels.[28] However, during the period between the EU's launch of its Wider Europe-New Neighbours concept in the autumn of 2002 and the formalising of its Communication in March 2003, a route other than the pentagonal negotiation process for the resolution of the Transnistrian issue began to be discussed among the leaders of Russia, Moldova and Transnistria. This was carried out in parallel with official pentagonal negotiations. It is said that on 7 February 2003 Moldovan President Voronin asked President Vladimir Putin for his support in resolving the Transtrian issue as soon as possible. As a result, a mixed constitutional committee was organised by the representatives of Chisinau and Tiraspol, and that the following schedule was settled upon. A draft constitution was to be drawn up within six months; it was to be open to public debate for two months; then a referendum was to be organised in February 2004 and a general election held in February 2005.

Mr Dmitrii Kozak, the Russian Deputy Head of Presidential Administration, made an unofficial visit to Chisinau to consult with President Voronin's counsellor in May 2003. He then returned to Chisinau in August with the Russian draft of the resolution and undertook a bout of shuttle diplomacy between Chisinau and Tiraspol. Then, on 17 November 2003, the Russian draft on the federalisation of Moldova, the so-called Kozak memorandum, which emerged through this process, was suddenly handed over to the participants of pentagonal negotiations. It was also made available to the public on the internet at a later date.

Immediately after that, the struggle among several political actors concerning the Kozak memorandum began. Mr Kozak himself met the leaders of the political parties in Moldova. President Voronin met two former presidents of Moldova – Mr Snegur and Mr Lucinschi, leaders of political parties and also the foreign diplomatic representatives in Chisinau, and made efforts to persuade them to accept the memorandum. Opposition parties, however, considered the Kozak memorandum as a danger to the Moldovan state and society. Thus they organised the "Committee for the Defence of Independence and the Constitution of

---

[28]   N. Popescu, *op. cit.*, p. 12.

the Republic of Moldova" (Comitetul pentru Apararea Independentei si Constitutiei Republicii Moldova) and large-scale anti-government meetings. They also started to protest loudly against the Kozak memorandum. On the other hand, Mr Smirnov, "President" of Transnistria, asked to add a clause on the stationing of the Russian army for thirty years in the Kozak Memorandum. Immediately, the Russian Minister of Defence, Mr Sergei Ivanov, declared at a press conference that they were preparing a draft on the stationing of the Russian army in Transnistria until 2020.

It was against this background that the press secretary of President Voronin declared on 23 November that President Putin would come to Moldova to observe the signing of the document by Mr Voronin and Mr Smirnov the following day (24 November, 2003). This statement escalated the anti-Kozak memorandum movement to such a degree that a large number of demonstrators gathered in front of the Russian embassy in Chisinau and burned the portrait of President Putin, as well as the Russian flag.

The international community intervened at last in the increasing tension of Moldovan society. It was reported that both the OSCE Chairman-in-Office, Dutch Foreign Minister Jaap de Hoop Scheffer and the High Representative for the CFSP, Javiar Solana called President Voronin. The American ambassador also met President Voronin. The American embassy in Chisinau has not disclosed the content of their conversation but the meeting is believed to have been tense. It was rumoured that the ambassador persuaded Mr Voronin to abandon signing the document by showing the President the foreign bank account of his son. The Dutch Foreign Minister told Moldovan President Voronin, "Our consultations with participating states show there is no consensus to support this document." In addition, he informed President Voronin that several participating states had expressed serious reservations regarding some of the provisions of the memorandum, such as the lack of clarity on the proposed division of powers between the central and regional authorities, the *de facto* veto power of Transnistria in the Senate until at least 2015, and the absence of a satisfactory multinational guarantee system.[29]

The international community – the EU, the OSCE, the US embassy and the embassies of other Western states in Chisinau – had analysed the Kozak memorandum cautiously, and all arrived at the conclusion that it included several serious defects. First of all, it specified the continued stationing of the Russian army until 2020, which was in direct

---

[29] Press Release: Organisation for Security and Cooperation in Europe, Chairman-in-Office, 24 November 2003.

contradiction of the Istanbul decision specifying the withdrawal of Russian troops by the end of 2002. According to one western diplomat, the US seems to have been the most sensitive regarding this issue. The American standpoint was that the Istanbul decision of the OSCE summit should be respected, and that it constituted a prerequisite for the ratification of the CFE treaty.

Secondly, according to the Kozak memorandum, the Republic of Moldova was to be composed of three constituent republics, including not only Transnistria but also Gagauzia, which would make it possible for Transnistria and Gagauz together to reject all the decisions of the Parliament of Moldova. Because 13 of a total of 26 seats in the Upper House would be assigned to these two proposed republics (9 and 4 seats, respectively), they would, between them hold exactly half of the total votes of Upper House, effectively a veto on all bills, potentially blocking all legislation. That is to say, there was a hidden possibility in the Kozak memorandum that the Moldovan legislature would cease to function, precipitating administrative paralysis and turning the country into a failed state.

Thirdly, the international community was concerned that if President Voronin were to sign the Kosak memorandum, an extremely serious situation could develop in Chisinau because large-scale anti-government demonstrations were frequently organised in the capital.

The international community therefore expressed opposition to the signing of the Kozak memorandum just before the visit of President Putin to Chisinau. On the night of 24 November, just hours before President Putin's visit, President Voronin suddenly announced that he was no longer minded to sign the document, and the visit of President Putin was cancelled. It appears that President Voronin became worried that signing the document could lead to a deterioration in relations with the Western community and could even disrupt the negotiations for Moldova's accession to the EU. It is also likely that he was mindful of the internal confusion which signing the document could have caused in Moldova. Furthermore, he may have taken into consideration what was happening in Georgia at that moment. It is hardly fanciful to suggest that he may have pondered the parallels between his destiny and that of President Eduard Shevarnadze, who was forced to resign from his post, under pressure from anti-government demonstrators and the US administration. Whatever the exact reasons, President Voronin decided in the end not to sign the Russian document. The Italian Presidency of the EU, in a statement three days later, welcomed President Voronin's final decision.[30]

---

[30] Permanent Council, No. 479, 27 November 2003, EU Statement on Moldova.

D. Repercussions of the Failure to Sign the Kozak Document

As a result of the Modovan president's failure to sign the Kozak document, relations between Russia and the Western states were chilly at the OSCE ministerial meeting in Maastricht on 2-3 December 2003. The meeting ended with a unilateral declaration by the Western states, demanding the withdrawal of the Russian army from Transnistria and Georgia. Russia opposed the declaration. US Secretary of State Colin Powell said that the United States regretted that it had not been possible to reach agreement on a regional statement on Moldova and Georgia and stressed the need for the fulfilment of Russia's Istanbul commitments relating to Georgia and Moldova without further delay.[31] In opposition to this, Russian Foreign Minister Igor Ivanov stated, "the Memorandum prepared with Moscow's mediation was accepted by the parties. We are convinced that its signing would make it possible to solve the Transnistrian problem within the framework of a single State. Unfortunately, however, it was not signed, owing to pressure from certain States and organizations."[32]

In the introduction of this paper we evoked the possibility that the "New Neighbour" policy of the EU and the "Near Abroad" policy of Russia might clash over the Western CIS, as the interests of the EU in the traditional zone of Russian influence increase as a result of its enlargement. The evidence analysed above indicates this scenario is no flight of fancy but already a reality in the case of Moldova, where the EU and Russia have faced exactly these difficulties. Russia has tried to increase its influence over Moldova by completing an official agreement with the country prior to the EU New Neighbour policy taking concrete shape. Russia hurried to resolve the Transnistrian issue before the Maastricht ministerial meeting of the OSCE in order to assure the continued stationing of the Russian army in Moldova and to exclude any possibility that the EU and the Western states would intervene concerning the status of Transnistria and the form that the PKF might take. The aim of stationing the Russian army might have been partly as a counter-measure in reaction to the rumour that NATO troops would be relocated in the "New Europe" – Poland, Romania etc.[33] – and partly as a method of further strengthening Russian influence over Moldova. Russian success in Moldova could bring successive gains to Moscow in

---

[31] Statement in response to the Chairman's Statement, MC.DEL/64/03, 2 December 2003.

[32] MC.DEL/11/03, 1 December 2003.

[33] Defence Minister Ioan Pascu said on 3 December 2003 that a US military delegation would visit Romania to discuss the possibility of establishing military bases on Romanian territory, Radio Free Europe, Daily News, 4 December 2003.

the other areas of the "New Neighbour"/"New Abroad" region. This may be the reason why Russia endeavoured to resolve the Transnistrian issue alone, and in advance of the Maastricht ministerial meeting of the OSCE.

To this Russian attitude, however, the EU and the other Western states responded firmly, and without any concessions. On the contrary, judging that Russia would try to bring Moldova not only further into the Russian orbit, but also into a fragile, unstable, and even dysfunctional state, the EU endeavoured to break these Russian intentions. The EU asserts from time to time its willingness to cooperate with Russia in the resolution of its new neighbours' conflicts, but it emphasises, at the same time, its intention to pursue its own interests. The Communication on EU-Russia relations issued on 9 February 2004 declared that "the EU should demonstrate its readiness to engage with the NIS on the basis of its own strategic objectives, cooperating with Russia whenever possible."[34] Furthermore, it has been reported that the EU European Council in June 2004 will discuss whether the Caucasus is suitable for inclusion among the beneficiaries of the EU's New Neighbours Initiative.[35] This demonstrates that, although the EU has shown its willingness to cooperate with Russia in relation to surrounding regions, it also has firm intentions to pursue its security and economic interests in relation to its new neighbours without recognising Russia's concept of its influence zone, the "New Abroad". The above-mentioned Communication mentions that "the EU should be ready to discuss all the matters with Russia and should not hesitate to defend EU interests vigorously". It remains to be seen whether such a firm EU policy will bring about a cooperative Russian attitude in dealing with conflict resolution in the CIS states, or whether it will lead to deterioration in EU-Russia relations. The Transnistrian issue will be a test case for future relations.

IV. The Japanese Position Regarding EU Enlargement and the Possibility of Japan-EU Cooperation in Relation to the EU's New Neighbours

The Japanese Ministry of Foreign Affairs has made it clear that it welcomes EU Enlargement. This response is based first on the fact that enlargement has contributed to solving ethnic problems in the Central and East European states, and to promoting their democratic reforms,

---

[34]   The Communication from the Commission to the Council and the European Parliament on relations with Russia, COM(2004)106, 9 February 2004, p. 5.

[35]   The Council of the European Union decided to include Armenia, Azerbaijan and Georgia in the ENP. Press Release, 2590th Council Meeting, General Affairs, 14 June 2004, 10189/04 (Press 195), p. 12.

bringing them relative stability. This is a tremendously welcome development for Japan because regional peace and stability promotes global peace and stability, something which corresponds to Japanese national interests. Secondly, as "Japan shares with the EU common values and special responsibilities in international society"[36] EU enlargement – with its concomitant values such as democratisation, the central place of the market economy, human rights and the humanitarian dimension – helps to promote cooperation with Japan as a strategic partner contributing to peace and stability in a globalised international society. Thirdly, Japan values highly the increased voice of the EU in the world, as the possibility of Japan-EU cooperation to solve world issues and to promote common diplomacy towards the US and Russia will very likely continue to increase in the future. The Japan-EU diplomacy towards the US and Russia regarding the Kyoto Environment Protocol is a typical example. Fourthly, EU enlargement produces not just positive political outcomes, but also brings economic advantages for Japan. As the Euro Zone and EU markets expand to the Baltic and Central and East European states, it will increase business opportunities for Japanese enterprises, promote the production of high quality goods with cheaper labour in the new EU member states, and enhance sales in an enlarged market without burdensome customs procedures.

It is true, however, that EU enlargement may also have a negative impact on Japan. Although Japanese enterprises have made considerable investments in the Czech Republic, Poland, Hungary, and Slovakia, they will not be able to continue doing so after these states have become members of the EU. This is because EU norms of trade, which are different from those of these central European states, will be extended to these new member states as well. To take an example, the preferential treatment given to Japanese enterprises which have invested in the Central and East European states will be withdrawn as the laws of these states are put in harmony with those with the EU after accession. Therefore, Japan has been negotiating with the EU and these Central and East European states to prevent an abrupt halt in this preferential treatment after accession, pressing for appropriate transitional measures to be taken. In addition, there is also the issue of customs. While internal customs laws within the EU will be abolished, common customs laws will be introduced in relation to outside countries. As a result, increases in customs duties will be levied by some of the EU's new member states. In such cases, Japan will propose consultation according to the procedures of the WTO Agreement. In addition, if the EU becomes less operationally effective due to any newly introduced and more compli-

---

[36] Speech by Minister of Foreign Affairs Kawaguchi, 14 December, 2002, COM(2004) 106, 9 February 2004, p. 5.

cated decision-making processes as a result of EU enlargement, Japan may not be able to continue in its cooperative relations with the EU. It is also possible that the EU may become more confident because of its successes in enlargement, and may attempt to increase its influence over international policy formation and rule-making processes, which might not be compatible with Japanese interests.

Under these circumstances, the necessity of Japan-EU cooperation will be even greater. So far, Japan and the EU have stabilised guidelines on cooperative fields and types, according to which they have promoted cooperative relations. Information on issues such as the Iraq problem, the situation on the Korean Peninsula, Afghanistan, the peace process in the Middle East, Asian situations such as Ache and Burma, weapons of mass destruction, terrorism, human rights, and relations with great powers such as Russia and China has been exchanged at regular consultative meetings. Above all, excellent results were obtained in Balkan stabilisation through Japan-EU cooperation. While the EU has already been promoting military activity in Macedonia and Bosnia-Herzegovina as a replacement for NATO troops, Japan has also given support to the reconstruction process in some Balkan states through Official Development Assistance (ODA), and sent election-monitoring groups to the area as OSCE observers. Japan is said to have given assistance totalling more than 1.8 billion dollars to the Balkans since 1990. In this way, Japan has contributed to preventive diplomacy in the Balkans in cooperation with the EU.

This year is expected to see a great leap in Japan-EU cooperation because the strength of the EU's voice will certainly increase with its fifth enlargement in May, and Japan, for its part, has made clear its intention to contribute to the stability of the world politically and militarily, as well as economically, by sending national defence forces to Iraq. If this turns out to be the case, it would not be surprising to see Japan-EU co-operation promoted in relation to issues of peace and stability in the new neighbours of the EU. From a geopolitical point of view, Eurasia might be more significant for Japan than the distant Balkans. Eurasia has the abundant natural resources necessary for Japanese economic development. Indeed, the Hashimoto government made it clear that it would promote Eurasian diplomacy and would actively involve itself in Eurasian international politics, sending a well-known expert on Eurasia, Professor Yutaka Akino, to Tajikistan in order to show internally and externally the enthusiasm of the Japanese government for establishing peace and stability in the region. On the other hand, the interests of the EU in the Caucasus have recently increased, just as the EU is about to decide in the European Council in June 2004 if the Caucasus should be included in the EU's New Neighbours Initiative[37] We might comment that although one does not choose one's neighbours, one can choose whether or not to include them in an Initiative. The EU has strong political and economic interests at stake in the stability of areas surrounding the Azerbaijan-Georgia-Turkey oil pipeline. Such EU interests in the region were reflected in the Council's decision on 7 July 2003 to appoint an EU Special Representative for the South Caucasus, as well as in several high-level visits to Tbilisi. The President of the EU Commission, Romano Prodi met interim President Nino Burjanadze in December 2003; High Representative Javier Solana visited Georgia in January, 2004 and Irish Foreign Minister Brian Cowen, attended Saakashvili's inauguration on 25 January 2004 in his capacity as the Chairman of the Council of EU Foreign Ministers.

This evidence demonstrates that Japanese Eurasian diplomacy and the New Neighbours policy of EU will overlap in Eurasia: Japan-EU relations will be not only competitive in relation to natural resources and economic interests, but also cooperative in relation to strengthening democracy and stability in this region, including regional conflict resolution. Japan and the EU have not, however, consulted on any issues concerning the CIS region in their regular meetings. This is, firstly, because there have been a lot of points to be discussed on the agenda at their regular bilateral meetings, and there has not been sufficient time to spare for the exchange of information on specific regional issues. Secondly, Japan's Ministry of Foreign Affairs may not have given priority to this region. Relations with the US and the other great powers like China, Russia, and the United Nations have had priority over this region in Japanese foreign policy. In addition, Japanese diplomacy has been obliged to pay more attention to Iraq, the Korean Peninsula, Afghanistan, Sri Lanka, Indonesia, ASEAN, etc. It is understandable under these circumstances that Japan should question the need to deepen relations with states in an area as complicated as the CIS, something that could even cause Japan troublesome relations with Russia. Therefore, the Japanese position is that it should contribute to regional stability through economic support, without getting involved deeply in the political issues of the region, limiting its activities to collecting information on political affairs so as to gain a better understanding of the regional situation.

Accordingly, there is little possibility that Japan and the EU will actively cooperate to resolve conflicts in the CIS region, at least in the near future, as long as the EU fails to approach the Japanese government regarding this matter. This kind of phenomenon is not uncommon

---

[37] The Council of the European Union decided to include Armenia, Azerbaijan and Georgia in the ENP. Press Release, 2590th Council Meeting, General Affairs, 14 June 2004, 10189/04 (Press 195), p. 12.

in Japan-EU relations in general. When Japan asked the EU about the possibility of Japanese participation in the Middle East peace process, it is said that the EU paid little attention to the Japanese proposal. Similarly, when the EU expressed an interest in joining the consultative meetings on the North Korean issue composed of six states – the US, Japan, China, Russia, the Republic of Korea and the Democratic People's Republic of Korea – Japan is said to have been reluctant to accept this request. There are understandable reasons, however, for the negative attitudes of both states: the more participants there are in an international conference, the more difficult it is to reach a consensus. Here we can see the geopolitical limits of further Japan-EU cooperation when each party tries to influence situations in distant regions.

In view of these facts, the Japanese Ministry of Foreign Affairs is reforming its organisation in order to adapt itself precisely to the new international situation produced by the EU enlargement. As a result, Ukraine, Belarus and Moldova, which were dealt with by the New Independent States Division of the Ministry, will be integrated into the Central and South Eastern European Division on August 1, 2004.[38] Therefore, novel ideas for further Japan-EU cooperation regarding the EU's new neighbours and Eurasia might arise from the newly transformed structure of the Ministry of Foreign Affairs. Moreover, we cannot discount the possibility that Japan and the EU may begin consultations on the regional situation, including conflict issues concerning the EU's new neighbours if EU interest in the Caucasus and Central Asia increases. In this context, it is noteworthy that, as far as the relations between the EU and its new neighbours are concerned, the EU has been collaborating with the OSCE and NATO in formulating policy towards these states. This is a desirable situation for Japan, because Japan, as an observer at the OSCE, has cooperated with the organisation to maintain peace and stability among OSCE member states, in Central Asia in particular. Therefore, it is very likely that Japan will cooperate with the Union, not only bilaterally, but also in terms of the OSCE framework in working for peace and stability in Eurasia, just as Japan has done in Asian areas such as Afghanistan and Sri Lanka.

---

[38]   Indeed, the WNIS has been dealt with in the Central and South-Eastern European Division in the Ministry since July 2004.

PART TWO

PROMOTING TOGETHER
SUSTAINABLE DEVELOPMENT

CHAPTER 6

Japanese Environmental Foreign Policy and the Prospects for Japan-EU Cooperation

The Case of Global Climate Change

Hiroshi OHTA

Aoyama Gakuin University

During the negotiation of the UN Framework Convention on Climate Change (UNFCCC), Japan and the EU attempted to persuade the United States to join a collective effort toward reducing emissions of greenhouse gases (GHGs). However, during and after the negotiation of the Kyoto Protocol, Japan became increasingly reluctant to take on a leadership role, reflecting domestic differences between the objectives of policy-makers concerned with the environment on the one hand and considerations related to the economy, on the other. The US government's rejection of the Kyoto Protocol in March 2001 was a major blow to the international initiative, which had been led by the EU with the help of vulnerable developing countries and environmental NGOs to effectively mitigate global climate change (known more commonly in Japan by the term global warming).[1]

Ironically, the US breakaway from the Kyoto framework encouraged a rebuilding of Japan-EU cooperation aimed at mitigating climate change. During the resumed sixth conference of the parties (COP6-Part 2) in July 2001, the EU compromised with Japan over the effort to reduce GHGs by preserving forests. As a result, Japan obtained a greater reduction allowance for carbon sequestration by forests than it initially requested. Japan eventually ratified the Kyoto Protocol in June 2002, right after the EU ratification. Even though Japan may be reluctant to take the initiative in mitigating global warming, it has shown its com-

---

[1] I use the terms global warming and global climate change interchangeably since in Japan the term "global warming" is more popular than "global climate change."

mitment to reducing the GHGs by articulating climate change policies. These include the Guideline for Measures to Prevent Global Warming of 1998, and its revised Guideline of 2002, in preparation for Japan's ratification of the Protocol. Nonetheless, the fact that (at the time of writing) the Kyoto Protocol has not yet entered into force (due to hesitation to ratify on the part of Russia) encourages the advocates of a cautious approach to the implementation of climate change policy.

The purpose of this paper is to present the policy options that determine the Japanese government posture toward the issue of global climate change and their implications for the construction of more steadfast cooperation between Japan and the enlarged EU. The most distinctive structural factor that shapes Japanese policy is the country's energy supply-demand structure. Another factor is the organisational setting in which climate change policy is generated and implemented. Although a specialised unit has been set up to address the issue of global warming under the Prime Minister's Office, the substantive policy is articulated and implemented through intensive negotiations between the Ministry of the Environment (MoE) and the Ministry of Economy, Trade, and Industry (METI).

This paper begins with a general introduction to Japanese environmental foreign policy and goes on to describe the Japanese energy supply-demand structure and environmental performance as pertains to the issue of climate change. After a summary of the main features of the Guidelines for Measures to Prevent Global Warming, I will analyze the policy options for Japan mainly focusing on the domestic policy discourse between the environment and economic ministries. The conclusion analyzes the prospects for constructive cooperation beyond 2012 between Japan and the enlarged EU on this important global problem.

I. Japanese Environmental Foreign Policy: An Overview

Japan's environmental diplomacy began to form in the 1970s, catalysed by various international events. The first report of the Club of Rome's project on the predicament of humankind was alarming. However, it was the United Nations Conference, held Stockholm in 1972 (or the Stockholm Conference) that first brought the damage being done to the global environment to the attention of Japanese policy-makers. Then, the US government's *The Global 2000: Report to the President* further influenced Japanese policymakers, who thereupon began institutionalising efforts to tackle global environmental problems.[2] Soon after

---

[2]   D. H. Meadows, D. L. Meadows, J. Randers and W. W. Behrens III, *The Limits to Growth*, New York: Universe Books, 1972; Gerald O. Barney, *The Global 2000 Report to the President of the United States*, Oxford, Pergamon, 1980.

the publiccation of *The Global 2000*, the Japanese government began to articulate its environmental foreign policy.[3]

A. Responding to International Developments

The first product of this policy was Japan's contribution to the creation of the World Commission on Environment and Development (WCED or also known as the Brundtland Commission). As one of its achievements, the WCED helped publicise the notion of "sustainable development," which means to "ensure that [development] meets the needs of the present without compromising the ability of future generations to meet their own needs."[4]

The importance of Japan's role as a member of the world community was a strong rationale for the initiation of Japan's international contribution in the field of the environment and development. The Japanese government proposed the creation of the WCED at the tenth anniversary for the Conference on Human Environment held in Nairobi in 1982. In the following year, with Japan's contribution of ¥1 billion for its creation, the WCED was established by the General Assembly of the United Nations.[5] The WCED launched its activities in May 1984 in pursuit of a vision for the global environment as the 21st century neared. The WCED had seven meetings in Geneva, Jakarta, Oslo, São Paulo, Ottawa, Harare, and Moscow before it completed its mission at the close of the final meeting in Tokyo in February 1987. The Tokyo Declaration of the WCED called upon the nations of the world to "build a future that is prosperous, just, and secure." Nations were urged to integrate the concept of "sustainable development" into their goals and to implement the principles of the new policy.[6]

---

[3] For more detailed account on the genesis of Japan's environmental foreign policy, see Hiroshi Ohta, "Japanese Environmental Foreign Policy," in Inoguchi Takashi and P. Jain (eds.), *Japanese Foreign Policy Today*, New York, Palgrave, 2000, pp. 96-121.

[4] The World Commission on Environment and Development, *Our Common Future*, Oxford, Oxford University Press, 1987, p. 8. This concept itself, however, had already been capitalised in *The World Conservation Strategy* that was constituted and publicised in 1980 by the International Union for the Conservation of Nature and Natural Resources (IUCN) and the United Nations Environment Programme (UNEP).

[5] Interview with Bunbei Hara, Speaker of the House of Councilors (or former Director of Environment Agency) on September 2, 1993. The Environment Agency (EA), *The Twenty-Year History*, p. 366; and the EA, *The Quality of the Environment*, 1992, p. 236.

[6] The Tokyo Declaration states that a bright and constructive future depends upon whether or not all states adopt "the objective of sustainable development as the overriding goal and test of national policy and international cooperation." (WCED,

After receiving the final WCED report, entitled *Our Common Future* in 1987, the Japanese government established the Headquarters of Policy Planning and Promotion for Global Environmental Protection under the Office of Administrative Deputy Minister in the Environment Agency in August 1988. Meanwhile, the Environment Agency's annual white paper, the *Quality of the Environment* (known in Japan as the *Kankyo hakusho*) of May 1988 featured global environment issues as its main theme for the first time.

The speed of Japan's environmental initiative was accelerated and its scope widened by ever-growing international diplomatic concerns about destruction of the global environmental. By 1989, the contest for leadership or "jockeying for position" in international environmental diplomacy and politics had intensified, especially among West European countries. In March 1989, the then British Prime Minister Thatcher hosted a three-day international conference on the issue of the depletion of the stratospheric ozone layer. The following week, the governments of France, the Netherlands, and Norway jointly held an international conference in The Hague. The main subjects of this conference were the depletion of the stratospheric ozone layer and climatic change caused by global warming.[7] In June, the Greens gained 19 seats in the election of the European Parliament. This brought them to a total of 39 seats in the 518-seat assembly.[8] In addition to these developments, the Group of Seven's annual meeting, held in Paris in July 1989, symbolically highlighted environmental diplomacy. The economic declaration of this G7 meeting devoted 19 out of 56 paragraphs to environmental issues, including climate change, ozone depletion, and deforestation.

In 1989, the wave of environmental diplomacy rolled into Japan. The Tokyo Conference on the Global Environment and Human Response toward "Sustainable Development" was held from September 11 to 13. This conference was jointly hosted by Prime Minister Kaifu Toshiki, Secretary General Mostafa Tolba of the UN Environment Programme (UNEP), and Secretary General G.O.P. Obasi of the World Meteorological Organisation (WMO). Other participants were representatives of

---

Our Common Future, p. 363). Eight principles are listed as the guidance for each state's policy. The headings of these principles include: (1) Revive Growth; (2) Change the Quality of Growth; (3) Conserve and Enhance the Resource Base; (4) Ensure a Sustainable Level of Population; (5) Reorient Technology and Manage Risks; (6) Integrate Environment and Economics in Decision-Making; (7) Reform International Economic Relations; and (8) Strengthen International Cooperation (WCED, *ibid.*, pp. 364-65).

[7]   L. Brown, "The Illusion of Progress," in L. Brown *et al.*, *State of the World: 1990*, New York, W. W, Norton & Company, 1990, p. 13.

[8]   "Is Europe Turning Green?" (editorial), *The New York Times*, June 22, 1989.

international organisations, widely respected scientists and experts on global environmental problems. The main themes of the conference were the issues of the changing atmosphere and development and the environment in developing countries.[9]

Corresponding to the emerging environmental diplomacy during the Arche Summit of 1989, the Japanese government launched its environmental ODA policy. The main features of the policy include: (1) the expenditure of about 300 billion yen in bilateral and multilateral environmental assistance for the three years beginning in 1989; (2) emphasis on forest conservation and related research programs, especially for tropical rain forests; (3) emphasis on capacity building in ODA recipient countries; and (4) the enhancement of environmental considerations in its assistance programs.

One year prior to the UNCED, international environmental diplomacy maintained its momentum and the Japanese government added some extra features to environmental ODA. At the London Summit of 1991, on top of Japan's mission for developing countries to share its past experience in overcoming industrial pollution problems, the policy objective of dealing with the linkages among poverty, population growth, and environmental degradation was added to the focal policy areas in Japan's environmental ODA.

The 1992 UNCED (or the Earth Summit), held in Rio de Janeiro, adopted the UN Framework Convention on Climate Change and the Convention on Biological Diversity. The former Convention became effective as of December 1993 and the latter in March 1994. Another Convention to Combat Desertification was adopted in June 1994. These conventions helped strengthen the existing international legal framework for the protection of the environment.

Responding to these international developments and, at the same time, aiming to further articulate Japanese environmental foreign policy, the Cabinet adopted the ODA Charter, one of whose principles addresses improvement of the environment, on 30 June 1992.[10] Further-

---

[9] Kankyo-cho, chikyukankyo-bu kikaku-ka (Planning Division, Global Environment Department of the Environment Agency) (EA), *Chikyukankyo-no jidai* (*The Era of Global Environment*), Tokyo, Gyosei, 1990, pp. 247-263.

[10] The Official Development Assistance Charter of June 1992 specifies some nature of Japanese ODA in the address of "Japan's ODA in relation to military expenditure and other matters of the developing countries," or the four ODA principles. They include: (1) Environmental conservation and development should be pursued in tandem. (2) Any use of ODA for military purposes or for aggravation of international conflicts should be avoided. (3) Full attention should be paid to trends in recipient countries' military expenditures, their development and production of mass destruction weapons and missiles, their export and import of arms, etc., so as to maintain

more, under the Basic Environmental Law of 1993 (hereafter, the Basic Law), the Basic Environmental Plan (the Basic Plan) was established within the purview of the Basic Law's call for initiatives for protecting the global environment and assisting developing countries in the field of environmental protection.

The activities of ODA-funded international environmental cooperation have various aspects. They include research on desirable projects, developmental studies, as well as the dispatch of technical experts to, and acceptance of trainees from, developing countries. In terms of the manner of giving, there are grants, loans, and financial contributions to international organisations, such as the UNEP and the International Tropical Timber Organisation (ITTO). In 1991, the Global Environmental Facility (GEF) was founded to provide developing countries with financial resources to tackle the problems of global warming, loss of biological diversity, problems relating to international waters, and depletion of the stratospheric ozone layer.

At the UNCED, Japan pledged to significantly expand its environment-related ODA between ¥ 900 billion and ¥ 1 trillion over five years, starting in FY 1992. By the end of the fourth year, Japan had disbursed about ¥ 980 billion, thus meeting its target a year ahead of the original schedule. The contents of this environmental ODA include grants, loans, along with technical and multilateral assistance, among which loans are the largest element.

At the June 1997 Special Session of the United Nations General Assembly on Environment and Development, Prime Minister Ryutaro Hashimoto announced Japan's comprehensive medium- and long-term plan for environmental cooperation. This plan, called the Initiatives for Sustainable Development toward the Twenty-first Century (ISD), indicated the ways in which Japan would support programs in developing countries to address a wide variety of environmental problems, including global warming, air and water pollution, waste disposal, deforestation, and loss of marine and terrestrial biological diversity. Furthermore, as the host of the Third Conference of Parties to the UNFCCC (COP3) which was held in Kyoto in December 1997, Japan presented the Kyoto Initiative. It consists of strengthened environmental support that focuses on assisting developing countries in arresting

---

and strengthen international peace and stability, and from the viewpoint that developing countries should place appropriate priorities in the allocation of their resources on their own economic and social development. (4) Full attention should be paid to efforts for promoting democratisation and introduction of a market-oriented economy, and the situation regarding the securing of basic human rights and freedoms in the recipient country. MOFA, *Japan's ODA: Official Development Assistance, 1992*, Tokyo, Association for International Cooperation, 1993, pp. 193-94.

global warming in the policy framework of the ISD. The Kyoto Initiative, like the ISD, will be implemented mainly through the Japanese government's ODA program.

B. The Climate Change Regime and Japan

Japan ratified the UNFCCC on 28 May 1993 and the Kyoto Protocol on 4 June 2002. During the final stage of intensive negotiations about the Kyoto Protocol, Japan agreed to reduce greenhouse gases by 6 percent below the 1990 level during the first commitment period of 2008-2012. While the UNFCCC became effective in December 1993, the Kyoto Protocol still lacks one condition for coming into effect. The rule (Article 25 of the Kyoto Protocol) for entry into force of the Kyoto Protocol is that 55 Parties to the Convention must ratify (or approve, accept, or accede to) the Protocol, including Annex I Parties (developed countries) accounting for 55 percent of that group's carbon dioxide emissions in 1990.[11] As of 26 November 2003, 119 countries (87 non-Annex I and 32 Annex I countries) and the EU had ratified the Protocol, clearing the condition of 55 countries' ratification. These countries, however, include Annex I Parties accounting for just 44.2 percent of that group's CO_2 emissions in 1990, so that the other condition has not yet been met. Under the current George W. Bush administration, the United States, whose CO_2 emission rate in 1990 was 36.1 percent, rejected ratification of the Kyoto Protocol in March 2001. The Russian Federation, which emitted 17.4 percent in 1990, holds the key to the success of the Kyoto Protocol. However, Russia did not ratify the Protocol when the COP9 was held in Milan, Italy on 1-12 December 2003. The future of the Protocol remains uncertain at the time of writing.

The implementation of climate change policy, such as the introduction of a carbon tax at a significant rate, would have an enormous impact on any given country's economic performance and the international competitiveness of its industries. Accordingly, policy-makers concerned with relative gains and losses seek to avoid placing their own country in an unfavorable situation in comparison with other countries.[12] Although Japan is firmly committed to the reduction of GHG emissions,

---

[11] Article 25 (1) reads "This Protocol shall enter into force on the ninetieth day after the date on which not less than 55 Parties to the Convention, incorporating Parties included in Annex I which accounted in total for at least 55 percent of the total carbon dioxide emissions for 1990 of the Parties included in Annex I, have deposited their instruments of ratification, acceptance, approval or accession."

[12] See for instance, J. M. Grieco, "Anarchy and the Limits of Cooperation," *International Organization* (Vol. 42, No. 3, 1988), pp. 485-508 and D. Baldwin (ed.), *Neorealism and Neoliberalism*, New York, Columbia University Press, 1993.

concern with the absolute gain of arresting global climate change is now being contested more overtly than before by concern with relative gains.

Japanese policy on climate change today, therefore, reflects policy discourse on the absolute and relative gains and losses. Before advancing to an examination of Japan's climate change policy, we need to look at the fundamentals of current Japanese GHG emission trends, the basic structure of energy supply and demand, as well as energy policy in general. It is because climate change policy is closely related to energy policy and that consideration of relative gains and losses is influenced by the performance and characteristics of such fundamentals. Thus, we will now turn to an overview of Japan's energy requirements and environmental performance.

II. Japanese Energy Use and Its Environmental Performance

Since Japan lacks almost all domestic sources of energy, it imports substantial amounts of crude oil, natural gas, uranium, and other energy resources. In 2001, Japan depended on imports for more than 79 percent of its primary energy needs. Oil provided Japan with 50.1 percent of its total energy needs, coal 16.8 percent, nuclear power 14 percent, natural gas 13.5 percent, hydroelectric power 4 percent, and renewable sources 1.1 percent (see Diagram 1).

A. The Supply-and-Demand Structure of Energy in Japan

The industrial sector uses about half of Japan's energy, the transportation sector about one-fourth, with nearly all the rest used by the residential, agricultural, and service sectors. As for the proportions of carbon emissions produced by these fuels, oil accounts for 57 percent, coal 28.8 percent, and natural gas 13.5 percent.[13]

With regard to electricity, Japan generated 1,037 billion kilowatt-hours (Bkwh) on 235 gigawatts of capacity in 2001. Of Japan's total generation in 2001, about 60 percent came from thermal – oil, gas, and coal – plants, 30 percent from nuclear reactors, 8 percent from hydroelectric dams, and less than 2 percent from renewable resources such as geothermal heat, solar-, and wind-power (see Diagram 2).

---

[13] Energy Information Administration (EIA), "Japan Country Analysis Brief," July 2003. http://www.eia.doe.gov/emeu/cabs/japan.html (10 December 2003).

Diagram 1: Japanese Energy Sources in 2001

Source: Energy Information Administration (EIA), "Japan Country Analysis Brief",
July 2003 [The total energy consumption in 2001 was 21.9 quadrillion (10^{15}) Btu.]

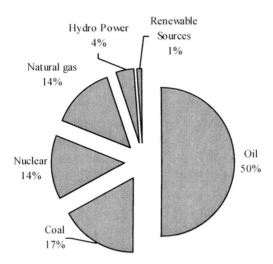

Diagram 2: Japan's Electricity in 2001

EIA, "Japan Country Analysis Brief", July 2003

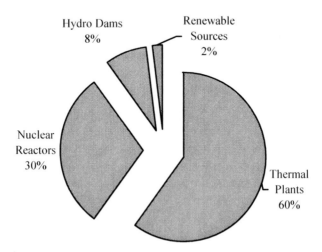

Japan maintains a strong commitment to the use of nuclear power as the national energy strategy for decreasing its dependency on imported oil. The government of Japan now emphasises an additional rationale for maintaining nuclear energy development: nuclear energy's contribution to the reduction of CO_2 emissions. Japan's current ten-year energy plan, approved in March 2002, calls for the expansion of nuclear generation by about 30 percent by 2010, or the construction of between 9 and 12 new nuclear power plants.[14] Japan currently has 51 nuclear reactors with an installed capacity of 45 GW, which is the third largest capacity after the United States and France. However, national nuclear policy has been facing strong political opposition with the development of new plants, particularly since the Tokaimura nuclear accident in 1999.[15]

Compared with nuclear energy, the development of renewable energy such as from solar, wind, and geothermal sources, is still insufficient, but it has now obtained some serious attention. METI's 1998 long-term projection for energy use calls for a threefold increase in the use of renewable energy sources, including solar and wind energy, by 2010 through a "Green Credit System" designed to give electricity producers incentives to purchase energy from renewable sources. Moreover, financial assistance to businesses was introduced in order to encourage the use of unconventional energy sources. The Revised Energy Savings Law, adopted in 1999, also calls on central and local governments to offer effective economic incentives to promote wider use of environmentally friendly products and technologies including solar cells and lower-emission and multi-fuel vehicles.[16]

The Japanese government set targets to increase the development of solar, wind, geothermal energy, and other sources. One such policy target for solar energy was to increase photovoltaic power generation to 5,000 MW by 2010 from its 1996 level of 55 MW. Regarding wind energy use, in 1999, Japan added 43.4 megawatts (MW) of wind capacity, increasing its total to 75.1 MW. The government has set a target to install equipment to produce an additional 300 MW by 2010.[17] In

---

[14] The Japanese government also plans to offer subsidies for nuclear power plant construction in order to offset expected cost-cutting pressures on utilities due to deregulation.

[15] Energy Information Administration, "Japan: Environmental Issues," July 2001, http://www.eia.doe.gov/emeu/cabs/japan.html#envir (11 December 2003).

[16] EIA, *ibid.* (2001), http://www.eia.doe.gov/emeu/cabs/japanenv.html# RENEWABLE (11 December 2003).

[17] Wind power capacity is currently insignificant in Japan's electricity generation, but is now facing strong challenges to growth. Some obstacles for wind power generation development in Japan include unreliable weather, inaccessibility of suitable, and thus relatively expensive transmission costs.

comparison with wind, the Japanese government set a much higher policy target for geothermal energy use: namely, 32 percent increase in thermal energy use over the same period. The country currently has 533 MW of installed capacity. Another method of using renewable energy is the utilisation of waste to generate solid fuel. The capacity for waste-generated power will be upgraded to 5,000 MW by 2010 from the 1996 level of 890 MW.[18]

B. Energy Consumption and Environmental Performance

Total energy consumption in Japan in 2001 was 21.9 quadrillion (10^{15}) Btu, 5.4 percent of total world energy consumption. Energy-related carbon emissions in the same year for Japan were 315.8 million metric tons, 4.8 percent of world total carbon emissions. According to OECD/IEA data, for CO_2 emissions from fuel combustion, the largest emitting country was the United States, accounting for 24.0 percent of the world total in 2001. In second and third place were China and Russia, with 13.0 percent and 6.4 percent, respectively. Japan's 4.8 percent put it in fourth place, followed, for instance by India with 4.3 percent, Germany with 3.6 percent and Great Britain with 2.3 percent (See Diagram 3).[19]

Diagram 3: CO_2 Emissions from Fuel Combustion in 2001
Source: OECD/IEA, 2003

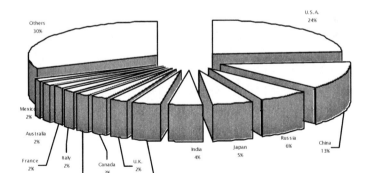

[18] EIA, *ibid.* (2001), http://www.eia.doe.gov/emeu/cabs/japanenv.html (11 December 2003).

[19] International Energy Agency, *CO₂ Emissions from Fuel Combustion: Highlights 1971-2001*, Paris, OECD/IEA, 2003, p. 31.

In terms of energy efficiency, Japanese performance well exceeds other developed countries' performance. As of 2001, Japan has consumed 6,523 Btu per dollar of GDP (measured in 1990 USD), which is about half the US energy consumption of 12,638 Btu/$1990. Carbon intensity is 0.06 metric tons of carbon/thousand $1995, which was much better than the US figure of 0.17 metric tons/thousand $1995. Japan's energy intensity (energy use per unit of GDP) is among the lowest in the developed world. The sense of unfairness arises from the fact that different countries have different levels of energy efficiency so that the same level of reduction entails different costs. This is true of Japan, which had carried out the energy shift from coal to oil in the 1960s, and achieved a high level of energy efficiency, especially after having overcome the two oil crises of 1973-74 and 1979-80.[20] Diagram 4 shows one such feature of efficiency in Japanese energy consumption in comparison with other major developed countries. Unlike Japan, coal consumption declined in the United Kingdom only in 1990 and in Germany only after reunification due to the de-industrialisation of East Germany.[21] In this context, it is understandable that Japan might consider the 1990 base year for assessing emission reductions unfair and unjust.

---

[20] The Japanese negotiation team often pointed out these facts in critiquing the validity of the 1990 base year emission. See, for instance, T. Toshiaki, *Chikyu ondanka to kankyo gaiko* (*Global Warming and Environmental Diplomacy*), Tokyo, Jiji Tsushin, 1999.

[21] E. Weigrandt, "Climate Change, Equity, and International Negotiations," in U. Luterbacher and D. F. Sprinz (eds.), *International Relations and Global Climate Change*, Cambridge, MA, The MIT Press, 2001, p. 139 and M. Grubb with C. Vrolijk and D. Brack, *The Kyoto Protocol: A Guide and Assessment*, London, Royal Institute of International Affairs, 1999, pp. 81-87.

**Diagram 4: End Energy Consumption
per GDP Unit in Major Developed Countries**
(The numbers are indexes with Japan's level in 2000 as 100)

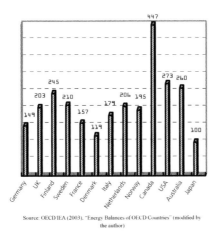

Source: OECD IEA (2003), "Energy Balances of OECD Countries" (modified by
the author)

III. Japanese Climate Change Policy

Throughout negotiations for the conclusion of the Kyoto Protocol, numerous proposals were put on the negotiation table to address the issue of fair allocation of burdens among Annex I countries. An agreement was reached on the numerical reduction target at the very end of the two-week session of COP3, when Al Gore, then vice president of the United States, intervened in the negotiation process and helped strike a deal. Japan, the United States, and the EU finally agreed to reduce the GHG emissions by 6 percent, 7 percent and 8 percent, respectively, below the level of 1990. However, since these targets were not based on scientific and objective criteria, and also imposed no obligation for reductions on some Annex I countries such as Russia, a sense of unfairness about the burden-sharing arose, especially in some Japanese policy circles and among many US law-makers. For instance, US Senate Resolution 98, known as the Byrd-Hagel Resolution, which was unanimously adopted in July 1997, urged US delegates at COP3 not to sign any international agreement that would not place responsibility for reducing GHG emissions on developing countries or that would result in serious harm to the economy of the United States.[22]

---

[22]   *Congressional Record* (S. Res. 98), "Expressing Sense of Senate Regarding UN Framework Convention on Climate Change" (Senate – 25 July 1997), S8138.

Both Japan and the EU had accepted the differentiated targets, and Japan had proposed a lower level of the reduction target and the EU a higher level. More importantly, however, both Japan and the EU agreed to the US proposal for the utilisation of the Kyoto mechanism, or emissions trading, a joint implementation and clean development mechanism that is considered efficient and cost-effective for reducing GHGs. The EU, Japan, most developing countries, and environmental NGOs were unwilling to accept the utilisation of emissions trading and overseas reduction projects because they would discourage domestic efforts to reduce GHG emissions in developed countries, particularly in the United States. However, since the US participation in GHG emission reductions was essential to making the climate regime effective and legitimate, Japan and the EU conceded this point to the United States.

A. Guidelines for Measures to Prevent Global Warming

After the Kyoto Protocol was adopted in December 1997, on 19 June 1998, the Japanese government established the Guideline for Measures to Prevent Global Warming: Measures towards 2010 to Prevent Global Warming, published by the Japanese government's Global Warming Prevention Headquarters. This policy program relies on, above all, the role of forests in absorbing CO_2, supported through additional activities such as forest management, suggested in Article 3.4 of the Protocol. With regard to forestry activities, the proposed "essential measures" to prevent global warming aimed at the reduction of 3.7 percent out of 6 percent, or an assigned target for Japan. The policy to reduce domestic GHG emission by 2.5 percent consists of energy conservation, introduction of new energy and more construction of nuclear power plants "with rigid nuclear safety measures." However, the Guideline estimated a 2 percent GHG increase due to the emissions of CFC-alternative gases. Therefore, Japan would have to rely on the Kyoto mechanism to the extent to which it could gain credits equivalent to 1.8 percent of emissions reduction.

The 2002 Amendment of the Guideline

This initial policy was amended in March 2002 when accord on the detailed legal documents of the Protocol was reached in November 2001 at COP7. The path to conclusion of the detailed rules for the Kyoto Protocol was not easy. A full agreement was not reached at COP6, held in The Hague in November 2000, so COP6 was reconvened in Bonn in July 2001. Three months before the second session of COP6, the declaration of the new Bush administration that the United States would not ratify the Kyoto Protocol was tantamount to a death sentence for the Protocol. However, the US abandonment of international cooperation inadvertently united the rest of the world and induced the EU, during the resumed session of COP6, to make a large concession to Japan and the Russian Federation, particularly on the role of forests for their role in sequestration of CO_2. In the end, the EU succeeded in securing political agreement on the key features of the Kyoto Protocol such as a flexible (or Kyoto) mechanism and on special funds for the most vulnerable developing countries. The prospect for revitalising the Protocol came in sight at COP7 in November 2001, when the detailed legal aspects of the Protocol were finalised in the Marrakesh Accord.

Steps to Fulfillment of Japan's Obligations

Having obtained more leeway for carbon sinks,[23] the Japanese government began to prepare for the ratification of the Kyoto Protocol. About one month after the EU ratification, the Japanese government finalised its process of ratification on 4 June 2002. In March, prior to the ratification, it had also adopted a new policy guideline to alleviate global warming. The special feature of the new guideline is its step-by-step method. There are three steps in this policy scheme. During the first step period of 2002-2004, the government entrusts voluntary reduction efforts to industry. During the second step period of 2005-2007, the government will review the performance of current policies and, if necessary, introduce legal institutional reforms, including the introduction of an environment tax as one policy choice. Finally, Japan will keep its international commitment of 6 percent reduction.[24] The largest emitter within Japan is manufacturing industry, which accounts for roughly 60 percent of entire CO_2 emissions. Whereas CO_2 emissions from the manufacturing sector during 1990 and 1999 increased just by 1 percent, during the same period, the household sector increased by 17 percent and the transport sector by as much as 23 percent. Therefore, the objective of the new policy guideline, or "7 percent reduction by industry, 2 percent by households and 17 percent by transportation,"[25] is quite difficult, if not impossible.

The current trend across different sectors within Japan regarding emissions adds a new dimension relating to distributional justice. How to allocate emissions reduction among different industries is a vital issue to some industries and, at the same time, the utilisation of the Kyoto

---

[23] Japan's ceiling for forest sequestration of CO_2 as a part of domestic efforts to reduce greenhouse gases was raised to 13 million carbon tons, which in turn enabled Japan to rely on carbon sinks for 3.9 percent (up from 3.7 percent) of its target of 6 percent below the level of 1990 during 2008-2012.

[24] Division of Global Warming Prevention Headquarters of the Japanese government, "The Guideline for Measures to Prevent Global Warming," 12 March 2002.

[25] *Ibidem.*

mechanism may generate new commercial activities. While some eco-businesses may be able to grasp this opportunity to invent energy saving technologies and create new markets for them, others may suffer from emission regulations. Possible losers are the raw materials industries such as steel, chemical, paper, and cement industries.[26] In addition, some environmental NGOs have begun to stir up policy debate regarding a carbon tax as a legal instrument that could distribute reduction costs and responsibilities to all sectors, namely, manufacturing, transportation, and households.[27]

B. The Basic Features of the Guideline for Measures to Prevent Global Warming

Japan has committed itself to reducing GHGs by 6 percent below the 1990 level during the first commitment period of 2008-2012. The Guideline divides the overall objective of 6 percent reduction into four categories. The first category is to reduce 2.5 percent of CO_2, CH_4, and N_2O. The second is to reduce 3.9 percent by sequestration of CO_2 through forests. The third category actually allows the increase of HFC, PFC, and SF6 by 2 percent. The rest of the reductions will be achieved through the utilisation of the Kyoto mechanism. The following section summarises the content of each category according to the Guideline.[28]

Reduction of 2.5 Percent of CO_2, CH_4, and N_2O

The first category of objectives consists of three further subdivisions. The first consists of the CO_2 emission reduction from energy sources (approx. 0%). The second subdivision is the combination of CO_2 reduction from non-energy sources and the reduction of CH_4, and N_2O (-0.5%). The third is innovative technological development and efforts by all sectors of society (-2.0%).

(1) Reduction of CO_2 Emissions from Energy Sources (± 0%)

The main objective of the policy for reducing CO_2 emissions through energy sources is to contain the increase of CO_2 emissions as a whole, while setting differentiated goals for different sectors of Japanese society. Putting aside concerns about fairness in the allocation of burdens among the different sectors of society, the assigned amount for

---

[26] "Haisha to shosha" (Winners and Losers), *Nikkei Ecology*, July 2002, pp. 24-37.

[27] Tanso-zei kenkyukai (Carbon Tax Study Group), *Chikyu-ondanka taisaku sokushin-no tameno "tanso-zei" no sokidonyu-ni muketa seido-sekkei an (An Institutional Design Proposal toward the Early Introduction of Carbon Tax for Promoting Measures to Arrest Global Warming)*, 31 March 2002.

[28] This section refers to the Guideline of 2002 (see footnote 25 *supra*).

reducing CO_2 emissions from energy use differs for the industrial, residential and commercial, as well as transportation sector.

The industrial sector will reduce emissions by 7 percent or by approximately 462 million metric tons of CO_2 through the incremental implementation of voluntary Action Plans and their follow-up activities. The residential and commercial sector will take steps to reduce emissions by 2 percent or by approximately 260 million tons of CO_2, particularly through energy conservation measures. The latter include the introduction of energy management systems for large office buildings, in line with those in place in large factories, through revision of the Law Concerning the Rational Use of Energy; better distribution and use of high-efficiency water heating appliances; and the promotion of widespread use of energy management systems for households and businesses. As for the transportation sector, an increase in CO_2 emissions by 17 percent, or approximately 250 million tons of CO_2 will be allowed during the first commitment period. The distinctive measure adopted for the transportation sector is the introduction of the "top runner" approach, which will require all cars in the future to be at least as energy efficient as today's most fuel-efficient car. Other measures are the development and diffusion of low-emission vehicles, including clean energy vehicles, the improvement of efficiency in freight services through means such as a modal shift to marine transport, and promotion of the use of public transportation.

Other measures relate to all three sectors. The promotion of the use of alternative energy sources – solar, wind, thermal, biomass energy, fuel cells – will result in the reduction of 34 million tons of CO_2. Fuel conversion from coal to natural gas for power generation, for instance, will result in a reduction of 18 million tons of CO_2. The most controversial measure to reduce GHGs *via* energy sources is the promotion of nuclear power generation.

(2) Reduction of CO_2, CH_4, and N_2O
from Non-Energy Sources (-0.5%)

The reduction of CO_2 emissions from non-energy sources can be achieved through the implementation of waste-reduction legislation, policy innovations, and the promotion of recycling. Those measures include the implementation of the Waste Disposal Law and recycling-related laws, expansion of the use of timber and wood materials, cultivation of green manure on farmland, and promotion of recycling through composting. Emissions of methane (CH_4) will be reduced by half through direct landfill of wastes through the implementation of the Food Recycling Law and improvements in farmland management. In addition, it is expected that the development of emission-reduction technology for agriculture will reduce CH_4 emissions. The emission reduction of N_2O, the source of which is fertilisers, fossil fuel burning, and land conversion to agriculture, will be realised by upgrading the treatment of waste water sludge, through sewerage facility planning, and the like.

(3) Innovative Technological Development
      and Efforts by All Sectors of Society

A considerable portion of Japan's CO_2 reduction, or 2 percent, is assigned to innovative technological development and further promotion of activities to prevent global warming undertaken by Japan in all sectors of society. Innovative technological development includes new energy efficient steel production processes, new energy efficient chemical processes, development of materials for lighter vehicles, electronic equipment with low power consumption, and power transmission and distribution systems with low power loss.

All sectors of Japanese society are asked to take measures to prevent global warming. People are encouraged to change incandescent lighting to fluorescent lighting and to conserve energy when they use refrigerators. The Guideline recommends that office workers turn off lights during breaks and curtail unnecessary photocopying.

Checking the Increase of HFC, PFC, and SF6 (+ 2%)

Another major category for reduction of GHG emissions aims at cutting back emissions of HFC, PFC and SF6 to a level of a 2 percent increase, as opposed to the projected 5 percent increase if no countermeasures had been taken. Some of the measures are the development of new alternative substances, low-cost and compact technology for recycling and break-down of fluorocarbons, as well as implementation of the Home Appliance Recycling Law and Fluorocarbon Recovery and Decomposition Law.

Forest Sequestration (-3.9%)

The largest portion of Japanese governmental reduction scheme belongs to forest absorption of CO_2. Although the 1998 Guideline initially requested a 3.7 percent reduction by forests, Japan obtained 3.9 percent, or 0.2% more than that allocated to it at the COP7. This gain was obtained mainly because EU member states were anxious for Japan to remain within the framework of the Kyoto Protocol.[29] Some measures include development of healthy forests through planting, weeding and thinning, promotion of the use of wood and wood biomass, and promotion of tree planting in urban areas.

---

[29] The same thing may be said for Russia's gain for forests sequestration.

The above are the main components of Japan's policy guidelines for mitigation of global warming.[30] Some other programs and initiatives include climate technology initiatives, the promotion of studies on ocean sequestration of carbon dioxide, geological sequestration of carbon dioxide and large-scale solar power generation. There are also substantial international R&D projects in process, such as International Cooperation for Energy and the Environment (Green Aid Plan: $ 89.76 million; the provision of the Foundations for International Facilitation of Clean Coal Technology: $ 21.66 million; and the promotion of International Joint Research Projects with the Oil-Supplied Countries: $ 20.35 million).

Japanese environmental NGOs are critical of Japanese government policy, particularly its heavy reliance on nuclear power, innovative technologies, and carbon sinks. The EU and most developing countries were also hoping for more assertive Japanese leadership in mitigating climate change. Japanese leadership can be a crucial force since a country like Japan, which has already achieved the highest rate of energy efficiency among the developed countries, could become a role model for the rest of the world. The short-term costs of implementing measures for alleviating climate change loom disproportionately large for Japan in comparison with other industrial countries. What, then, is the rationale for Japan's taking a leadership role in mitigating climate change? What is the major policy discourse on climate change? The next section deals with these questions.

IV. Policy Discourse and the Prospects for Japan-EU Cooperation

After COP6, policy wrangles between the Ministry of the Environment (MoE) and the Ministry of Economy, Trade and Industry (METI) gradually became more noticeable, particularly over the issue of introducing environmental tax. The issue of climate change has become such a central item of Japanese foreign policy that Prime Minister is in charge of policy-making under the leadership of the Global Warming Prevention Headquarters. However, METI traditionally places greater priority on protection of industrial interests than on environmental protection. There are no clear policy guidelines for the utilisation of the Kyoto mechanism, such as for assigning specific targets to each industry. Because of this, METI (and the energy intensive industries) may be unwilling to adopt a policy for a "cap-and-trade" emissions reduction system but rely on voluntary reduction efforts by industry.

---

[30] The remaining 1.6 percent will be reduced overseas through the utilisation of the Kyoto mechanism.

Moreover, METI is not fully supportive of the idea of imposing an environmental tax. When the MoE made public its interim draft report and solicited public views on proposed policies, including an environmental tax, METI's deputy-minister criticised the proposal. He stated that it was too early to talk about such a policy in concrete terms and there were other policy options for dealing with global warming.[31] Shunichi Suzuki, the then environment minister, countered this argument by stating that the timing was not at all too early, for it would be too late to start an inquiry into the introduction of an environmental tax as an economic policy measure only should the 2004 policy review arrive at the conclusion that additional measures to arrest global warming were necessary.[32]

A. Proposal for an Environmental Tax

Aiming at its introduction in 2005, the MoE's policy draft on a carbon (or global warming) tax was presented on 17 July 2003 to the special committee within the Central Environmental Council, an MoE policy advisory body.[33] A portion of the new tax revenues would be allocated to local governments to arrest global warming. With regard to measures to reduce rapidly increasing CO_2 emissions from the household sector, a policy is advocated of financial assistance for newly built energy-saving houses and the promotion of energy conserving household appliances along with the replacement of energy consuming ones. As for the transportation sector, the dissemination of fuel-cell automobiles is the main feature of the policy proposal.

The proposed global warming tax is a new category of taxation levied according to the carbon content of fossil fuels such as coal and oil. The imposition of the carbon tax seeks simplification through "upstream imposition," where the number of taxpayers is small. Referring to the current oil tax and taxes on volatile oils such as benzene and naphtha, the global warming tax would be imposed on importers of crude oil and the manufacturers of petroleum-related products. Since petroleum used for the production of synthetic fibers does not produce CO_2, this sector would be considered to be exempt from this tax. Taking international competitiveness into consideration, tax reduction measures would be applied to the steel, cement, and other industries, which consume vast quantities of petroleum-based energy. In short, according to the MoE trial calculation, a tax of at least ¥ 3,400 per ton of carbon would be

---

[31] Jiji tsushin sha (the Jiji Press) and Kyodo tsushin sha (the Kyodo News Service), 17 July 2003.

[32] Jiji tsushin sha (the Jiji Press), 22 July 2003.

[33] Kyodo tsushin sha (the Kyodo News Service), 18 July 2003.

required in order to fulfill the international commitment under the Kyoto Protocol.[34]

However, Russia has not yet initiated the process of ratification so that the Protocol is not likely to become effective in 2004. This current development is now encouraging METI's cautious position to the early imposition of carbon tax, which is to be introduced during the second step phase (2005-2007) of the Guideline. Nonetheless, as the Guideline is the policy decision made by the Cabinet, this fact suggests that this policy will be implemented regardless of the delay of the effectuation of the Protocol.[35] More importantly, if a new global warming tax is introduced, even at the modest rate of taxation of 3,400 yen per carbon ton, it could generate a substantial amount of revenue (about ¥950 billion according to MoE's trial calculation) that could be used as subsidies for the implementation of climate change policy. The allocation of this new revenue must be in the interest of all concerned ministries such as Ministry of Agriculture, Forestry and Fisheries, Ministry of Land, Infrastructure and Transport and even METI.[36] In the end, a policy coalition for the new taxation may become a majority within the policy circle, unless a strong drive leads to the use of the market system by establishing a "cap and trade" emissions trading system in Japan.

B. Prospects for Japan-EU Cooperation Beyond 2012

An interim report of METI's Industrial Structure Council of July 2003, entitled "Perspectives and Actions to Construct a Future Sustainable Framework on Climate Change," represents METI's stance on global climate change.[37] Although the METI report admits the difficul-

---

[34] Chuo Kankyo Shingikai (Central Environment Council of Ministry of the Environment), "Ondanka-taisaku-zeisei no gutaiteki-na seido no an" (A Draft on Specifics for Global Warming Taxation), 29 August 2003, p. 7.

[35] An interview with Ms Kimiko Hirata of Kiko (Climate) Network (a Japanese environmental NGO that specialises in issues of global climate change) on 4 November 2003.

[36] The budget for the Guideline to Prevent Global Warming in the fiscal year of 2003 was about 1.32 trillion yen in total. The largest amount of about 390 billion yen was allocated to forestry related projects such as forest environment conservation projects. The second largest share of about 320 billion yen was measures for the promotion of nuclear energy. The third largest amount of about 200 billion yen was allocated to the provision of waste treatment facilities, non-energy source CO_2 and methane emissions reductions through the improvement of water drainage systems in rural communities and the like. In addition, about 126 billion yen was allocated for the establishment of an environmentally friendly transportation system, and about 122 billion for new energy development. [A draft policy paper of August 2003 issued by the MoE Central Environment Council, p. 11 (see footnote 2 *supra*).]

[37] The following description of METI policy on climate change is from a summary of the Interim Report entitled "Perspectives and Actions to Construct a Future

ties for Japan of achieving the emissions reduction target stipulated in the Kyoto Protocol, because Japan has already achieved high energy efficiency, it promises Japanese efforts to implement various measures steadily under the new national program to arrest global warming in a step-by-step approach. The report also stresses the importance of creating a new international framework in which both the United States, the world's largest greenhouse gases (GHGs) emitter, and developing countries, themselves emerging major-GHG emitters, take responsibility for reducing GHG emissions. Accordingly, a truly meaningful climate regime beyond 2012 must take into account each country's energy supply and demand structure. This implies the importance of cost effectiveness for adopting various policy measures. With the reflection of differences in an energy supply-and-demand structure, the marginal costs of greenhouse gas reductions differ greatly from country to country, from region to region and from sector to sector. Therefore, it is suggested that future agreement on the allocation of responsibilities among states must be made fair and just by taking into consideration the different marginal costs of reducing GHGs.

Aside from the 1990 base-year problem, METI's interim report expresses some reservations about the so-called "EU Bubble"[38] and, at the same time, points to the need for a special consideration of the redistribution of new EU members' emissions allowance for the framework beyond 2012. Although the EU as a whole has committed itself to 8 percent reduction during the first commitment period of 2008-2012, some EU member states can be exempt from reduction and even can increase their emissions. Whereas Luxembourg, Germany, and the United Kingdom will substantially reduce GHG emissions by 28, 21, and 12.5 percents respectively, France is not required to reduce at all and Portugal, Greece, and Spain can even increase their emissions by 27, 25, and 15 percent respectively. It is not so easy for Japan, for instance, to accept that France should be exempt from reducing GHG emissions, given that both Japan and France belong to Annex B of the Kyoto Protocol. Moreover, according to the METI interim report, each EU member state has sole responsibility for reducing GHG emissions and can utilise the Kyoto mechanism more flexibly than can non-EU Annex B countries of the Kyoto Protocol. This is another source of discontent since non-EU countries' utilisation of the Kyoto mechanism

Sustainable Framework on Climate Change," Global Environmental Subcommittee, Environmental Committee of Industrial Structure Council, July 2003.

[38] Article 4 of the Kyoto Protocol allows the Parties to redistribute their emissions commitments in ways that preserve their collective goal. According to this agreement, while the EU as a whole committed to 8 percent reduction, its member states set up different goals. This is called the EU Bubble.

is constrained by the norm of supplementarity to domestic reduction efforts.[39]

With regard to the enlarged EU and a future sustainable framework on climate change, the METI interim report calls for special consideration of the redistribution of emissions allowances generated by new candidate states for the enlarged EU. As we can see in Table 1 (Appendix I), the total GHG emissions of most candidate states for the enlarged EU (or EU-25) substantially declined from the level of 1990 to that of 2000. Although the scope of the EU Bubble is strictly limited to the present 15 countries, the METI report suggests that a future framework beyond 2012 eliminate the "hot air" of the additional ten EU member states, or their excess emission allowances over the business-as-usual emissions.[40]

Finally, with the recognition of the nature and value of a stable global climate as indispensable to the global public good, the METI report emphasises the significance of technological breakthroughs in order to cope with the long-term challenge of arresting global warming. For instance, alternative energy sources capable of replacing fossil fuels or much more energy-conserving technologies than state-of-the-art technologies are the key to success. In addition, the dissemination of appropriate existing technologies to developing countries is also essential for the success of international efforts to tackle the long-term challenge.

While agreeing on the importance of technology, another policy report of the MoE stresses the absolute gain of mitigating global climate change. A policy report delivered during COP9 in Milan presented seven points for basic consideration on a climate regime beyond 2012.[41] For instance, this interim report calls for continuous progress to meet the ultimate objective of achieving stabilisation of greenhouse gases in the atmosphere "at a level that would prevent dangerous anthropogenic interference with the climate system" (Article 2 of the UNFCCC), bringing the Kyoto Protocol into effect, and achieving global participation including the United States and developing countries. This report goes on to focus on the importance of ensuring equity based on the principle of common but differentiated responsibilities (CBDR) (Article 3.1 of the UNFCCC).[42] In order to ensure equity between developed

---

[39] METI Interim Report of July 2003, pp. 28-29.

[40] *Ibid.*, p. 29.

[41] Global Environment Committee, Central Environment Council of Ministry of the Environment, "Climate Regime beyond 2012: Basic Considerations, Interim Report (Draft)," December 2003.

[42] See footnote 4 of this paper.

and developing countries based on the CBDR principle, the report calls on developed countries' leadership in combating climate change and, at the same time, for special consideration to be given to the circumstances of developing countries, which lack capabilities to address climate change. It also calls for taking different circumstances among developed countries and among developing countries into consideration for more equitable burden sharing *vis-à-vis* a climate regime beyond 2012.

All in all, despite some different policy preferences between the MoE and METI, both are in keeping with the Japanese government position of supporting the Kyoto Protocol together with the EU. Thus, for instance, METI reservations about EU collective efforts should be understood in the context of building a sustainable climate change regime into the future, or beyond 2012.

V. Strengthening Climate Change Regime Beyond 2012

Both Japan's Ministry of the Environment (MoE) and Ministry of the Economy, Trade and Industry (METI) regard a stable global climate system as an international public good. Both recognise Japan's responsibility for mitigating global warming and are willing to help the most vulnerable developing countries to adapt to the adverse consequences of climate change. However, while the MoE emphasises the importance of the principle of "common but differentiated responsibilities," the METI emphasises the fair and just distribution of costs and efficient ways of alleviating global climate change. With regard to policy implementation, whereas the MoE is attempting to take the initiative in introducing a global warming tax as a fair and effective means of sharing costs, METI's preference is to solicit voluntary efforts by industry and reluctant to promote both the introduction of a new environmental taxation or a "cap-and-trade" emissions trading system at home.

The abandonment of the Kyoto Protocol by the United States inadvertently united the rest of the world and forced the EU to make a concession to Japan and the Russian Federation during the resumed COP6. As a result, both Japan and Russia obtained more allowances for the sequestration of CO_2 by forests than they had previously demanded. The defection of the United States thus indirectly raised Japan's (and Russia's) negotiating position high enough to obtain substantial relative gains, while reducing absolute gains in terms of the stabilisation of global climate system. Some may argue that the unyielding stance of the EU during COP6 was a diplomatic blunder since it was forced to make substantial compromises at the resumed COP6 and COP7. In any event, it seems fair to say that the great importance of the Kyoto Protocol to Japanese foreign policy can be seen in the fact that Japan finally decided to step forward with the EU and the rest of the world by ratifying the Kyoto Protocol, thereby leaving the United States behind.

Ever expanding and deepening Japan-EU relations support this move. With a combined population of 500 million, Japan and the EU comprise less than 10 percent of the world's population. Yet their combined GDP accounts for more than 40 percent of the world's total. The scope and domain of their economic relations are increasingly broadening and deepening over such areas as trade, foreign direct investment, and regulatory reform. The wider and deeper their relations become, the more important it will be for both Japan and EU to promote stability in each region of the world. Furthermore, their prominence entails regional and global responsibilities for the promotion and main-tenance of peace and security. Accordingly, Japan and the EU promul-gated the 1991 Joint Declaration and the Action Plan for EU-Japan Cooperation of 2001,[43] which together laid the foundations for Japan-EU relations into the 21st century.

Aiming to strengthen their cooperation, the 10th Japan-EU Summit adopted the Action Plan. Its four basic objectives include: (1) promoting peace and security; (2) strengthening the economic and trade partner-ship; (3) coping with global and societal challenges, and (4) bringing people and cultures together.[44] Under the third objective of coping with global and societal challenges, the Action Plan called for additional efforts to ensure the entry into force of the Kyoto Protocol by 2002.[45]

This immediate goal has yet to be met. However, various mid-term and long-term collective efforts can be pursued in order to mitigate global climate change, in the meantime persuading the Russian govern-ment to ratify the Kyoto Protocol. In concluding this chapter, I would like to present some suggestions for future Japan-EU cooperation beyond 2012. I suggest that mid-term policy objectives involve techno-logical cooperation and efforts to enhance the sense of fairness about the climate regime. As to technological cooperation, the "top runner" program may be a good way of achieving environmental goals through technological innovation.[46] International technological cooperation

---

[43]   The Joint Declaration on Relations between the EC and Its Member States and Japan was signed in The Hague on 18 July 1991. The Action Plan entitled "Sharing Our Common Future" was adopted at European Union-Japan Summit in Brussels in 2001.

[44]   "Sharing Our Common Future," *ibid.*

[45]   *Ibid.*, p. 15.

[46]   This program was introduced for the transportation sector (and now expanding to other sectors) to set high fuel efficiency standards for automobiles. This program will require all cars in the future to be at least as fuel efficient as today's most fuel-efficient car. The government intends to tighten the standard every few years to ensure continued gains in efficiency. If fully implemented, the current "top runner"

among Japan, the EU (hopefully also with the United States), and key developing countries like China and India is indispensable to the mitigation of climate change. However, this type of technological cooperation should not be limited to advanced technological development such as fuel cell technology. We should pay more attention to the joint reinvention of alternative or traditional technologies for sustainable development. As to enhancing the sense of fairness about the climate regime, we need to maintain the authority or legitimacy of international cooperative frameworks. In other words, Japan and the EU should continue to make strenuous efforts for broader participation in GHG emission reductions. If possible, efforts should be made to cooperate with pro-action states and other non-state actors in the United States and the key developing countries – China, India, and Mexico – in restraining or reducing GHG emissions. Moreover, for strengthening the cooperative framework beyond 2012, it is essential to narrow the perception gaps on the fair distribution of emission reduction targets between Japan and the EU or the enlarged EU.

Finally, a broad range of long-term efforts is important as well. Japan and the EU can continuously work to reduce uncertainties about global climate change through scientific and administrative cooperation. At the same time, they can work together closely to search for models of genuine sustainable development between the developed and developing countries through technological cooperation. Within the framework of the Kyoto Protocol, both can continuously utilise overseas incentive mechanisms (ET, JI, and CDM), as initiatives supplementary to domestic efforts for reducing GHG emissions. It is also indispensable to enhance partnership among multi-stakeholders, including local governments, private corporations, and environmental NGOs. In short, with their strongly shared sense of global responsibility, Japan and the EU together should take the initiative in mitigating climate change beyond 2012. The prospects for fair weather in the future lie, indeed, in the success of Japan-EU cooperation.

---

standard will mandate significant improvements in automobile efficiency (on average a 22.8% improvement by 2010 over 1995 levels).

Appendix I

Table 1: Total GHG Emissions of Annex B Countries
(Million-ton CO_2)

Country	Total GHG (1990)*	Total GHG (2000)	% Change	Kyoto Target
Austria	85.8	89.2	3.9	-13
Belgium	141.3	158.5	12.2	-7.5
Denmark	68.9	67.9	-1.5	-21
Finland	74.9	71.8	-4.2	0
France	545.4	547.7	0. 3	0
Germany	1,202.3	992.6	-17.4	-21
Greece	101.3	122.1	20.6	25
Ireland	54.6	67.0	22.7	13
Italy	514.1	538.6	4.8	-6.5
Luxembourg	11.8	9.3	-21.0	-28
Netherlands	214.1	223.9	4.6	-6
Portugal	65.2	87.2	33.8	27
Spain	290.3	389.4	34.1	15
Sweden	70.4	70.5	0.1	4
United Kingdom	748.8	659.0	-12.0	-12.5
EU-15 sub-total	**4,198.2**	**4,094.0**	**-2.3**	**-8**
Czech Republic	185.9	142.0	-2.3	-8
Estonia	39.0	17.2	-55.8	-8
Hungary	104.2	83.8	-19.6	-6
Latvia	29.5	11.0	-62.8	-8
Lithuania	45.2	20.8	-54.0	-8
Poland	532.8	376.3	-29.4	-6
Slovakia	72.7	49.5	-31.8	-8
Slovenia	18.4	19.8	7.7	-8
EU-25 sub-total**	**5,216.9**	**4,814.4**	**-7.7**	
Australia	415.8	497.5	19.7	8
Canada	608.1	736.7	21.2	-6
Iceland	2.8	3.2	12.9	10
Japan	1,256.7	1,381.5	9.9	-6
New Zealand	72.9	81.2	11.4	0
Norway	50.7	57.8	14.0	1
Switzerland	54.1	54.4	0.5	-8
United States of America	6,167.2	7,020.7	13.8	-7
Non-EU Annex B countries sub-total	**8,628.3**	**9,833.0**	**14.0**	

Country	Total GHG (1990)*	Total GHG (2000)	% Change	Kyoto Target
Russian Federation	3,031.1	2,006.9	-33.8	0
Bulgaria	144.7	76.3	-47.3	-8
Croatia	27.8	25.6	-7.6	-5
Romania	267.4	121.2	-54.7	-8
Ukraine	907.4	457.5	-49.6	0
Economies-in-Transition sub-total	4,378.4	2,687.5	-38.6	
Annex B total	**18,223.6**	**17,334.9**	**-4.9**	**-5.2**

Source: IEA/OECD, CO$_2$ Emissions from Fuel Combustion, UNFCCC National Communications

* Base year for HFC's, PFC's and SF6 is either 1990 or 1995, whichever is larger, and base year of some EIT countries (Bulgaria, Hungary, Poland and Romania) for CO$_2$, CH$_4$ and N$_2$O is also 1995.

** The data for Malta and Cyprus are not included in EU-25.

CHAPTER 7

The Doha Development Agenda and Its Impact on Enlarged EU-Asia Relations

Willem VAN DER GEEST

Director, European Institute for Asian Studies, Brussels[1]

I. Introduction

The European Union (EU) is a unique institutional structure integrating and creating a union of countries with as many as twenty-five member states by May 2004. This recent enlargement is an unique historical occasion and must be seen as a quantum leap, certainly compared to the four earlier enlargements of the Union. The EU develops its own systems of supra-national governance through its 'common policies' as well as its common European Union institutions. This feature distinguishes it from other initiatives of regional integration, such as the ASEAN or the South Asian Association for Regional Cooperation (SAARC) – the EU exhibits 'deep' integration, whereas that of others is, at best, shallow.

In response to the request of the organisers, I will focus on one particular implication of the forthcoming enlargement – its impact on the EU's economic cooperation and development partners in Asia. I will place this in the context of the multi-lateral process of the WTO Doha Development Round, which stalled following the failure to reach any tangible agreement at the 5th Ministerial in Cancún.

---

[1] The European Institute for Asian Studies is an independent think tank on EU-ASIA relations for the European Union institutions, supported by the European Commission. It seeks to inform the European Union institutions about recent political, economic and security developments in Asia and encourage scholarly enquiry regarding relations between the European Union and Asia. All views expressed are those of the author alone and can in no way be attributed to EIAS or its sponsoring EU institutions.

II. Globalisation, Regionalisation and Competitive Markets

'Globalisation' implies an intensification of competition through multiple channels. As I have emphasised in previous presentations at this distinguished University, as well as in my presentations to the Asian International Forum in Fukuoka, Japan,[2] three of these channels are particularly important:

I.   increased competition with low wage countries (North-South trade);

II. increased competition in product and capital markets (especially through endogenous technical changes within the OECD); and

III. increased volatility of financial flows and portfolio investments (with the risks of contagion and economic instability).

Promoting greater trade and investment flows are the main objectives of the WTO Doha Development Round, actively supported by the EU and Japan. In this context, the EU and Japan are 'active globalisers' – as indeed is China, as well as other countries of East Asia.

The first type of global competition is essentially regulated through the market access rules and trade policy regime of the European Union. However, openness to external trade and investment alone does not necessarily ensure a competitive economy. For example, Hong Kong and Singapore are extremely open economies, with the highest scores for openness to trade, irreversibility of this policy and predictable trade and investment policy regimes. Nevertheless, this does not mean that one does not find cartels and oligopolies in these countries. Openness to trade and investment is beyond doubt a necessary condition for economic efficiency, but it is not the only one.

The second type of global competition, driven by innovation and technology, is played out at the level of the EU, US, Japan, Korea, China etc. Enterprises do not operate in a static way, but make relocation and restructuring decision throughout, including cross-border mergers. It is for this reason that un-regulated open markets may drift towards forms of monopoly, albeit usually of a temporary and limited nature. Therefore, the EU's approach to openness of its markets is complemented by developing and practising its own unique competition policy.[3]

---

2   The Asian International Forums I – III were organised in Fukuoka, Japan by the Kyushu University and the city's Prefecture in order to assess the regional integration in response to globalisation.

3   It is unique because the EU, as a supra-national institution, acts as an arbiter between national interests of its member states, each of which has its own economic structures as well as its own regime and 'best practices' for regulating competition.

It is increasingly recognised that the EU's economic structures are perhaps best characterised by 'imperfect competition'. The ideal-type of the purely competitive market in which numerous atomistic enterprises compete with equal information and resources for well-defined markets simply does not apply to major segments of the EU's industrial and services sectors.

The 'normal model' for high-tech and high-value added industry and services in the mature economies of the EU is perhaps that of a 'weak' or 'Cournot' monopolist, in which the enterprise can respond to a market demand function with a range of price-quantity choices. Unlike the context of 'pure competition', the Cournot monopolist can extract higher profits than the firm operating in the purely competitive environment. However, this gain is realised through a re-distribution or transfer of welfare from consumers to producers. EU competition policy is designed to minimise the 'deadweight loss' or 'social cost of monopoly' which results from this.

The recent EU enlargement may bring several dominant players from individual member states together through cross-border mergers and acquisitions. This provides a heightened need to ensure that competitiveness within the Union is maintained and indeed, strengthened.

But most fundamentally, to ensure a smooth process of enlargement, it is essential that the economic benefits from the larger and more integrated market may be captured by all players competing on equal terms. In particular, it is important that dominant firms from the EU-15 do not reap windfall profits by buying out smaller firms in the acceding economies characterised by less advanced R&D and less efficient technology, lower factor productivity etc.

This is in particularly important for those industrial sectors characterised by considerable economies of scale such as the chemical processing industry or the industrial pharmaceutical sector. However also in the services sectors, one finds the economies of scale, usually related to the existence of chains and networks which can supply additional services for a very low marginal cost. The banking and telecom industries are two classic examples of this.

To achieve this equitable competition, a neutral and respected referee is needed, placed above the national interests. The EC Treaty gives that role to the European Commission, which, under the control of the Court of Justice, can establish Community law on competition. These European laws take precedence over those of the national governments.

The Commission can also take direct decisions and the member states cannot oppose Commission decisions.[4]

III. The Failure of Cancún and the Implications for EU-Asia Partnership

Mr Pascal Lamy, the European Commissioner for Trade, noted on his personal website prior to the Cancún Ministerial meeting that it was not going to be an exotic holiday. Indeed, he doubted very much that he would have any time to go to the beach. The Cancún agenda covered some twenty complex international trade issues, related to agricultural and industrial goods, trade in services, intellectual property rights and medicine and, finally, the so-called 'Singapore issues'. Competition was one of the 'Singapore issues', perhaps second in sensitivity only to investment. Added to these were other pressing problems such as transparency in government procurement and trade facilitation. Mr Lamy referred to these as the 'less sexy' topics and it may be argued that, if nothing else, at least one outcome of the failure of the Cancún Ministerial has been to 'sex them up' a bit.

It became clear that not only the EU and its partners in Asia, but also the US have different positions on market openness and competition. There was no sign of any genuine convergence at Cancún in this area. The US agrees that international cooperation on anti-trust is desirable, but should not be done through the WTO. In contrast, the EU, in order to complement its common competition policy for the enlarged European Union, seeks to move towards a WTO multilateral agreement on competition policy. Indeed, the issue of competition was brought onto the agenda of the WTO by the EU, along with others, as long ago as 1995-1996. The EU was keen to see progress towards the adoption of a WTO agreement on the core principles of a multilateral competition policy.

Mr Lamy had already conceded prior to Cancún that the EU would not be taking a 'maximalist position', accepting that developing countries in Asia and elsewhere would have to move at their own pace and that 'flexibility' was called for. At the first bi-annual Singapore Ministerial a specific Working Group had been set up to:

> ... study ... the interaction between trade and competition policy, including anti-competitive practices, in order to identify any areas that may merit fur-

---

[4] The types of anti-competitive practices specifically prohibited include (i) price fixing and market-sharing arrangements (ii) artificial limits on production and investment (iii) price-discrimination and the application of dissimilar conditions to equivalent transactions; and (iv) the imposition of supplementary obligations, unrelated to the original purchase or product.

ther consideration in the WTO framework. (Singapore Ministerial Declaration, Article 20)

The formation of this Working Group was in no way going to prejudge the question of whether or not negotiations should be initiated in the future – this would only happen after an 'explicit consensus decision' among WTO Members regarding such negotiations.[5]

The Doha Declaration at the end of the 4th Ministerial meeting in November 2001 reaffirmed this approach. However, it went beyond the Singapore statement in the sense that it clarified that it was 'agreed that negotiations *will* take place' after the 5th Ministerial session (in Cancún) on the basis of an 'explicit consensus' on the modalities of the negotiation (Doha Declaration, Article 23). In the period prior to Cancún, there was to be further work on core principles for trade and competition, modalities for voluntary cooperation and the need for capacity building in this field within developing countries, especially the LDCs (Doha Declaration, Article 25). The Chairman of the Doha Ministerial, Qatari Trade and Finance Minister Yussef Hussain Kamal, clarified in his closing statement prior to the adoption of the Doha Declaration that 'explicit consensus' meant that each WTO member had the right to

> take a position on modalities that would prevent negotiations from proceeding after the 5th Session of the Ministerial Conference until that member is prepared to join in an explicit consensus. (quoting from WTO website[6])

Followingup the Doha meeting, the European Commission submitted a communication to the WTO's Working Group on the Interaction between Trade and Competition Policy. It sets out the 'core principles' at stake in competition policy, from a European point of view. Despite these constructive efforts at clarification, the EU position and its approach in Cancún seemed to be characterised by a considerable inflexibility as well as an inability to communicate clearly its willingness to shift its position on the Singapore issues.

---

[5] It may be remembered that the OECD had been forced to withdraw its proposal for a multi-lateral investment agreement, under pressure from consumers, industry and developing countries – of course the EU was keen to avoid such an embarrassing situation on any of the four issues.

[6] www.wto.int.

According to one insider with Green Room access,[7] during Cancún there was no narrowing of the vast divisions between the WTO members. According to this source while some said that negotiations should continue on all four issues, others suggested negotiations in some areas but not others, and still others 'were adamant that none of these areas should be the subject of negotiations'. The Singapore issues had been 'the most inflammatory' and inspired the 'greatest degree of anger' between Members at the Head of Delegations meeting, which took place the night before the collapse of the Cancún Ministerial.[8]

In his de-briefing at the European Parliament, Mr Lamy pointed to the LDC group's refusal of the Chair's compromise to negotiate on only one of the Singapore issues – transparency in commercial transactions and in public procurement.[9] He noted that South Korea's position was 'diametrically opposed' to this suggestion as it insisted that investment and competition remain on the table. However, his speech to the European Parliament's plenary did not indicate that the EU itself was ready to accept the 'one issue' compromise. A clear, strong and positive endorsement by the EU of the Chair's compromise proposal might quite easily have persuaded the LDC group. They had too much to loose from the delay and interruption of the Doha trade negotiations. Nevertheless, the Doha Development agenda is now in intensive care and on a life-support machine, probably not to be resuscitated before the Hong Kong Ministerial some time late 2004 or early 2005.

In my personal assessment, the LDC coordinator Bangladesh would have been able to forge some unity amongst its sub-group on such a compromise approach, all the more so because greater transparency in public procurement tends to be consistent with the efficiency and equity objectives of low income countries. The opposition of South Korea to restricting the negotiations to just one single issue could easily have been deflected by the EU and/or US. Indeed, it would seem disingenuous for the EU Commissioner to hide behind South Korea's insistence on competition and investment – what about the EU itself?

---

[7] The Green Room is the consultative subcommittee in the WTO which prepares decisions – the major players and a selected number of other members participate. For example the 49 LDC countries were at Cancún represented by three Trade Ministers in the Green Room process.

[8] Rockwell, K. M. (2003), 'China and Chinese Taipei – the challenge that confronts them', paper delivered at the European Alliance for Asian Studies workshop held at the School of Oriental and African Studies, University of London, 17 October 2003.

[9] P. Lamy, European Commissioner for Trade and the EU's Chief Negotiator at Cancún; text of his speech at the European Parliament, Strasbourg, 24 September 2003. Re-printed in full in *EurAsia Bulletin*, Vol. 7, Nos 8&9, pp 18-20.

IV. Longer Term Perspective on EU Trade and Enlargement[10]

Today's world does not even remotely look like the early post-war years, which had been characterised by Europe's trade deficits, financed by concessional borrowing from the US through the Marshall plan. Indeed, today's world consists of trade surpluses in Asian countries, leading to reserve accumulation used to finance US twin deficits in both its public finance and current account.

Simultaneous to the deepening of European integration, the Eurostat trade time-series from 1958-2001 tell a different story. These speak of the fast emergence of Asia, and in particular, China, rather than the EU, as a global trading power. The data also demonstrate why ASEM is important. I shall review the evidence through a few selected facts:

- world trade grew from the equivalent of €70 billion in 1958 to well over €5 trillion in 2001 – some 72 times in monetary terms over just 42 years;
- nevertheless, 2001 was the first year which saw a substantial decrease in global trade value (-5.5 percent), after decades of continuous growth;
- neither the US nor the EU (despite its enlargements) were the fastest growing – indeed they both lost in terms of their share of world trade; the US share fell from 24 to 16 percent and in the case of the EU, from 29 to 20 percent;
- some 10 Asian countries had become major global players by 2001 – in order of importance of exports these were Japan, China, Hong Kong, South Korea, Malaysia, Thailand, Indonesia, India and the Philippines. *EurAsia Bulletin* readers will recognise that this list (except for India) offers a striking resemblance to the Asian membership of the ASEM;
- of these Asia-10, some five countries did not even register just one-tenth of one percent in world exports when the Treaty of Rome was signed – these were China, Korea, Malaysia, Indonesia and the Philippines;
- the global trade share of these Asia-10 started very modestly at 7 percent in 1960, to double by 1970 and once again to (nearly) double by 1990 to 27 percent of global trade – by which time the Asia-10 had surpassed both the EU and the US;
- in 2000 more than 30 percent of global export value originated in the Asia-10 – which was close to the sum of EU plus US exports – which together traded 33 percent of global exports in value terms. The graph below sums up these selected facts, also presented in Table 1, which will appear as Annex 1.

---

[10] An earlier version of this section of the paper was first published in the *EurAsia Bulletin*, Vol. 7, No. 3, pp. 30-31.

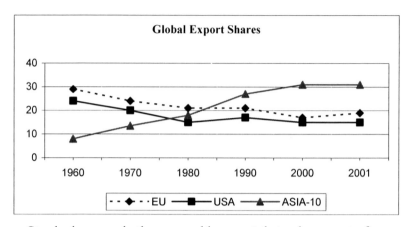

Standard economic theory would suggest that enlargement of a customs union would stimulate trade within its area, diverting trade away from imports from outside the free trade region. Whereas the EU-6 posted trade deficits, these grew in size during the EU-10. However, by 1986 the EU had expanded to twelve member states and during four out of the nine years between 1986 and 1995, the Union recorded trade surpluses. With the further expansion to EU-15 since 1995, the EU had a modest trade surplus during 3 out of 6 years. These amounted to between €20-€50 billion, while deficits during the other three years were comparatively manageable – certainly not greater than those experienced during the 1980s. If we aggregate over the six years for which we have EU-15 data, it is not unreasonable to argue that the EU-15 is now genuinely close to a zero-trade balance. Hence, the EU times-series evidence seems generally supportive of this basic notion of economic integration.

If we look at the pattern of inter-regional trade balances, we can note the following selected/pertinent/salient facts:

- the EU has always had significant trade deficits with the USSR, Japan and China;

- while those with Russia and China have continued to grow, those with Japan, as well as the four Asian tigers, appear to have remained stable since the late 1990s; and

- since the most recent enlargement of 1995, the EU trade surplus with the North American Free Trade Area (NAFTA) has grown significantly, reaching some € 55 billion in 2001.

A thorough analysis of the economic impact of enlargement on the rest of the world remains a topic of policy research requiring serious investigation. In particular, an analysis of the likely impact of the forthcoming enlargement to EU-25 on patterns of global and inter-regional trade is imperative. Will the Asia-10 continue to support substantial trade surpluses with the EU, while the EU achieves trade surpluses with NAFTA? Or will trade-diversion cause downward pressure on EU imports? If so, what will be the impact of enlargement on EU-Asia trade and investment flows?

V. Concluding Remarks

At present, it is inconceivable that multilateral or international agreements in East Asia should become an effective arbiter for competing national interests, for example between China and Japan or between Korea and China. At best, the EU can provide some useful support in the right direction. The EU-Japan agreement on anti-competitive practices, signed in July 2004, is an important step in the right direction. It makes explicit provision for information-sharing and notification, e.g. on hard-core cartels; in short, it enhances global competition. Why not seek to replicate this between the EU and other countries, or for that matter, promote such agreement amongst third parties, such as Japan and China?

The EU competition and investment policy regimes inside its borders are vital for several reasons indicated above (Section 2). However, the insistence on multilateralising EU principles and competition and investment to a heterogeneous world in Asia and Latin America would appear misguided. The EU went a step too far in Cancún with its insistence on fully-fledged negotiations on the Singapore issues. This risks a harmful upset of multilateral trade relations with Asia. In short, some bilateral approaches to the Singapore issues may be appropriate and feasible, but the multi-lateral approach is bound to have to wait.

References

European Commission (2001), "Europe and Asia: A Strategic Framework for an Enhanced Partnership," COM(2001), 469, 4.09.01 final.

European Commission, DG Competition (various), IP/00/906; IP/01/1232; IP/03/1150.

Eurostat (2002), *Commerce Extérieur et Intra-Union Européenne – Annuaire Statistique: Données 1958-2001.* The volume covers global trade, trade with major partners, trade by product type and trade by EU member states.

Moussis, N. (2002), *Access to the European Union; Law, Economics, Policies* (11th revised edition), Rixensart, European Study Service.

Van der Geest, W. (2001a), "Pause or Fast Forward for East Asia?," in E. Diener (ed.), *2000 Austrian Handbook for International Relations*, Vienna, Austria.

Van der Geest, W. (2001b), "EU and ASEAN Integration," in *Panorama*, Singapore, Konrad Adenauer Stiftung.

World Bank (2003), *Global Economic Prospects 2004*, World Bank, Washington DC.

World Trade Organisation (2002), *Communication from the European Community and Its Member States*, WT/WGTCP/W/222, Geneva, World Trade Organisation, November 19, 2002.

Annex: Table 1

Evolution of Global Exports 1960-2001 (Euro Billion Equivalent)

	1960	1970	1980	1990	2000	2001
World Exports	**84.1**	**211.6**	**1016.1**	**1885.4**	**5342.6**	**5044.3**
% of which						
European Union*	28.7	24.3	20.7	20.7	17.6	19.5
United States	24.4	20.4	15.6	16.3	15.6	15.7
Asia-10	7.4	13.8	17.9	26.8	30.7	30.7
Of which						
Japan	4.6	8.9	9.2	11.9	9.6	8.3
China	0	0	1.2	2.6	5.0	6.9
Hong Kong	0.7	1.1	1.3	3.4	4.0	3.7
South Korea	0	0.3	1.2	2.7	3.4	3.2
Singapore	0.2	0.7	1.3	2.1	2.8	2.5
Malaysia	0	0.7	0.9	1.2	1.9	1.9
Thailand	0.4	0.3	0.4	0.9	1.3	1.3
Indonesia	0	0.5	1.5	1.0	1.2	1.3
India	1.5	0.9	0.5	0.7	0.8	0.9
Philippines	0	0.4	0.4	0.3	0.7	0.7

* *Exports from EU member states to non-EU countries*

FDI flows EU-Asia: Impact of EU Enlargement
Preliminary Qualitative Assessment

Motivation Driving FDI	Pre-Enlargement Situation within the EU	Likely Impact of EU-25 Enlargement	Optimal Responses from Asian Partners
Market Access	*EU Outflow:* Predominant focus on OECD-countries, plus China (ASEAN and India lagging behind), total € 235 bn. *EU Inflow:* Primarily from OECD source countries; slow-down after Asian Financial Crisis Overall: Large Net Outflows approx. € 125 bn	*EU Outflow:* Extra-EU investment now becomes Intra-EU investment – but EU's investment into Asia for reasons of market access not directly affected *EU Inflow:* Likely to increased due to GDP effects (+€ 625 bln, approx + 8 %) Overall: Size of the net EU outflows bound to be reduced	Encourage deeper Asian integration and intensify compliance with WTO-style regulatory frameworks Intensify market research with focus on FDI to accession countries (consumer preferences, production costs, technical regulations, retail & distribution structures)
Low Cost Production Base and International Production Networks	Accelerating Outflow and Out-sourcing from EU to Asia in production and services sectors	*EU Outflow:* Some limited reduction due to lower-costs alternatives in accession countries *EU Inflow:* Some limited increase due to lower-cost alternatives in accession countries Overall: Size of the net EU outflows bound to be reduced	Improve supply-chain management and implementation of international production standards
Natural Resource Extraction and Exploitation	Looming resource shortages esp. in the energy sector and land-based production sectors	*EU Outflow:* Bound to continue as accession countries are not either natural resource-rich (relative to Asia and Africa) *EU Inflow:* Limited new opportunities in accession countries Overall: Growth of EU outflows for resource seeking bound to be continue	Scope for attracting additional inward investment
Logistic and Transport Linkages	Strong EU-linkages with, for example, Hong Kong and Singapore	*EU Outflow:* Bound to continue *EU Inflow:* Considerable new opportunities in accession countries vis-à-vis Greater Russia Overall: Growth of EU outflows bound to be continue	Examine BOT and BOO opportunities in accession countries for infrastructure Develop global networks and internationalisation of Asian businesses

137

CHAPTER 8

Harmonisation of the Norms of International Development

The Japanese Approach to Common Goals

Juichi INADA

Professor, Senshu University

I. Introduction: Global Governance and the International Framework for Aid

Progress has been made in global governance regarding international aid. "Global governance" can be defined as "the system in which the common norms and rules exist among many actors across many issue areas in the global level".[1] Common values and norms should be shared for better collaboration in development aid. What are the shared values and norms in recent trends in international development? Does Japan share such "universal" values and norms in its policy? In this paper I will draw a comprehensive picture of how Japan shares common values and norms in respect of international development.

The most prominent feature of the international development regime after the end of Cold War is the progress of global governance. There are many aspects and definitions of global governance[2], but it is clear that some common goals, values and norms, such as democracy, human rights, good governance, free market, sustainable development, poverty reduction, etc. have gained acceptance among the international community, or at least among the major donors of the OECD, throughout 1990s in international development arguments. Those goals and

---

[1] For instance, J. N. Rosenau, E.-O. Czempiel (eds.), *Governance without Government: Order and Change in World Politics*, Cambridge University Press, Cambridge, 1992; O. R. Young, *Governance in World Affairs*, Cornell University Press, Ithaca, 1992.

[2] See Hiroshi Okuma's chapter hereafter.

values are basically shared among donors, although their approaches still vary, an aspect I will return to presently.

Another important feature of the international regime after the Cold War is the overlap of international development and international security issues. In the past decade, internal, rather than inter-state conflicts were at the heart of most of the situations where there was resort to arms. The "failed states" post-conflict reconstruction and peace-building became major issues of international development. Poverty, hunger, human rights and oppression are all regarded as important components of "human security".

In line with these international community trends, Japan's foreign aid policy also has undergone a rapid transformation during the last decade. As the Japanese foreign ministry has often said, Official Development Assistance (ODA) has long been a main pillar of Japanese foreign policy, and continues to be so. Given that international development issues overlap with questions of international security, Japan's ODA and international cooperation policy are now the main tools of Japan's involvement in international security matters. What has been the Japanese approach in its ODA and international cooperation policy? Are they the same as other advanced western countries, or are there differences?

Before talking about these goals and values, I should explain briefly the core institutions of the international aid regime. As is already well-known, there are two different kinds of international organisations, namely the Breton Woods Institutions, such as the World Bank and the IMF, and the United Nations Group on the other hand. The World Bank and the IMF initiated economic and social reforms in many developing countries through their structural adjustment lending (SAL) in the 1980s and 1990s, and the Poverty Reduction Strategy Paper (PRSP) framework after 2000.[3] On the other hand, the UN took initiatives in international community "peace building" in the 1990s. In recent years, the mandates and missions of these two groups have overlapped, a fact often referred to as the World Bank's mission creep into poverty and conflict-related areas.[4]

---

[3] See C. Jayiraah, W. Branson, *Structural and Sectoral Adjustment: World Bank Experience 1980-92*, The World Bank, 1995; G. Mohan, E. Brown, B. Milward, A. B. Zack-Williams, *Structural Adjustment: Theory, Practice and Impacts*, Routledge, London, 2000.

[4] See J. Einhorn, "The World Bank's Mission Creep," *Foreign Affairs*, Sep-Oct. 2001.

The G7/G8 regime and the OECD/DAC are also play a very important role at the core of this system.[5] Basic policies in development and economic assistance are formulated among G7, and the OECD/DAC agreements and consensus are the basis of all discussions among the international community.

Japan has given almost $ 10 billion in aid to developing countries every year in the 1990s, making it one of the largest aid donor of the last decade. Japan's contribution has been very large in monetary terms, but its basic stance has been strongly influenced by trends in the international community, which have also shown a high degree of coordination with the stance of the United States. On the other hand, although Japan shares common goals and values with the international community, there have been heated arguments over what kinds of approach Japan should take in each case.

In the next section, I will summarise some common goals which have been formulated among donors in the 1990s, and explain what kinds of arguments have been made in each agenda among the Japanese aid community.

II. Prevailing Norms of International Development and the Japanese Approach

A. Market Economy

The most important common goal among donor countries is the spread of, and support for a market economy. Aid donors have been assisting the transition from a planned economy to a market economy in Eastern Europe, Russia, and also in Asia, in countries such as Mongolia, Vietnam, Laos, China and the Central Asian republics. The World Bank/IMF and other major donors have been promoting economic reforms toward a more liberalised and free market system through SAL in the 1980s and 1990s,[6] the response to the Asian financial crisis in 1997-1999, and HIPCs (Highly Indebted Poor Countries) Initiative after 2000.

Japan has been deeply involved in this framework of assistance for the establishment and support of a market economy in the developing world, even though there have been some criticisms against the WB/IMF approach. The WB/IMF prescriptions are often described as

---

[5]   See P. I. Hajnal, *The G7/8 System: Evolution, Role and Documentation*, Ashgate, Aldershot, 1999.

[6]   See The World Bank, *From Plan to Market: World Development Report 1996*, Oxford University Press, Oxford, 1996.

the "Washington Consensus," based on neo-classical economics that emphasises the liberalisation and globalisation of the economic system. The so-called "Washington consensus" is almost considered to be the common sense procedure of economic reform by the World Bank and the IMF, both of which are located in Washington DC. The following ten elements are included.[7] 1) fiscal discipline; 2) prioritisation of public expenditure; 3) tax reform; 4) financial liberalisation; 5) market-based exchange rate system; 6) trade liberalisation; 7) liberalisation of foreign investment; 8) privatisation of state-owned enterprises (SOEs); 9) deregulation; and 10) establishment of private property rights.

Typical criticisms of the WB/IMF approach are summarised in the following three points. 1) Their prescriptions offer a universal analytical paradigm but often neglect social aspects of economic development and the unique characteristics of specific countries and areas;[8] 2) the WB/IMF conditionality interferes too much with the domestic political and societal affairs of the recipients. Donors should think much more about the "ownership" of the recipients;[9] and 3) the Breton Woods Institutions are strongly controlled by the United States, especially by Wall Street, the Treasury Department and the World Bank/ IMF.[10] Some maintain, for instance, that an Asian-centered institution (such as the Asian Monetary Fund) should be established to assist Asian countries.

We can also find a "Revisionist Approach" which emphasises the role of government and gradualism in comparison with the "Washington Consensus." I have summarised the differences between the two arguments in Table 1.

[7] J. Williamson, "Democracy and the Washington Consensus," *World Development*, Vol. 21, No. 8, 1992.

[8] For instance, S. George, F. Sabelli (eds.), *Faith and Credit: The World Bank's Secular Empire*, Penguin Books, Harmondsworth, 1994.

[9] For instance, K. Danaher (ed.), *Fifty Years are Enough: The Case against the World Bank and the International Monetary Fund*, South End Press, Boston, 1994.

[10] J. Bagwati, "The Capital Myth," *Foreign Affairs*, Vol. 77, No. 3, May/June 1998.

Table 1. Comparison of the Washington Consensus and Revisionist Approach

	Washington Consensus	Revisionist Approach
Role of government	Small (response to market failure)	Large (leading development)
Industrial policy	Ineffective, market mechanism	Necessary and effective at the beginning of development
Pace of reform	Big Bang (shock therapy) Drastic comprehensive liberalisation	Gradualism Emphasis on sequence and the establishment of institutions
Privatisation	To be rapidly promoted at an early stage	Improvements in operation and unemployment measures before promoting privatisation
Trade and exchange	Liberalisation and deregulation at an early date	Gradual liberalisation depending on the conditions of domestic industries
Administrative organisation	Priority on transparency and efficiency Elimination of corruption and 'kickbacks'	Emphasis on the role of highly competent bureaucracy
Political liberalisation	Civil society as a prerequisite for a market economy	Gradual liberalisation in parallel with economic growth

In brief, the Washington Consensus (WC) advocates the elimination of government intervention as far as possible and allowing market forces to work, while the Revisionist Approach (RA) considers that the role of government in development is important, in light of the success of the past development of Japan and Asian NIEs (newly industrialising Economies).

The Washington Consensus argues that a government industrial policy of supporting certain industries will impair market discipline. The RA claims that it is useful to concentrate limited resources in certain industries or to strategically develop certain industries that may be competitive in the export market.

The Washington Consensus often argues that the privatisation of state-owned enterprises should be made promptly and drastically to achieve economic efficiency. The RA refutes those arguments: if rapid privatisation leads to costly structural changes such as the increase of unemployment, and if there are no industries to absorb such unemployment, privatisation should be undertaken over a long period of time while to avoid turbulence.

Those are examples of the arguments of the Washington Consensus and the Revisionist Approach. There are many kinds of arguments, even within the World Bank and Japan. We can find a lot of arguments similar to the Revisionist Approach in Japan, but mainstream opinion is shifting to a more liberal neo-classical approach, even in Japan, because of the long-lasting economic stagnation in Japan and the fall of economies of the Asian NIEs in the Asian financial crisis.[11]

B. Democracy

The second common goal and value among the donor community is the promotion and support for democracy and human rights.[12] Around 1990, democratic movements burgeoned in many countries and areas, typically in Eastern Europe. In such circumstances, the promotion of democracy and human rights became the common goals of major donors.[13] Even in Asia, there are some cases of democratic movements as in Myanmar (1988), and China (1989).[14]

In all these cases, the US and the EU initiated support for democracy and were followed closely by Japan. The Japanese government announced that Japan shared this common value with other western donor countries, but that they were maintaining a cautious attitude to aid being tied to democratic conditionality and domestic political intervention. Some Asian countries criticised Western democratic values, and claimed to follow the so-called "Asian Way".[15]

Japan's stance was ambivalent in the first half of 1990s. There were some controversial cases, such as that of Thailand (outburst of military oppression, February 1991), Indonesia (the East Timor incident, November 1991), and Peru (President Fujimori's suspension of the constitution, April 1992). In all these cases, some major donors stopped their aid because of the undemocratic conduct of the governments.[16] Japan however, requested the recipients to improve their conduct, but contin-

---

[11] I argued more in detail in the next: J. Inada, "The Liberal Universal Values and Asian Responses: The Case of the Asian Economic Crisis," in C. Otsuru & R. Oshiba (eds.), *American Nationalism and Citizenship in a Global Age*, Minerva Shobou, Tokyo, 2003, chapter 6 (Japanese).

[12] See F. Fukuyama, *The End of History and the Last Man*, Avon Book, New York, 1992.

[13] "Securing Democracy," in *Political Declaration*, The 16th G7 Summit Meeting at Houston, July 1990.

[14] See J. Inada, "Democracy and Stability: Political Considerations in Japan's ODA to Myanmar and China," in L. C. Chen & T. Matsumae (eds.), *In Pursuit of Common Values in Asia: Japan's ODA Charter Re-evaluated*, Tokai University Press, Tokyo, 1997.

[15] See K. Mahbubani, "The Dangers of Decadence," *Foreign Affairs*, Vol. 72, No. 41, Sept./Oct. 1993, pp. 10-14.

[16] The US suspended aid to Thailand after the military crackdown, the Netherlands halted aid to Indonesia after the East Timor Incident.

ued its aid It justified this position by pointing out that democracy is a universal value and Japan shares the value, but the way to democracy is not always simple and linear, depending on the social and historical background of the countries concerned.

However, Japan's stance has been changing in the latter half of 1990s. Strong international trends that emphasise the factor of "good governance" in developing countries have been prevailing, and Japan has begun to coordinate its stance in line with the tendency in the international community.

The concept of "good governance" in development first emerged in the World Bank report on Africa (1989), in which the World Bank raised the problems of institutions and public sector management as the major causes of African economic failure.[17] The definition of good governance still has a wide spectrum. In a narrow sense, it means accountability, transparency, rule of law, and efficient economic management.[18] Later, the concept began to contain the factors of participation, civil society, and an absence of corruption.[19] In a wide sense, the concept also includes more political factors such as democratic systems, reduced military spending, etc.[20]

Japan's stance is in line with other major western donors, but still hesitates to step into such political agendas, especially in the aid agencies. In a JICA report of 1995, authors divided the governance factors into administrative factors and democratic factors, and proposed to engage in administrative governance factors but took a cautious stance on political factors.[21] Regarding the OECF, which is responsible for concessional loans of Yen, there is no official report, but some academic papers which have been published as OECF periodicals showed negative opinions on the World Bank governance policy.[22]

---

[17] The World Bank, *Sub-Saharan Africa: From Crisis to Sustainable Development*, 1989.

[18] The World Bank, *Governance and Development*, 1992.

[19] The World Bank, *Governance: The World Bank Experience*, 1994.

[20] OECD/DAC, *Orientations on Participatory Development and Good Governance*, OECD, Paris, 1995.

[21] JICA (The Japan International Cooperation Agency), *Participatory Development and Good Governance*, JICA, 1995 (Japanese).

[22] For instance, Shigeru Ishikawa, in *Kaihatsu Enjo Kenkyu* (*Journal of Development Aid Studies*), OECF (The Overseas Economic Cooperation Fund), Vol. 4, No. 1, 1997.

C. Conflict Prevention (Human Security)

The third common goal of the international aid community is that of conflict prevention and peace building.

The international aid community shifted its stance to link its aid with world disarmament after the Gulf War (1990-91), and began to set conditions on military spending, nuclear (and Bio-Chemical) weapons development and arms trading on the part of the aid recipients. The Japanese government also adopted "ODA 4 guidelines" in April 1991 (just after the outbreak of the Gulf War), which contain the above-mentioned three disarmament factors.[23]

After that, Economic sanctions were imposed by the Japanese government on a number of occasions, as in the case of China (1995) and India and Pakistan (1998). In each of these cases, the Japanese government suspended its aid to the country concerned, following on the carrying out of nuclear tests which Japan had denounced in the strongest terms and from which Japan had called on them to desist. Japan's aid to China resumed in late 1996, because China announced that it was to sign the Comprehensive Test Ban Treaty (CTBT). Japan's aid suspension to India and Pakistan, on the other hand, continued until late 2001, when both countries took stances in support of the US military attack in Afghanistan, despite both of them having not yet signed the CTBT.

To summarise, the effectiveness of aid as a policy tool in influencing the decisions of the recipient is something to be assessed on a case-by-case basis. The most important consideration is what to say to the recipient, what conditions to attach to aid resumption. In short, we need an appropriate and clear strategy. Aid-giving and aid-suspension or sanctions are only a tool to achieve our goals. In those cases, Japanese decisions were basically initiated by domestic politics affected by sentiments of the public, which was strongly opposed to nuclear weapons and thus, diplomatic considerations seemed to have been pushed into second place.

Another important topic of international aid community is the post-conflict reconstruction and peace building of war-torn economies and "failed states".[24] After the end of the Cold War, there were many regional conflicts, as there are still. International assistance to the peace process of those countries and areas was a key issue in international development and security in the 1990s. The UN groups (through PKO,

---

[23] S. Yasutami, J. Nakagawa, J. Saito, *The Political Economy of the ODA Charter: Applications and Principles of Aid*, Yuhikaku, Tokyo, 1999 (Japanese).

[24] There is no clear definition of the "failed states." It is often used as "the situations that the central government does not exist or lost its effective control on its territory."

UNHCR, etc.), the WB, and the G7(8), are all core international institutions which have been making great efforts in this area.

Japan's role has been increasing in those agendas through its financial assistance, its involvement into the PKO, its diplomatic efforts, by sending personnel, etc. Firstly, in Cambodia (Japan hosted the peace conference and reconstruction meeting in 1991, and joined in UNTAC in 1992-93), and there are many cases of Japanese active contributions, such as Palestine (reconstruction efforts after 1993), Bosnia and Herzegovina (Japan joined the peace and reconstruction efforts after 1995), Kosovo (Japan supported UNMIK after 1999), East Timor (joined into UNTAET and UNMISET after 1999), Afghanistan (Japan hosted a reconstruction conference in 2002), and Iraq (Japan announced an offer of \$ 5 billion in total and sent its Self Defense Forces in 2003).

The level of involvement can vary greatly, depending on the case, but these have led to Japan having close and in-depth talks with other donors and international organisations in order to optimise the division of labour among the international community.

One of the key concepts in this agenda is "human security". This term originally came from the UNDP's "Human Development Report" of 1994.[25] It is a term that has achieved great popularity among aid professionals and in the wider community, as the concept involved emphasises non-military factors in security: poverty, hunger, unemployment, disease, oppression, human rights, environment, etc. It also emphasises individuals instead of states, and transnational cooperation, including NGOs.

This concept is now more widely used, and in a broader sense. For instance, "Human Security" figures in the foreign ministers' statement of the Cologne (Köln) G8 Summit in 1999, in which democracy, human rights, good governance, terrorism, small arms, etc. were mentioned as components of "human security."[26] In other words, this term is now used as a 'cover-all' diplomatic word, applicable to any kind of international issues with a common action dimension.

The Japanese government's stance has also been favourable to this policy concept since 1998, when Japanese Prime Minister Obuchi announced his strong support for the "Human Security Fund" established by the UN. I suppose the reasons for the positive Japanese attitude to this word are: 1) it matches the liberal and "pacifist" public opinion of Japanese people and it is easy to get public support for a Japanese contribution to the world human security agenda; 2) it is also a

---

[25]   UNDP (United Nations Development Program), *Human Development Report 1994*, UNDP, 1994.

[26]   *Political Declaration*, The 25th G7/8 Summit Meeting at Köln, Germany, July 1999.

logical concept to justify Japanese active support for the UNHCR and refugee issues; 3) the view for UN-initiated concepts and funds (such as Human Security Fund) is favorable, even in the context of the perceived need for UN reform, which the Japanese government has been advocating for a long time.

III. The Norms of "De-politicisation" and "Non-Interference" in Japan's Post-War ODA Policy

Looking at these trends in international development and security, and the efforts of the international community, we can find common features: the spread of democratic value in the world, and the formulation of norms to justify international interventions in domestic issues. Both characteristics are the signs of spreading of global governance.

However, there are still some factors which constrain Japanese behaviour and policy, some of which are international constraints and the others of which are domestic in nature. Domestically, Japan still carries the legacy of historically formulated norms.

Over the course of nearly half a century since the inception of Japanese ODA program in 1954, Japan's ODA has undergone substantial change, both in terms of the concepts underpinning Japanese aid and the financial amounts involved. It might be argued, nevertheless, that there exist *de facto* policy norms which have hardly changed at all during this period. These are the *de facto* policy norms of "non-interference" in internal affairs of the recipients and the "de-politicisation" of its aid.

These are policy norms, moreover, which have exerted considerable influence, not only on Japan's ODA but also on its post-war diplomacy as a whole, as often referred to as the "Yoshida Doctrine."[27] In the case of Japanese economic diplomacy, for example, the principles of non-interference and de-politicisation can be seen to have played a prominent role as *de facto* norms circumscribing Japan's post-war economic diplomacy. With respect to the former, Japan has attempted, as far as possible, to refrain from intervention and/or involvement in the domestic politics of those countries that have received aid, and with respect to the latter, Japan's economic diplomacy has sought to ensure minimal overlap between its political aims and its economic activities. The question we might ask, then, is whether or not this is still the case.

---

27 There are many books on the "Yoshida Doctrine." One of the positive arguments to it is: M. Kosaka, *Saisho Yoshida Shigeru*, Chuo-kouron-sha, Tokyo, 1968 (Japanese). One of the negative critics against it is: H. Okazaki, *Yoshida Shigeru and His Days*, PHP Kenkyusho, Tokyo, 2002 (Japanese).

A. ODA and Involvement in Internal Affairs

Those involved in the sphere of Japanese aid (including both the bureaucracy and non-governmental specialists) have, generally speaking, frowned upon close involvement in issues related to political systems or internal affairs. It might be argued that the reason for this stance lies in the existence in Japanese diplomacy of the vaguely-defined ideology of non-intervention that has taken shape during the post-war period, an ideology that has as its core tenet the avoidance of entanglement in the internal affairs of foreign countries.

Japanese ODA from the early post-war period through the 1970s and into the 1980s was closely linked to Japan's economic interests; however, over time the relative weight of Japan's short-term economic interests has decreased *vis-à-vis* political and diplomatic considerations.[28] Nevertheless, in those places on the receiving end of Japanese aid, the understanding that aid is for the purpose of economic development alone and that political factors should be kept from the agenda as a matter of course remains deeply entrenched.

The request-based system (*yôsei shugi*) in Japanese ODA policy, by which, in principle, ODA is granted in response to an official request from the recipient, has served to tone down the extent of involvement in the receiving country's internal affairs. While this principle has been somewhat revised in accordance with more recent emphasis on policy dialogue (*seisaku taiwa*) and policy-based lending (*seisaku shien*), it continues to be a fundamental principle of Japanese ODA. In 2003, Japan's ODA Charter (drawn up in 1992) was revised and the new ODA charter emphasised the "policy dialogue" with the recipient, but the "request basis" principle still remains.

On the other hand, in recent years an emphasis on good governance in the receiving country, together with the concomitant view that even with respect to aid the political and social system of the receiving country should come under scrutiny, has been gaining international currency. Japanese aid officials have increasingly found themselves unable to ignore this prevailing trend, but there remains considerable scope for discussion of the criteria by which such governance might be best evaluated and assisted.

A number of approaches exist internationally, such as those that emphasise administrative function favoured by the World Bank, and those that focus on democratisation, favoured by the USAID (United States

---

[28]   J. Inada, "The Meaning of Japan's ODA in International System," *Kokusai Seiji (International Politics)*, No. 93, The Japan Association of International Relations, March, 1990 (Japanese).

Agency for International Development). Japan has tended to be extremely wary of the latter type, which is bound up with overt political implications.[29]

However, the arguments that the principles of de-politicisation and non-interference to which Japan has hitherto adhered are anachronistic, and that Japan should become actively involved in the domestic political and social issues of the Third World have been garnering support, even within Japan. In actual fact, as Japan increases its ties to international bodies and NGOs, it is gradually increasing the degree of its intervention in the political affairs of the developing world.

B. The Linkage between ODA and National Security

Post-war Japanese ODA policy, furthermore, has steered clear of involvement, not only in the receiving country's domestic politics, but also in its military and national security affairs. This traditional norm remained in full force until the 1990s, since when, however, there have been a number of significant changes.

The watershed between the estrangement of ODA and national security concerns and their subsequent linkage can be traced to the "ODA 4 Guidelines" released in April 1991. This was a landmark development, where political considerations were publicly linked to ODA guidelines for the first time. As for how to apply the designated four *caveats* to the actual distribution and implementation of ODA, however, the Japanese approach has been to treat each case on an individual basis "taking into account the overall situation". How to balance these new considerations against such factors as the development needs of the beneficiary country and its economic and historical links with Japan has constituted a thorny issue with each new case.[30]

For example, China's nuclear tests in May and August of 1995 severely tested Japan's ability to respond in a manner that preserved the balance between expression of opposition to China's development of nuclear weapons and yet took into account the close historical and economic links between the two countries.[31] On the other hand, in response to the nuclear tests carried out by India and Pakistan in May 1998, the Japanese government suspended economic aid across the board almost without exception. The freezing of aid to both countries in

---

[29] *Op. cit.*, JICA, *Participatory Development and Good Governance.*

[30] J. Inada, *Democratization Marketization, and Japan's Emerging Role as a Foreign Aid Donor*, USJP Occasional Paper 93-03, Harvard University, 1993.

[31] S. Katada, "Why Did Japan Suspend Foreign Aid to China? Japan's Foreign Aid Decision-making and Sources of Aid Sanction," *Social Science Japan Journal*, Vol. 4, No. 1, pp. 39-58, 2001.

this case can be said to have expressed the Japanese government's stance of opposition to nuclear testing, but was implemented on the grounds that economic links between the two countries and Japan were not so close as those with China.

Furthermore, in recent years, Japanese ODA has become increasingly involved with aid programs of an unmistakably political hue, related to national security and regional stability, in the form of conflict management and post-conflict reconstruction aid.[32]

The prototypes for this kind of reconstruction aid were the Indochina reconstruction assistance in the late 1970s after the Vietnam War, and the Cambodia reconstruction assistance following the establishment of the United Nations Transitional Authority in Cambodia (UNTAC) in 1992. In both these cases, the tangible involvement of Japan in economic support with its significant political and diplomatic overtones, was groundbreaking.

Towards the end of the 1990s, the sequential need for post-conflict reconstruction aid in, for example, Kosovo and East Timor, occasioned much debate in Japan.[33] Consequently, the newly-formulated ODA medium-term goals of August, 1999, cited "Conflict and Development" as a priority issue, and emphasised the need for Japan to henceforth assume a leading role in the areas of conflict prevention and post-conflict reconstruction support. In December 2001 (just after the US attack on Afghanistan), Japan modified the "PKO Law" and made it possible for Japanese forces to engage in the "main activities" of the UN Peace Keeping Forces. Subsequently, by way of example, Japan sent its Self Defence Forces to the PKF in East Timor in 2002, and adopted a stance of active involvement with respect to Afghanistan reconstruction efforts since the international conference held in late November 2001, and has become deeply involved in the very controversial reconstruction process in Iraq since 2003.

C. Have the "Traditional Norms" of the Post-War Period Changed?

Have, then, the "traditional norms" of Japan's post-war aid diplomacy changed, or do they remain unchanged?

Since the 1980s, Japanese ODA has become increasingly linked to international politics, and even the Japanese government, under the

---

[32] JICA, *Peace Building: Towards the Realization of Human Security*, JICA, April 2001 (Japanese).

[33] J. Inada, "Conflict Prevention and Post-conflict Assistance," in Y. Shimomura, K. Tsuji, J. Inada, Y. Fukagawa, *International Development Cooperation: Its New Trend*, Yukikaku, Tokyo, 2001, Chapter 6 (Japanese).

concept of "comprehensive security," has officially redrawn the line between politics and economics as goals of aid.[34] The official declaration that political considerations might be linked even to the use of aid, as set out in the ODA 4 Guidelines of 1991, was a development of no little significance. The fact of the matter is, however, that Japan remains disinclined to interfere in the receiving country's internal affairs or political and social systems. The continuing influence of the norm of non-interference would seem, as before, to owe much to the bitter experience of the path to defeat in the Second World War.

Nevertheless, the view that international society should take precedence over national sovereignty in order to support and achieve the universal values and goals such as a minimum standard of living and the guarantee of basic human rights has been rapidly gaining currency throughout international society. It is in this context that "international norms" have been developing apace in recent years. Indeed, international society has been increasing its involvement, not only in post-conflict reconstruction in the developing world, but also in the conflicts themselves, and aid donors, by means of their assistance, have come to exert significant influence on governance in developing countries.

In conclusion, it might be said that Japan has been compelled to gradually review and revise the "traditional norms" of its post-war ODA in accordance with the development of new norms of behaviour evident throughout international society.

IV. Conclusions: Toward Deeper Partnership in Global Governance

A. *Limitations of Japan's Role in International Arena*

One of the international constraints of Japan's international role is basically unchanged: international regimes such as the Permanent Five system of the UN Security Council and the overwhelming US influence on the WB/IMF. As a late-comer to those UN and the Breton Woods systems, Japan's influence is still weak, and the number of Japanese staff in those international organisations is still small in comparison with its large financial contribution.

In addition, the Western paradigm has been initiating the arguments on democracy and a market economy in international development. The Japanese or Asian intellectual community has not yet succeeded in

---

[34] D. T. Yasutomo, *The Manner of Giving: Strategic Aid and Japanese Foreign Policy*, Lexington Books, Lexington, 1986.

finding a more persuasive alternative paradigm than of the western model.

However, relatively large financial support from Japan within a co-ordinated scheme of international community, although its amount is now levelling off, is still a big contribution to the promotion of global governance in the areas of development, post-conflict reconstruction, etc. On the other hand, there are still many intellectual efforts in Japan, in collaboration with our Asian partners in some cases, to find and formulate a good alternative approach to promote more liberal and prosperous political and economic systems in the developing world. Many people believe that Japan has some advantages when it comes to taking leadership, especially in the areas of the arms control (non-nuclear policy) and as regards environmental protection.

B. What Is Necessary for Closer Partnership between Japan and the EU?

We can find some regional architectures both in Asia and Europe such as the EU, the OSCE, the APEC, the ARF, ASEAN+3, and the inter-regional forum between them such as ASEM, KEDO etc. Those institutions have been strengthened and have been increasing their roles towards global governance in order to realise common goals. The EU-Japan dialogue can be an important part of such constructive intra-regional architectures. I believe there should be a lot of common agendas between EU and Japan.

For instance, we can work together in foreign aid programs to realise common goals of respect for human rights, promotion of democracy, and good governance. Both the EU and Japan can develop their capacity to play a larger role in conflict prevention, peace building and post-conflict reconstruction, and also can cooperate in strengthening the international community's institutions and instruments for those goals especially in the developing world.

Although there might be some differences of their approaches, we can share our common goals and values through, for instance, joint comparisons and assessments of each other's policies for development, stability and peace building in the third world.[35]

To converge our goals, values, perspectives and approaches, we need to strengthen not only governmental level links but also civil society links between the EU and Japan, and deepen the contacts and exchanges of people.

---

[35] These are also mentioned in *Shaping our Common Future: An Action Plan for EU-Japan Cooperation*, EU-Japan Summit, Brussels, 2001.

Through those efforts, the arguments and the "norms" of Japanese people who are relatively cautious about involvement in the domestic politics of developing countries and conflict-related issues in the world, may change further in the near future. We are still on the way toward "global governance."

CHAPTER 9

New Directions in Japan's Official Development Assistance

Hiroshi OKUMA

Professor, Seijo University

Japan made the biggest contribution to the rise in ODA in 1999. Its total net ODA disbursements reached USD 15.3 billion – the largest annual figure ever recorded by a single donor. It included continuing generous help to the countries most affected by the Asian financial crisis, especially a USD 3 billion contribution to the Asian Development Bank and substantial rises in bilateral aid, particularly to Indonesia, Thailand and Vietnam (OECD/DAC, *Development Cooperation 2000 Report*, p. 95).

Japan began its supply of ODA to China following that country's shift to a route of reform and liberalisation from the end of the 1970s. Behind this decision was the judgment that prosperity for China and its assimilation into the international community would lead to stability in Asia, and contribute to Japan's own national interests as well. [...] The Japanese government has reacted to its current fiscal pinch with the decision to slash next fiscal year's ODA budget by 10 percent. To make effective use of the pared-down funds, the priority ranking of recipients must be reviewed. For China, factors to be considered include the importance of Sino-Japanese relations, China's relinquishing of demands for wartime reparations in the normalisation of diplomatic ties and other realities. Even taking such elements into account lowering the value of ODA to China is the natural course of evolution, given that it is now a more developed country in its coastal areas. The Japanese Foreign Ministry has said that last year China itself channelled $ 450 million (¥ 54 billion) in assistance to 58 countries. Japan has received no explanation from the Chinese with regard to such aid, an issue that has the potential of undermining the relations of mutual trust between the two nations. Likewise, the Chinese government has yet to suitably explain to its people the nature of the ODA coming from Japan[1].

I. Introduction: Going Beyond Top Donor

In the past decade, or in the 1990s, Japan has become a major player in the field of North-South development cooperation. In terms of total ODA disbursed, Japan has been the world's largest donor among 22 OECD/DAC member countries, including the Commission of the European Communities, for nine consecutive years. In 2001, due mainly to the terrorist attacks in the United States on September 11th, the United States ODA volume increased by 14.8% to USD 11.43 billion (22% of total DAC ODA) and became the world's largest aid donor for the first time since 1992, when it was overtaken by Japan's ODA boom. In 2002, the United States further increased its ODA by 16.3% to USD 13.29 billion (23% of total DAC ODA). Thus Japan relinquished its position as the top donor to the United States, a status it had held for a decade. Japan's ODA fell by 16.6% in real terms in 2001, and it decreased by 1.2% in real terms in 2002. Its net ODA volume of USD 9.8 billion in 2001 (19% of total DAC ODA) and USD 9.3 billion in 2002 (16% of total DAC ODA), as the second largest aid donor, still constituted the predominant share in the total ODA from DAC members, however.

In parallel with such quantitative developments in official aid, Japan has been seeking, since the mid-1990s, to obtain a position in the international community commensurate with the volume of aid it provides. That is to say, Japan has been trying to transform its role in the global donor community, from that of the "Top Donor" to "Leading Donor" in which it provides guidance in the formulation of basic philosophy and strategy in development cooperation. This move is, in part, a response to previous characterisation of Japan's ODA policy as *Faceless Japan*, *International ATM*, and *Chequebook Diplomacy*, might be represented by the following remarks in the article entitled "Japan and the Third World: Co-prosperity by Peaceful Means," *The Economist* (June 17, 1989, p. 16):

> Yet without a clear notion of what it hopes to achieve, Japan's aid can be only a blunt tool of diplomacy. And so far the bureaucrats seem to have found no successor to the idea of aid-as-export-promotion. Official reports on the aid programme are full of vague, grandiose notions. When they turn to detail, the interest seems to be more in the quantity of money laid out than in what it does, for the recipients or for Japan itself. Take the knotty ques-

---

[1]   "The Realities Have Changed, So Must Japan's ODA to China," *Asahi Shimbun*, October 28, 2001.

tion of how far aid-givers can interfere in the politics of receiving countries. Japan takes the noble aim of non-interference to extremes.

This chapter is an attempt, based mainly on primary sources, to trace and describe Japan's search for the way to "Leading Donor" status in the 1990s. An emphasis is placed on interrelationships between Japan's development cooperation strategy and new directions in development thinking, or development paradigm in the global donor community. In other words, its chief objective is to shed light on the logic of Japan's new aid strategy within the total context of historical evolution of North-South relations in the post-Cold War era of globalisation.

II. The Preliminary Step Towards Leading Donor: ODA Charter in 1992

On June 30, 1992, after the end of Gulf War, the Japanese cabinet adopted Japan's Official Development Assistance Charter (ODA Charter). It was a landmark event in the evolution of Japan's ODA policy. Since its beginning in the mid-1950s, Japan has continued to take a very cautious stance towards intervention in the domestic affairs of recipient developing countries, and Japan has deliberately avoided insisting on economic and political conditionality in its aid program. For Japan, political and diplomatic use of ODA has been *taboo* for a long time, and the Japanese government has repeatedly stressed the non-political nature of Japan's development cooperation.[2] This tradition of Japan's foreign aid policy is aptly captured by Professor Dennis Yasutomo as follows:

> Japan's economic assistance policy developed throughout the post-war period as a component of foreign economic policy. Beginning with reparation payments to Southeast Asian nations in the 1950s and 1960s, Japan's recovery from wartime devastation and the subsequent 'economic miracle' received a boost from the extension of aid to develop overseas markets and secure needed raw materials. In the 1970s Tokyo utilised foreign aid to stabilise the flow of energy resources in the wake of the first oil shock, and this entailed a globalisation of aid allocation to Africa, Latin America, and the Middle East. Throughout these years the Japanese retained the primacy of economic and resources rationales rather than a strategic justification for aid. Japan consciously separated politics from economics. (Yasutomo, 1986, p. 111)

---

[2] In this regard, OECD/DAC argues its historical background as follows: "[...] Japan invaded several Asian countries during this century, an issue which still arises in its diplomatic relations. This sensitiveness towards non-intervention in the domestic affairs of recipient countries largely explains Japan's cautious stance towards conditionality and policy dialogue in its aid programme." (OECD/DAC, *Development Cooperation Review of Japan 1999*).

Traditionally the Japanese government has been reluctant to state basic principles and philosophy in its development cooperation policy at all. However, in the words of Mr Yoichi Funabashi, a diplomatic correspondent for the Tokyo daily *Asahi Shimbun,*

> The Gulf War was a unique phenomenon. The war itself crystallised and magnified issues that Japan should have addressed long ago. For Japan the crisis was, in a way, a day of reckoning. It broke out precisely when the gap was most pronounced between Japan's underdeveloped political capacity and its seemingly uncontrollable economic expansion. The outcome was shocking, rudely awakening Japan to its inability to cope with a crisis affecting its vital interests. The lesson was that the international environment in the 1990s will no longer allow Japan to follow the same one-dimensional economic strategy it has single-mindedly pursued for the past forty years. (Funabashi, 1991, p. 59)

Faced with the crisis over the Gulf, the Japanese government was forced to explicitly express its desire to use its enormous economic resources for political and strategic goals in a more explicit manner than in the past through the adoption of the ODA Charter in 1992, which drastically changed the *official* Japanese thinking on ODA. In the Charter, the following four key elements are identified under basic philosophy:

1) Humanitarian Considerations: many people are still suffering from famine and poverty in developing countries, and the international community can ill-afford to ignore this fact;

2) Recognition of Global Interdependence: the world is now striving to build a society where freedom, human rights, democracy and other values are ensured in peace and prosperity. Interdependence among nations and stability and the further development of the developing world are indispensable to the peace and prosperity of the entire world;

3) Environmental Conservation: it is a task for all humankind, which all countries, developed and developing alike, must work together to tackle; and

4) Importance of Self-help Efforts: Japan attaches central importance to support for the self-help efforts of developing countries, working towards economic take-off. Japan will implement its ODA programme to help ensure the efficient and fair distribution of resources and good governance in developing countries for globally sustainable development.

Under this philosophy, Japan commits itself to the following four principles:

(1) Environmental conservation should be pursued in tandem with development;

(2) Any use of ODA for military purposes or for aggravation of international conflicts should be avoided;

(3) Full attention should be paid to trends in recipient countries' military expenditures, their development and production of weapons of mass destruction and missiles, and the export and import of arms. Developing countries should place appropriate priorities in the allocation of their resources in their own economic and social development; and

(4) Full attention should be paid to efforts for promoting democratisation and the introduction of a market-oriented economy, and the situation regarding the securing of basic human rights and freedoms.

Thus, the basic philosophy and principles of Japan's ODA Charter faithfully reflect the dominant development thinking and development paradigm of the late-1980s which stressed, in addition to "economic reform" (Economic Structural Adjustment), the critical importance of "political and social reform" (Political and Social Structural Adjustment) in developing countries. In other words, the establishment Japan's ODA Charter was strongly encouraged by the growing international acceptance of political and social conditionality (Washington Consensus), and it was not necessarily a national statement based upon Japan's distinctive practices and experiences in the field of development cooperation. However, the explicit interjection of political and social elements into Japan's foreign aid policy marked a departure towards a new development strategy in Japan's ODA.

III. Launching the Initiatives: From Silent Partner to Active Participant

Since the establishment of the ODA Charter, Japan has moved to become an active participant in the formulation of fundamental development strategy in the global development arena. For almost four decades, Japan has been a reluctant partner. Now Japan has paved the way for a pro-active approach in proposing a basic development cooperation strategy, which might be illustrated as follows:

In October 1993, Japan organised the *Tokyo International Conference on African Development* (TICAD I). The Conference adopted *Tokyo Declaration on African Development "Towards the 21ˢᵗ Century"* in which "(the participants of TICAD) recognise that political, economic and social reforms must be initiated and carried out by African countries themselves, based on their visions, values and individual socio-economic background [...] We, the participants of TICAD, recognise that simultaneous implementation of political and economic reforms, while conducive to development, may often entail painful transition processes. [...] Africa's development partners, reaffirm our commitment to providing priority support to countries undertaking effective and efficient political and economic reforms."

In May 1996, OECD/DAC issued its New International Development Strategy, formally entitled *Shaping the 21ˢᵗ Century: The Contribution of Development Cooperation.* This New International Development Strategy identifies

1. economic well-being (a reduction by one-half in the proportion of people living in extreme poverty by 2015) and
2. social development (universal primary education, gender equality and the empowerment of women, a reduction in the mortality rate and access through the primary health-care system to reproductive health services) as the main objectives of development cooperation. In the Strategy's formulation, Japan assumed a leading role from the preparation stage.[3]

In the second half of 1997, many countries of Asia (Thailand, Indonesia, Malaysia and the Republic of Korea, for example), faced serious currency and financial crises. In response to the Asian Economic Crisis of 1997-98, Japan provided various types of assistance, and support for *Social Safety Nets* was one of the top priorities of Japanese assistance to Asia.[4] That is, in addition to assistance for economic structural reforms, Japan extended aid to socially vulnerable people through the development and improvement of medical services and health care systems. Additionally, assistance for human resource development and special measures for foreign students were other priority items.

In October 1998, Japan hosted the *Second Tokyo International Conference on African Development* (TICAD II). The Conference adopted *The Tokyo Agenda for Development,* in which the participants of TICAD-II declared:

---

[3] On Japan's leading role, see OECD/DAC, *ibid.*

[4] In March 1995, *World Summit for Social Development* held in Copenhagen, declares ten commitments to: (1) eradicate absolute poverty by a target date; (2) support full employment; (3) promote social integration based on the enhancement and protection of all human rights; (4) achieve equality and equity between women and men; (5) accelerate the development of Africa and the least developed countries; (6) ensure that structural adjustment programmes include social development goals; (7) increase resources allocated to social development; (8) create an economic, political, social, cultural and legal environment that will enable people to achieve social development; (9) attain universal and equitable access to education and primary health care; and (10) strengthen cooperation for social development through the UN.

[...] (4)The primary objective of this Agenda for Action for African Development is poverty reduction through accelerated economic growth and sustainable development, and effective integration of African economies into the global economy [...] (17) The experience of poverty reduction in East Asia demonstrates that rapid economic growth with equitable income distribution over a sustained period of time can help lift the poor above the poverty line.

The Conference reached an agreement on the following three areas as primary themes:

1) Social Development and Poverty Reduction: education, health, population and other measures to assist the poor;
2) Economic Development: private sector development, industrial development, agricultural development and external debt;
3) Basic Foundations for Development: good governance, conflict prevention and post-conflict development.

In August 1999, the Japanese government published *Japan's Medium-Term Policy on Official Development Assistance* to articulate a clear path for Japanese ODA over the next five years in terms of basic direction and priority issues and sectors. In the *Introduction*, it articulates the fundamental position of Japan's ODA as follows:

As the world's second largest economy and the largest donor of official development assistance (ODA), Japan shoulders the important responsibility of contributing to sustainable social and economic development in developing countries. This is a role through which Japan can win the confidence and appreciation of the international community. Furthermore, as a nation whose prosperity is closely linked to the world peace and stability and that is highly dependent on the importation of resources, energy, food and other basic materials, ODA plays a very significant role in ensuring Japan's own stability and prosperity. As such, economic assistance promotes Japan's best interests, including the maintenance of peace.

In Section I, *Basic Approaches*, the document expresses Japan's new approach of placing even greater emphasis on poverty alleviation and social development as follows:

Economic growth is a necessary measure for the improvement of welfare, and "human-centred" development is indispensable to the realization of sustainable development. Consequently, Japan will provide assistance for balanced economic growth and social development. Based on this human-centred approach, special attention will be given to the needs of the least developed countries. Due attention will also be focused on "human security" and the protection of individuals and communities.

In Section II, *Priority Issues and Sectors*, the following factors are cited for their special importance in the fight against poverty:

equitable distribution of the benefits of economic development, implementation of economic cooperation projects directly aimed at assisting the poor, and the sharing of Japan's own experiences of economic growth and poverty eradication with developing countries.

Thus, *Japan's Medium-Term Policy on Official Development Assistance* is a strategic statement which declares that Japan will undertake the fight against poverty in pursuit of social and economic development.

On August 29, 2003, the Japanese cabinet revised its ODA Charter of 1992 prompted by the recognition that "there is an urgent need for the international community, including Japan, to address new development challenges such as peace-building. Faced with these new challenges, many developed countries are strengthening their ODA policy, to deal with the serious problems that developing countries face." In the *Preface*, it articulates the fundamental position of Japan's ODA as follows:

> In line with the spirit of the Japanese Constitution, Japan will vigorously address these new challenges to fulfil its responsibilities commensurate with its national strength and its standing in the international community [...] the Government of Japan has revised the ODA Charter, with the aim of enhancing the strategic value, flexibility, transparency, and efficiency of ODA.

The document gives full details of Japan's new development objectives, policies, and priorities in the following section. Firstly, as to the objectives, it places stronger emphasis on political and strategic use of development assistance as follows:

> The objectives of Japan's ODA are to contribute to the peace and development of the international community, and thereby to help ensure Japan's own security and prosperity. [...] As the first nation in Asia to become a developed country, Japan has significantly contributed to the economic and social development of developing countries, especially in East Asia. [...] Preventing conflicts and terrorism, and efforts to build peace, as well as efforts to foster democratization, and to protect human rights and the dignity of individuals have become major issues inherent to the stability and development of the international community. Japan, as one of the world's leading nations, is determined to make best use of ODA to take the initiative in addressing these issues. Such efforts will in turn benefit Japan itself in a number of ways, including by promoting friendly relations and people-to-people exchanges with other countries, and by strengthening Japan's standing in the international arena. [...] Japan will proactively contribute to the stability and development of developing countries through its ODA. This correlates closely with assuring Japan's security and prosperity and promoting the welfare of its people.

Secondly, with regard to the basic policies, the document identifies the following five key elements of critical importance:

1) Supporting Self-help Efforts of Developing Countries based on Good Governance;
2) Perspective of "Human Security" focusing on Individuals;
3) Assurance of Fairness;
4) Utilisation of Japan's Experience and Expertise; and
5) Partnership and Collaboration with the International Community.

Finally, in accordance with these objectives and policies, the following four priority issues are identified in the document:

1. Poverty Reduction as a key development goal essential for eliminating terrorism and other causes of instability in the world;
2. Promotion of Sustainable Growth through a comprehensive package of aid, trade, and investment;
3. Addressing such global issues as global warming, infectious diseases, population, food, energy, natural disasters, terrorism, drugs, and international organised crimes. Japan will play an active role in the creation of international norms; and
4. Peace-building, Conflict Prevention, and Nation-building in post-conflict situations.

In September-October 2003, Japan organised the *Third Tokyo International Conference on African Development* (TICAD III) to review the achievements of the ten-year TICAD process and to discuss the future direction for African development. In his keynote speech, Japan's Prime Minister Junichiro Koizumi emphasised Japan's strong commitment to the TICAD process as follows:

> I would like to take this opportunity to announce the three pillars that comprise Japan's initiative for assistance to Africa. They are "human-centred development," "poverty reduction through economic growth," and "consolidation of peace." [...] Japan's appeal for an emphasis on African development through the convening of TICAD I ten years ago, has developed over the course of a decade into a mighty tide throughout the international community. Japan will move to institutionalise TICAD as a means of strengthening its follow-up structures to make the TICAD process more dynamic. [...] The key to TICAD's future is Africa's ownership and expansion of partnership. Japan hopes to act as a bridge between Asia and Africa. In so doing, by utilising Asia's experience and vigour, we would like to provide diversity and dynamism in African development.

At the conclusion of TICAD III, the Conference adopted *TICAD Tenth Anniversary Declaration* in which the TICAD process is illustrated as follows: "The TICAD process has also been playing a catalytic role in translating its philosophy and priorities into tangible projects in areas such as human resources development and socio-economic infrastructure [...] the TICAD process has contributed to enhancing owner-

ship and partnership to develop genuine solidarity that leads to expanded and multi-layered cooperation in support of African development."

IV. Challenges Ahead

In the past decade, Japan's ODA policy has taken a new direction. In
line with the New International Development Strategy, Japan shifted its
priority area from the development of economic infrastructure to poverty alleviation, social development, political and institutional reform,
and such highly politicised issues as conflict prevention, peace-building,
and post-conflict reconstruction. On the occasion of the Kyushu-
Okinawa Summit 2000, Japan, as a host, played a key role in the publication of a report entitled *Poverty Reduction and Economic Development*, which stresses the importance of poverty reduction and the social
dimension of development as follows:

> While growth is crucial in the fight against poverty, greater attention must
> be paid to a more equitable distribution of the benefits of growth. To this
> end, the right social policies are essential, including institution building,
> education and skills development, and the improvement of health, including
> the fight against infectious disease. These are the foundations for poverty
> alleviation and greater social equity. Social investment secures high returns
> over the longer term.

Moreover, at the time of the G8 Foreign Ministers' Meeting in
Miyazaki at the same Summit Meeting, Japan assumed a leading role in
the adoption of *G8 Miyazaki Initiatives for Conflict Prevention* which
aimed at providing a comprehensive response to conflict prevention.[5] In
other words, in the document the G8 articulates close linkage between
development and peace as follows:

> Peace and democratic stability are indispensable pre-conditions for eco-
> nomic growth and sustainable development. Moreover, economic and de-
> velopment cooperation has an important role to play in fostering peace and
> stability. The G8 can use its position as the major provider for the develop-
> ment assistance to pursue actively initiatives in this area. [...] The G8 also
> recognises that a recipient government's ownership of its development poli-
> cies and civil society's participation can contribute to mitigating tensions.

Thus, as a would-be leading donor, Japan has been actively involved
in the development policy dialogue and programming in the global
donor community.[6] Japan's ODA faces formidable challenges today,

---

[5] Taking this opportunity, Japan announced the *Action from Japan Initiative*, which
    was a package of undertakings on conflict prevention through development co-
    operation.

[6] In September 2000, the United Nations General Assembly adopted *United Nations
    Millennium Declaration* in which the following fundamental values are identified as

however. Faced with serious low economic growth rates and tight fiscal realities, the domestic environment surrounding Japan's ODA is not favourable. In the words of *Revised ODA Charter of 2003*, "The revision has also the aim of encouraging wide public participation and of deepening the understanding of Japan's ODA policies both within Japan and abroad." The Japanese people are questioning the need for continuing massive amounts of aid to foreign countries when corporate collapses and restructuring are forcing unemployment at home. Criticism in Japan against ODA to China, for example, is representative of the negative environment surrounding Japan's aid policy to developing countries.

In the document entitled *Economic Cooperation Program for China* in October 2001, the Japanese Ministry of Foreign Affairs stresses the need for a review of Japan's ODA to China and identifies the following points of critical importance:

1) It is in Japan's interest that China will progress towards a more open, stable society and take on greater responsibilities as a member of the international community;

2) It is indispensable for Japan to build broad, multi-layered relations with China, and ODA has an important role to play within this context;

3) In terms of greater effectiveness and efficiency in Japan's ODA programmes, some cast a sceptical eye on Japan's assistance to China;

4) Given China's economic development, Japan should encourage China's "self-help" efforts and provide complementary support for areas that China cannot reach;

5) There has been increasing criticism in Japan that Japan's assistance to China does not conform to the "Principles" articulated in the "ODA Charter" because of substantial increases in Chinese defence expenditures, China's development of nuclear weapons and missiles, China's imports and exports of arms, and questions about democracy and human rights protection;

6) Japan should make the utmost efforts to ensure deeper understanding on Chinese side of the principles of Japan's ODA Charter; and

7) Japan should encourage China to make greater efforts to enhance publicity activities on Japanese aid so that Japanese ODA is more widely known within China.

---

essential elements in the 21st century international relations: (1) Freedom; (2) Equality; (3) Solidarity; (4) Tolerance; (5) Respect of Nature; and (6) Shared Responsibility.

Public support for ODA is not what it was in the 1980s. According to an opinion poll conducted by the Office of the Prime Minister of Japan, in October 2000, 41.4 percent of respondents felt that Japan should maintain its efforts in economic assistance "at current levels;" 23.0 percent were of the opinion that it should be stepped up; 22.3 percent, that it should be reduced as much as possible; and 3.5 percent, that it should be stopped entirely. In the same opinion poll conducted by the Cabinet Office, Government of Japan, in October 2003, 43.5 percent of respondents felt that Japan should maintain its efforts in economic assistance "at current levels;" 19.0 percent were of the opinion that it should be stepped up; 25.5 percent, that it should be reduced as much as possible; 3.4 percent, that it should be stopped entirely. In other words, those who expressed support for the *status quo* or for expanded aid in 2003 together amounted for 62.5 percent of the total (compared to 78.7, 75.5, 70.0, and 64.4 percent in the 1996, 1997, 1998, and 2000 opinion polls). According to another opinion poll, conducted by *Yomiuri Shimbun* in October 2001, 48.1 percent of respondents felt that Japan should maintain its efforts in economic assistance "at current levels;" 4.2 percent were of the opinion that it should be stepped up; 39.3 percent, that it should be reduced as much as possible; and 4.2 percent, that it should be stopped entirely. Thus, more than 40 percent of respondents were concerned about the utility of Japan's ODA.

Responding to growing negative feeling toward Japan's development cooperation among the Japanese people, and also as part of the Koizumi Administration's fiscal rehabilitation initiative, the Japanese government declared that ODA was no longer to be considered "a sacred cow," and decided to slash ODA budget by 10 percent in 2001. In the OECD/DAC *Peer Review* conducted on December 12, 2003, severe domestic conditions surrounding Japan's ODA are illustrated as follows:

> There is clearly a sign of aid fatigue among the Japanese public. Although in part due to Japan's weak economic situation, the public is also becoming critical regarding the effectiveness of the aid programme and the commercial sector has become less supportive of aid. Simultaneously, the public is supportive of humanitarian efforts and responding to crises. [...] The continuing recession has had an effect on the gradually declining trend of ODA funds. At the 2002 Monterrey Conference, Japan was one of the few DAC members which was unable to commit to maintain or increase ODA.

In the same document, the following recommendations are made to the Japanese government:

1. In implementing the ODA Charter, Japan should highlight that the primary objective of ODA is for the development of the re-

cipient country and should ensure that, narrower national interests do not over-ride this objective;

2. Japan should make every effort to increase ODA levels as economic conditions improve, building broad-based public support to facilitate this.

On January 19, 2004, in the General Speech to the 159th Session of the Diet, Prime Minister Junichiro Koizumi reiterated Japan's strong commitment to the solution of the wider development problem as follows:

> As a responsible member of the international community, we have been providing assistance for "consolidation of peace and nation-building" in such countries as Afghanistan, the Democratic Socialist Republic of Sri Lanka and the Democratic Republic of Timor-Leste. We will work on the establishment of a structure in which Japan can more actively promote international peace and cooperation.
>
> Taking into consideration the perspective of "human security," in which we place emphasis on individuals, we will make strategic use of Official Development Assistance (ODA) to help developing countries overcome poverty and achieve sustainable growth and to solve global issues.

It might be understood as a sort of symbolic and political message, addressed not only to the Japanese public but also to the global donor community and developing recipient countries.

V. From Vision to Implementation: A New Area for Japan-EU Cooperation

In the words of the OECD/DAC *Peer Review of the European Community 2002*, "The European Community is a unique donor in that it plays a dual role in development, as a bilateral donor providing direct support to countries, and as a coordinating framework for European Union (EU) member states." In terms of ODA volume, the Commission of the European Communities provided USD 5.96 billion of net ODA in 2001, and it rose to USD 6.56 billion in 2002. The net ODA volume of EU countries combined was $ 26.29 billion in 2001, and $ 29.95 billion in 2002. All together, the European Union, or the Commission and the member states, provided USD 32.25 billion of net ODA in 2001, and USD 36.51 billion in 2002. This fact tells us that the European Union, as a region, provided some 60% of total DAC ODA, and along with the United States and Japan, the European Union is a major player in international cooperation and development assistance.

In addition to the substantial role in the quantitative dimension in official aid, the European Union, as a "Global Donor" has taken a strong leading role in the field of North-South development thinking and strategy in the past four decades. In February 1975, the European Community and its nine member states and 46 African, Caribbean, and Pacific States, or ACP States, signed the new and comprehensive co-operation agreement at Lomé, Togo. It marked the birth of *Lomé Regime* which aims to "establish a new model for relations between developed and developing states, compatible with the aspirations of the international community towards a more just and more balanced economic order."(*Preamble*). In June 2000, after twenty-five years of cooperation under the Lomé Conventions, the European Community and its fifteen member states and 77 ACP States signed the new *ACP-EU Partnership Agreement* at Cotonou, Benin, which is to cover the next twenty years of the relationship between the European Union and developing ACP countries. In the *Preamble* of the newly signed *Cotonou Agreement*, both Parties affirmed "their commitment to work together towards the achievement of the objectives of poverty eradication, sustainable development and the gradual integration of the ACP countries into the world economy." Then, both Parties reaffirmed "their willingness to revitalise their special relationship and to implement a comprehensive and integrated approach for a strengthened partnership based on political dialogue, development cooperation and economic and trade relations."

Furthermore, besides formal agreements with developing countries, the European Union has frequently demonstrated its strong political will to continue to take the leadership role in the North-South development cooperation. In October 2000, the European Union adopted the policy document entitled *The European Community's Development Policy – Statement by the Council and the Commission*, as the first tangible expression of the European Community's new development approach to the 21st century. It stresses the importance of development cooperation as follows:

> The European Union is a major player in the development sphere. It is the source of approximately half of the public aid effort worldwide and is the main trading partner for many developing countries. This declaration expresses the Council's and Commission's intent to reaffirm the Community's solidarity with those countries, in the framework of a partnership which respects human rights, democratic principles, the rule of law and the sound management of public affairs, and to begin the process of renewing its development policy based on the search for increased effectiveness in liaison with other players in the development sphere, and on the involvement of its own citizens.

In April 2001, the European Commission issued the *Communication from the Commission on Conflict Prevention*, in which it articulates the necessity to broaden the global development agenda and to include conflict prevention as a critical issue in development cooperation as follows:

> The ever-growing list of causes of conflicts calls for international co-operation and multilateral action of a new order. The EU, itself an on-going exercise in making peace and prosperity, has a big role to play in global efforts for conflict prevention. [...] Potential conflicts often cross borders. This demands international cooperation on long term prevention activities as well as coordination of responses to pre-crisis situations. The EU will therefore strengthen its cooperation with international partners active in the field of conflict prevention, such as US, Canada, Russia, Japan and Norway, main international organizations such as UN and OSCE as well as NGOs.

In May 2001, the European Community hosted the *3rd UN Conference on LDCs* in Brussels. It was intended to give a strong political signal about the significance it attaches to the problems of *marginalised* least developed countries in the era of *globalisation*.

In March 2002, just over six months since September 11, at the time of the *International Conference on Financing for Development* in Monterrey, Mexico, Mr Romano Prodi, President of the European Commission, addressed the following statement to demonstrate the European Union's determination towards international peace and prosperity as follows:

> We are conscious of the absolute moral imperative of combating the extreme poverty suffered by one fifth of humanity and we have fully endorsed the historic development goals written into the *Millennium Declaration*. [...] The European Union reaffirms its commitment to the target of 0.7% of GNP to be devoted to development aid, a target that several member states have already attained and overtaken. [...] The EU member states have collectively set themselves the interim target of 0.39% by 2006. This is a formal commitment which will allow a substantial increase in the amounts allocated to relieving poverty. Aid from the EU and its member states will increase by about € 8 billion (approximately USD 7 billion) per year by 2006 from its current level of € 27 billion, more than 50% of the world's ODA [...] Our future is a matter of political will and choice. Europe is opting for openness and solidarity. And I would call on our partners to work with in a global partnership for peace and sustainable development.

In parallel with the European Union's strong commitment to development cooperation, the Bush Administration of the United States, in *The National Security Strategy of the United States*, issued in September 2002, solemnly declared the following anti-terrorism development strategy:

> We will actively work to bring the hope of democracy, development, free markets, and free trade to every corner of the world. The events of September 11, 2001, taught us that weak states, like Afghanistan, can pose as great

a danger to our national interests as strong states. Poverty does not make poor people into terrorists and murderers. Yet poverty, weak institutions, and corruption can make weak states vulnerable to terrorist networks and drug cartels within their borders [...] the United States will deliver greater development assistance through the New Millennium Challenge Account to nations that govern justly, invest in their people, and encourage economic freedom.

As may be observed from these statements, "For the first time there is genuine consensus among rich and poor countries that poverty is the world's problem." "The need to eradicate poverty does not compete with the need to make the world more secure. On the contrary, eradicating poverty should contribute to a safer world – the vision of the Millennium Declaration." (UNDP, *Human Development Report 2003: Millennium Development Goals: A Compact among Nations to End Human Poverty*, p. 1 and p. 13).

Against this atmosphere which surrounding development cooperation, which "rediscovered" the importance of the solution of the wider problem of development within the new context of global peace and security, the fundamental question to be raised is this: what is the most promising area for development cooperation within the total framework of Japan-EU Cooperation? As influential members in the global donor community, Japan as an *aspiring* "Leading Donor" and the European Union, as an *established* "Leading Donor" share fundamental development thinking and strategy. The most difficult issues facing them are: how to translate vision into action; how to ensure implementation; and how aid should be delivered on the ground. The answer is to launch the Japan-EC Poverty Reduction and Conflict Prevention Initiative, which follows the model of the UNDP-EC Poverty and Environment Initiative, and aims at identifying concrete policy recommendations and practical measures based on the principle of a symmetrical division of labour. In this regard, what is of critical significance is how to ensure the implementation of *An Action Plan for EU-Japan Cooperation*, adopted at the European Union – Japan Summit in Brussels in 2001.

Major References

ACP-EU Partnership Agreement Signed in Cotonou on 23 June 2000, Courier, September 2000, Special Issue.

African Development Towards the 21st Century: The Tokyo Agenda for Action, Tokyo, October 1998.

Akaha, T., "Japan: A Passive Partner in the Promotion of Democracy," in P. J. Schraeder (ed.), *Exporting Democracy: Rhetoric vs. Reality*, London, Lynne Rienner, 2002, pp. 89-107.

Bush, G. W., *The National Security Strategy of the United States of America*, Washington, D.C., September 2002.

EEC-ACP Convention of Lome, Courier, No. 31 – Special Issue – March 1975.

European Commission, *The European Community's Development Policy: Statement by the Council and the Commission*, Brussels, 10 November 2000.

European Commission, *Communication from the Commission to the Council and the European Parliament on the 3rd United Nations Conference on Least Developed Countries*, Brussels, 11.04.2001 COM(2001) 209 final.

European Commission, *Communication from the Commission on Conflict Prevention*, Brussels, 11.04.2001 COM(2001) 211 final.

European Commission, *Development Co-operation with the Least Developed Countries: Fighting Poverty*, Brussels, DE 109, April 2001.

European Commission, *Communication from the Commission to the Council and the European Parliament: The European Union's Role in Promoting Human Rights and Democratization in Third Countries*, Brussels, 8.05.2001 COM(2001) 252 final.

European Commission, *Annual Report on the Implementation of the European Commission's External Assistance: Situation at 01.01.2001*, Brussels, 2002.

European Commission, *Annual Report 2003 on the European Community's Development Policy and the Implementation of External Assistance in 2002*, Brussels, 2003.

European Community, *Statement by Romano Prodi, President of the European Commission at the International Conference on Financing for Development*, Monterrey, Mexico, 22 March 2002.

European Union – Japan Summit, *An Action Plan for EU-Japan Cooperation*, Brussels, 2001.

Funabashi, Y., "Japan and the New World Order," *Foreign Affairs*, Vol. 70, No. 5, 1991, pp. 58-74.

G7 Finance Ministers, *Poverty Reduction and Economic Development: Report from G7 Finance Ministers to the Heads of State and Government*, Okinawa, 21 July 2000.

G8 Miyazaki Initiatives for Conflict Prevention, Miyazaki, July 2000.

UNESCO, "The Development Debate: Beyond the Washington Consensus," *International Social Science Journal*, December 2000, No. 166.

"Japan and the Third World: Co-prosperity by Peaceful Means, *The Economist*, 17 June 1989, pp. 15-18.

Japanese Government, *Japan's Official Development Assistance Charter*, Tokyo, 30 June 1992.

Japanese Government, *Revision of Japan's Official Development Assistance Charter*, Tokyo, 29 August 2003.

Koizumi, J., *Keynote Speech by Prime Minister Junichiro Koizumi at the Third Tokyo International Conference on African Development (TICAD III)*, Tokyo, 29 September 2003.

Koizumi, J., *General Speech by Prime Minister Junichiro Koizumi to the 159th Session of the Diet*, 19 January 2004.

Maxwell, S., "Heaven or Hubris: Reflections on the New 'New Poverty Agenda'," *Development Policy Review*, Vol. 21, No. 1, 2003, pp. 5-25.

Ministry of Foreign Affairs of Japanese Government, *Japan's Medium-Term Policy on Official Development Assistance (ODA)*, Tokyo, 10 August 1999.

Ministry of Foreign Affairs of Japanese Government, *Japan's ODA Annual Report 1999*, Tokyo, 2000.

Ministry of Foreign Affairs of Japanese Government, *Interim Report of the Second Consultative Committee on ODA Reform*, Tokyo, 1 August 2001.

Ministry of Foreign Affairs of Japanese Government, *Economic Cooperation Program for China*, Tokyo, October 2001.

Ministry of Foreign Affairs of Japanese Government, *Diplomatic Bluebook 2001*, Tokyo, 2002.

Ministry of foreign Affairs of Japanese Government, *Summary of the 2002 White Paper on Official Development Assistance (ODA)*, Tokyo, April 2003.

OECD/DAC, *Shaping the 21st Century: The Contribution of Development Co-operation*, Paris, May 1996.

OECD/DAC, *Development Co-operation Review of Japan: Summary and Conclusions*, Paris, 1999.

OECD/DAC, *Development Co-operation 2000 Report*, Paris, 2001.

OECD/DAC, *Development Co-operation 2001 Report*, Paris, 2002.

OECD/DAC, *Development Co-operation 2002 Report*, Paris, 2003.

OECD/DAC, *European Community: DAC Peer Review*, September 2002.

OECD/DAC, *Japan: DAC Peer Review*, Paris, December 2003.

TICAD Tenth Anniversary Declaration, Tokyo, October 2003.

Tokyo Declaration on African Development "Towards the 21st Century," Tokyo, October 1993.

UNDP-EC Poverty and Environment Initiative, *Chairmen's Report*, Brussels and New York, September 1999.

UNDP-EC Poverty and Environment Initiative, *Attacking Poverty while Improving the Environment: Practical Recommendations*, Brussels-New York, 1999.

UNDP, *Human Development Report 2003 Millennium Development Goals: A Compact among Nations to End Human Poverty*, New York, Oxford University Press, 2003.

United Nations, *World Summit for Social Development: The Copenhagen Declaration and Programme of Action*, New York, 1995.

United Nations General Assembly, *United Nations Millennium Declaration*, New York, September 2000.

USAID, *Foreign Aid in the National Interest: Promoting Freedom, Security, and Opportunity*, Washington, D.C., 2002.

Yasutomo, D., *The Manner of Giving: Strategic Aid and Japanese Foreign Policy*, Lexington and Toronto, Lexington Books, 1986.

PART THREE

ECONOMIC MODEL(S)
AND GLOBAL GOVERNANCE

CHAPTER 10

The EU Enlargement and
the EU-Japan Economic Relationship

Takayuki KIMURA

Visiting Professor, International Christian University

I. The EU-Japan Relationship

The relationship between Europe and Japan suffered periods of difficulty during the 1980s and early 90s and might justifiably be called the "Phase of Friction." During the course of this period, when Japanese annual economic growth was running at more than twice that of the average European Community country and Japanese exports to Europe were increasing rapidly,[1] the bilateral relationship was quite strained on economic issues. Under the then prevalent atmosphere of "Euro-pessimism," Europeans felt threatened by Japan, which looked so different from them. Many racially tinted accusations were made, not only by the media, but also by high-level political leaders in Europe.[2] At the demand of the European Commission and the member governments, the Japanese Government felt obliged to implement "voluntary" restrictions on ten major items of exports to Europe, including automobiles and electronic goods. In the so called "Battle of Poitiers" the French Government limited the customs processing of all Japanese video tape recorders to the custom house at the inland location of Poitiers. This city is also known to the Japanese as a famous battleground with the Barbarians, and the historical resonances of the location contributed to

---

[1]   OECD, *Main Economic Indicators, 1960-1990*, Paris, 1992.

[2]   The most vocal of them was Edith Cresson, then French Prime Minister and later European Commissioner until 1999, who made a number of emotional accusations against Japan. She was reported to have said, on the eve of Japanese Prime Minister Kaifu's visit to France in January 1990, "Japan is our enemy. The Japanese don't obey rules. They work like ants. They are aiming to conquer the world."

make this one of the most emotionally irritating of the many episodes of heightened friction.

During the course of the 1990s the situation changed gradually. The Japanese *per capita* GDP reached the level of the highest in Europe. The maturing of the Japanese economy, with a much slower annual growth rate, calmed the sense of rivalry towards Japan in the minds of increasingly self-assured Europeans. Substantial increases in two-way direct investment also promoted mutual understanding as well as the awareness of a mutually beneficial relationship. There has been increased scope for cooperation between Europe and Japan, both being modern societies with their own long historical and cultural traditions. In December 2001, at the 10th EU-Japan Summit in Brussels, the leaders of both sides agreed to an Action Plan for EU-Japan Cooperation[3] to launch a Decade of Japan-Europe Cooperation. The Action Plan covers a wide range of cooperation towards "shaping their common future," including promoting peace and security, strengthening the economic and trade partnership, utilising the dynamism of globalisation for the benefit of all, coping with global and societal challenges, and bringing together peoples and cultures. Following the Action Plan in the economic area, the EU-Japan Mutual Recognition Agreement was concluded and came into effect in January 2002 and the EU-Japan Competition Agreement was signed in August 2003. The Regulatory Reform Dialogue, which started in the middle of 1990s, became a more cooperative endeavour and an important number of requests were granted in the matter of regulation reform by both sides. For example, the activities of foreign lawyers and financial services have been further liberalised on the Japanese side, while procedures in a certain number of the EU states in issuing residence and work permits to Japanese and non-EU citizens have been improved. EU-Japan cooperation has become prominent in multilateral negotiations such as the global environment and the WTO. The EU-Japan Business Dialogue Round Table, established in 1999, has made joint proposals annually to both Japanese and EU leaders, which have been taken up in the following government-level talks.

Against this background, there follows is an examination of the effect of the EU enlargement to the EU-Japan economic relations.

II. Enlargement and Japanese Business

The 2004 EU enlargement will create an economic entity roughly the same size as the United States. As a result of the accession of the new ten member states, the GDP of the European Union will increase by

---

[3]   10th EU-Japan Summit, *An Action Plan for EU-Japan Cooperation*, December 2001.

4.8%, while its population will increase by 20%.[4] This is relatively small in terms of GDP, as compared to the previous enlargements. However, since the accession countries, in the process of the catching up, are expected to grow faster than the present member countries, the longer-term economic effects of the present accession and the coming accession of Romania and Bulgaria may be larger than the present figures suggest.

The enlargement will have a significant impact on the EU-Japan relationship, which, in general, is expected to further promote the mutually beneficial relations which exist between the two sides. At the 12th EU-Japan Summit held in Athens in May 2003, leaders of both sides welcomed the EU enlargement in their Joint Statement.[5] The Japanese side understands the benefits the enlargement would bring to Europe both politically, in terms of enhanced stability, and economically, through the creation of a larger single market and a reinforced growth dynamic in the acceding countries.

The Enlargement will create an environment which will benefit foreign firms doing business with the EU, including those from Japan. The accession countries, gaining stability under the EU rules, will provide better conditions to Japanese and international business. The new member states have the comparative advantage of their low cost skilled labour, their closeness to the market, not to mention their own potential purchasing power. With the prospect of the accessions, the number of Japanese companies establishing manufacturing facilities has doubled in the past three years.[6] Most of the Japanese direct investments to the new accession countries are in those sectors where proximity to the European market is a significant factor.

The future potential of Russia and other neighbouring markets is another factor. And the EU's increasingly closer economic ties with other European and non-European countries beyond the enlarged EU will be an added attraction for them. The future evolution of economic (and political) relations with these countries, especially the relationship of the Common European Economic Space with Russia, may give a large additional impetus to the positive effect of the enlargement. However, it also has to be pointed out that some part of new direct investment to the accession countries may be a diversion of the investments which would

[4] European Commission, *Enlargement of the European Union: The Implications for Japan*, September 2003, Basic data.
[5] 12th EU-Japan Summit, *Joint Press Statement*, Athens, 2 May 2003, p. 3.
[6] The number of Japanese companies in the five Central European countries of Poland, Czech Republic, Slovakia, Hungary, and Slovenia is 300, of which 120 have established or are establishing new manufacturing facilities. Nihon Keizai Shinbun, 1 January 2004.

have been located in the present member countries if the enlargement had not occurred. Their competitiveness, in terms of attracting globally oriented investment – which is less constrained geographically in deciding business locations – may not be as high as some other locations like China, where labour costs are much lower.[7]

Another important factor in attracting foreign investment is transparency and fair application of the rules and the treatment of foreign investments by the host governments. A survey of the Japanese companies operating in the accession countries revealed that the application procedures for investment in those countries are not sufficiently transparent. The application of laws and regulations is often arbitrary, depending on the individual local office dealing with the case. Complexity of procedure and unstandardised treatment for residence, work permits and driving licenses are also mentioned as sources of considerable difficulty.[8] It is expected that with EU accession and mutual competition to attract foreign direct investment, the new member countries' practices will converge with the standard of the present EU-15 or international standards.

The future enlargement of the Euro Zone will benefit not only those member countries directly concerned but also the rest of the world, including Japan and Japanese investment. It is obvious that the joining of the United Kingdom to the Euro Zone would have a larger impact and equally, that it is still a few years at least before the accession countries can meet the conditions for joining the common currency. However, the efforts of these countries to meet the required criteria will, of themselves, lead to the improvement of financial management and discipline, promoting fiscal stability and predictability, all of which is also beneficial to players from outside the EU. Any increase in the weight of Euro as another key currency would have an important effect in Asia and Japan. Already in 2003 the share of Euro bonds exceeded that of Dollar bonds in the medium and long-term bond market, according to the BIS.

III. A New Framework for Investment Promotion

Since mutual direct investment has become more important to both economies, a proposal from the Japanese side for a new framework for investment promotion between the EU and Japan is a logical course of action. In fact, one of the characteristics of EU-Japan economic rela-

---

[7]   S. Arai, Parliamentary Secretary for Foreign Affairs, *Japanese Investments in the Enlarged European Union*, Seminar on Japanese Investments in the Enlarged European Union, Brussels, 14 November 2003, p. 4.

[8]   Arai, *op. cit.*, pp. 5-6.

tions is that the weight of mutual foreign direct investment in relation to mutual trade is the highest among all bilateral economic relations of major industrial countries. The EU has been the biggest foreign investor in Japan in the last five years and in fiscal year (FY) 2002 Europe had a 29% share of the ¥ 2.2 trillion worth of the inward foreign direct investment in Japan.[9] The European side also regards foreign direct investment as a key element to promote the enlarged EU economy. Japan invested ¥ 1.8 trillion in Europe in FY 2002, up 40% on the previous year. This represents a 40% share of Japan's outward foreign direct investment. It is also worth pointing out that, while North American companies make largely portfolio investments, Japanese companies make new investments in such areas as automotive, consumer electronics, and telecommunication, which contribute to the creation of new jobs and employment in the host countries. In January 2003, Prime Minister Koizumi, in order to further promote inward foreign direct investment, announced an initiative to double the cumulative amount of inward foreign direct investment to Japan in five years.

The Framework will be an important follow up to the Action Plan and the EU-Japan Initiative on Investment, in which both sides committed themselves to making efforts to promote direct investment between Japan and the EU.[10] The expectation of the private sector on both sides to promote mutual direct investment is also very high. The EU-Japan Business Dialogue Round Table submitted recommendations to the leaders of both sides which call for the conclusion of a framework agreement for the promotion of mutual investment. The European Business Council in Japan, an association of European businesses operating in Japan, published a report calling for a similar framework. The joint efforts of Japan and the EU to include Investment in the negotiating agenda of the current Doha Round negotiations did not materialise because of the objection of developing countries. This has made possibility of future multilateral negotiations on Investment unlikely and gives added incentive to deal investment related matters on bilateral bases.

One of the difficulties in proceeding with the negotiation of the framework is that the competence of promoting direct investment is shared by both the European Commission and the individual member state governments, depending on which aspects are involved. The Commission seems to be reluctant to take the initiative in such subjects, for fear of intruding in the matters of individual governments' compe-

---

[9]   The figures are drawn from the statistics published by the Japanese Finance Ministry and EUROSTAT.

[10]   12th Japan-EU Summit, *Japan-EU Initiatives on Investment*, Athens, 2 May 2003.

tence. This is a typical example of the difficulties that beset any agreement or negotiations on matters of mixed competence with the European Union. Any third party like Japan is left in the situation in which neither the Commission nor individual governments are willing to get into negotiations on matters of mixed competence, even when both sides agree on its importance or desirability.

IV. Managing the Transition

While the general effect of the enlargement is positive to third countries like Japan, some of the economic impact could be more complex. There are a number of matters that have to be solved in the transition period of the enlargement, mismanagement of which could cause a substantial negative impact to Japan and to EU-Japan relations.

1. Compensation for the Accession Countries' Increased Tariffs

As a result of the accession, the common customs tariff of the present EU will apply automatically to the accession countries. Even though the EU claims that the general incidence of duties of the accession countries will be substantially lower than at present,[11] hundreds of items of traditional Japanese exports to the accession countries would be adversely affected by any sudden increase of the import tariff.[12] The WTO stipulates that third countries like Japan can request compensation from the customs union which may take the form of a tariff reduction on other items. Even though the EU has agreed to the principle of starting negotiations, the Commission has shown strong reluctance to pay any substantial compensation. It is important that the negotiations should be concluded swiftly, unlike the previous cases of EU enlargement.

2. Compensation for the Modification/Withdrawal of Commitments in the Service Sector

Most of the accession countries, through the negotiation under WTO (GATS), have specific commitments in the favorable treatment of foreign entities' activities in their domestic service sector such as audiovisual services, which are above the level of the European Union's commitments. The Japanese side believes that those commitments are not incompatible with their joining the European Union. However, if a decision is taken to withdraw the commitments, negotiations for compensation will be needed with any affected country including Japan.

---

[11] European Commission, *op. cit.*, p. 13.

[12] For example, Tariffs of Czech Republic and Poland on household electronic appliances will be increased from 0% to 14%, Hungary's tariff on trucks will be increased from 5% to 22%.

Here again, one of the problems is speed. The compensation negotiations regarding the accession of Austria, Finland and Sweden did not start until 2003.

3. Treatment of Investment Incentives Provided by the Accession Countries

Most Japanese companies that made direct investments in the accession countries are currently receiving investment incentives from the governments concerned. Even though incentives which are not compatible with the present EU rules will have to be altered, the incentives are part of contracts agreed upon by the host government and the companies concerned. The Japanese side believes honouring these commitments to be important. This could be done either by continuing the incentive for a certain period or through some alternative measures.

4. Continuation of the Treaties of Commerce and Navigation between Japan the Accession Countries

Japan has Treaties of Commerce and Navigation or Trade Agreements with six accession countries. The EU is insisting that those agreements are incompatible with the *acquis communautaire*, and should be discontinued. The Japanese side, while believing that these treaties are consistent with the *acquis*, just as are the similar treaties of commerce and navigation of Japan currently in effect with the United Kingdom and France, is willing to negotiate with the European Union in order to find the way to maintain the substance of the treaties with the accession countries.

5. Review of the Extension of Ongoing Anti-Dumping Tariffs

Some of the Japanese products exported to the European Union are the subject to the European Commission anti-dumping duties, but none of these same products are liable for anti-dumping duties in the accession countries. The Japanese companies concerned feel it unjustified that the items which had previously been accepted by accession countries as ordinary fair trade practice should suddenly attract anti-dumping duties only because those countries have joined the European Union. The Japanese side is requesting the reconsideration of the dumping status of individual items where the basis of calculation is substantially altered by accession.

6. Adjusting the Application of the EU-Japan Mutual Recognition Agreement to the Accession Countries

Some adjusting is necessary in extending the application of the bilateral agreements between Japan and the EU (EC). The Mutual Recognition Agreement (MRA) between Japan and the European Commission is a case in point. Legally, application of the MRA extends automatically to the territories of the enlarged European Union, including the accession countries. However, the Agreement does not become fully operational in the territories of accession countries until the necessary adjustments have been agreed upon by the two parties.

IV. The Enlarged European Union in the Multilateral Scene

The European Union and Japan together account for roughly 45% of the world GDP. The EU and Japan also share similar values and concerns in many international problems, as well as the similar approach of promoting a multilateral and rule oriented international order. Thus, the enlarged and strengthened EU could lead to a more effective EU-Japan partnership to deal with the global affairs. In fact, EU-Japan cooperation has already become a prominent factor in promoting rule-making and rule-improving in international economic and environmental forums, including the WTO. Other countries will also take further into account the views and ideas coming from the European Union, as its weight continues to increase in multilateral negotiations, with the added advantage of a larger number of the member states which will constitute powerful bloc votes.

Here the future effectiveness of EU-Japan cooperation is in large part dependent on whether the European Union can function effectively as a reliable partner. The problem is mostly whether decision-making in the European Union can function smoothly. If the enlargement leads to more difficulty in decision-making within the European Union, due to the larger number of members with substantially different economic conditions, it will have a negative effect not only on the European Union itself, but also on the rest of the world, including Japan. Another possible problem is whether the EU can give due regard to the positions of third countries. The difficulty of reaching agreement within the European Union may increase the stiffness of the EU position, being itself the result of laborious internal negotiations. This may, in turn, result in the agreed line being presented unilaterally and leave little room for compromise with other countries.

An example of this may be the case of the current WTO negotiations of the Doha Development Agenda. Because of the similarity of their interests and the necessity of enhancing their negotiating positions, a number of countries, including Japan, have allied with the European Union in the Doha Development Round. A great number of preparatory and strategy meetings, including joint or parallel approaches to non-participants of the group, were held by both the European Union and

Japan. However, as the European Union and the United States came to an agreement in agriculture in August 2003, some Japanese negotiators and parliamentarians closely involved in the matter complained that the EU had worked out a compromise position on agriculture with the United States, without involving Japan, which the European Commission had called their "ally" in these negotiations. They even called it as a second "Blair House Nightmare," the rather pithy sobriquet given to the compromise in the agricultural sector secretly agreed between the EC and the US, without the involvement of Japan, in the final stage of the Uruguay Round Negotiations. Similarly, on the final day of the Cancún Ministerial Meeting in September 2003, the European Union suddenly changed its position on the so-called Singapore issues without informing, let alone consulting with, other countries with which they shared positions. This left the partners of "the alliance" in a difficult situation. Korea could not adjust its position on the spot and was blamed by European negotiators as a cause of failure of the Cancún meeting, even though the most important reason for the Cancún failure was the developing countries' refusal to accept the Euro-American position on agricultural subsidies. The reason for not informing the allies was later explained as the difficulty of reaching timely agreement within the European Union and not the exercising of prerogative of an economic superpower to the rest of participants.[13] However, other countries will have to take into account that similar cases of difficulties of reaching an agreed position within the European Union may occur in the other important negotiations. And if the difficulty becomes more pronounced after the enlargement, it may reduce the influence of the increased power of the European Union, which would be, in general, an unwelcome development for Japan and many other countries.

At presently the obvious and immediate task which the European Union and Japan should take up cooperatively in the multilateral economic field is the restarting of Doha Developing Agenda negotiations of the WTO and leading it together to a successful conclusion. Whether it can be achieved or not may decide the workability of the EU-Japan cooperation in multilateral forums in general.

VI. Rule-Making and Administrative Decisions within the European Union

The European Union often goes ahead of the rest of the world in introducing new rules and systems in a wide variety of areas, including environment and social matters, which inevitably affect the interests of

---

[13] This was the explanation given to me by a high level official of the European Commission at a symposium held in Brussels in November 2003.

third country business concerns. In many cases when the EU introduces a new rule they seek to have the rule accepted as a global rule. This gives added importance to the third parties to follow the rule-making process within European Union and, if possible and appropriate, to propose a joint formulation of new rules. However, when introducing such rules and systems, third countries' interests are often given less regard in their deliberations. For the third countries, information on the new rules in the making is difficult to reach even though the rules may affect their interests or the interests of their companies. There is no established rule of public hearings and in fact, hearings are held only if the third country strongly approaches the Commission with the request.[14] This is not in line with the established practice in the United States or Japan. With the new enlargement the *de facto* discrimination between member and non-member governments will be automatically expanded to the accession countries.

Another difficulty to the third countries is the difficulty of following the evolution process of European integration, of clearly understanding which matters are currently under the jurisdiction of the European Union or individual member governments. Even though the *acquis* must stipulate it, it is actually quite difficult for outsiders to judge and there have been cases where the individual member governments claim that they are following the directives of the European Union while the Commission insists that the matter is under the competence of the member governments. The enlargement may mean that the long-suffering third parties will have to endure more of the same.

Decisions in the EU are often made by simple majority and even where the qualified majority is the rule, when the matter does not seriously affect member countries' interests, decisions are heavily influenced by the insistence of a few countries with strong views. Matters involving only a third country interest are often decided by the representatives of member governments which have no such interest, let alone industry, in that sector. The decision-making process is not necessarily transparent and therefore difficult for outsiders to get to know. However, there have been cases in the recent past where a government was strongly pressed by the Commission to vote for a dumping judgment in a tied '7-for, 7-against' vote. The case concerned the activities of a company from a third country and the government in question was not convinced of the judgement of dumping.[15] If the third country had been

---

[14] This is also a complaint I have often heard from my United States' counterpart while I was stationed in Brussels.

[15] I personally got knowledge of an anti-dumping case of a Japanese company specialising in transport parts. When approached by a Japanese officer for information, an officer in charge of the country concerned replied that they could have given a

represented in the Council, the result could have been different. In the case of Commission decisions, since the Commission is composed of at least one Commissioner for each member country, the same situation sometimes arises. Information on matters of serious concern to individual member governments are passed to them well in advance and appropriate action can be taken before the matter goes before the Commission for decision.[16] The enlargement could aggravate such situations unless a conscious effort is made and some institutional arrangements are introduced to alleviate *de facto* discrimination against the third parties.

VII. EU and Asian Regional Cooperation

ASEAN, which originally started as a means of increasing regional resilience against communist threat, is the oldest regional cooperation structure in eastern Asia. A grouping of ASEAN+3 has gradually evolved as an important forum, avoiding regional political sensitivities, as well as a very strongly negative reaction in the past from the United States. China has already agreed to a free trade agreement with ASEAN, which attaches the greatest importance to what is called the "early harvest program" in the area of trade in goods. Japan, breaking a long-standing position of avoiding bilateral trade agreements, has started moving towards economic partnership agreements (EPA), an extended form of conventional free trade agreements, concluding one with Singapore, currently negotiating with Korea, Malaysia, the Philippines and Thailand, aiming at an eventual agreement with the whole ASEAN and ultimately, at building an economic community of the whole region. Japan is looking for an economic partnership, not only with substantial trade liberalisation but also advancement on a wide range of other trade-related matters, as well as cooperation in various fields. Such a comprehensive and ambitious approach is expected to contribute to the improvement of the economic environment, which constitutes a more encouraging basis for long-term development of the region. In the

favourable reply if the Japanese approach had been two days earlier, the date they approved the case in response to a telephone call by the European Commission.

[16] There is a case of a Japanese company which the European Commission fined €1 million for not providing information on the possible impact of a merger case of two European companies. The Commission explained to me that the request for information was made to save the Japanese company from possible adverse effects of the merger to which the company was not a party. Since the Japanese company did not recognise the necessity of the help and did not provide information on the company, they were fined. The Commission proudly announced that this was the first case of a third party company not involved in the merger case being fined by the Commission. This is a typical case which would not have happened if the company were European.

financial sector, Japan is already a driving force in the Chiang Mai Initiative to stabilise regional financial markets.

With this recent advancement of Asian regional cooperation on a more structured base, there is an increasing expectation that the regional integration of the East Asian countries will soon be realised. The successful example of European integration is always in the mind of the advocates of East Asian integration. However, there is a wide difference between the European and Asian situation. The difference of economic level of development is far greater in Asia than in Europe. The *per capita* GDP of the richest country in the EU-25 is 13 times as high as that of the lowest, while in Asia the figure is more than 300 times. And the poorest 5 countries have a combined population of more than 78% of that of all ASEAN+3 countries. Some important countries are still under undemocratic regimes, even though their attitude has become considerably more outward-looking. Few countries besides Japan could pass the Copenhagen criteria, which are the conditions for starting accession negotiations to the European Union. If Asia were to adopt a collective decision-making process with some voting system reflecting individual countries' population, China alone would have 65% of votes.[17]

In spite of those fundamental obstacles, with the rapid increase of intra-regional trade and investment, the recent trend towards more institutionalised Asian regional cooperation will continue, partly as a response to the European Union's successful advancement of regional integration, partly because of the continuous expansion of free trade areas by the United States and the European Union respectively, while the global approach in the WTO and other organisations has become less promising in recent years.

ASEM (Asia-Europe Meeting) was first proposed in response to the strong desire of the EU countries to get more involved in Asian affairs in light of the rapid economic growth of East and Southeast Asia and the success of ASPAC (Asia Pacific Conference), a grouping including the US, Canada, Australia and New Zealand. ASEM, under the guidance of the head-of-states and head-of-government level meetings, has dealt with political, economic and cultural cooperation between Asia and Europe. As most of the Asian countries put more emphasis on economic cooperation and the European side on the political dialogue, Japan has been playing the role of the promoting balanced attention to

---

[17] Figures are drawn from the following data: World Bank, World Development Indicators database (http://devdata.worldbank.org/data-query/), ASEAN Secretariat (http://www.aseansec.org) and Asian Development Bank, Key Indicators 2002 of Developing Asian and Pacific Countries.

the three areas of cooperation. Even though the initial European enthusiasm cooled down after the Asian financial crisis of 1998, ASEM continues to be the only forum of dialogue and cooperation between the two regions.

The EU enlargement is expected to lead to ten new member countries joining the ASEM, which will encourage their involvement in cooperation and closer ties with Asian countries. However the prospect of their early joining in the ASEM is obscured by the European desire for 'automatic' membership of the accession countries and the Asian insistence on the admission of three ASEAN countries which are left out of the ASEM. Of these three countries, Myanmar is the country to which the European side objects because of its human rights situation. The Asian side has established a common position that the three countries have to participate in the ASEM simultaneously and without condition. Japan supports the Asian position, arguing that human rights and other progress can be made through inclusion rather than exclusion in the forum of discussion and peer pressure, while on the other hand continuing the bilateral direct approach to Myanmar.

VIII. Conclusion

The effect of the EU enlargement on the EU-Japan relations depends largely upon whether the European Union can manage internal differences and function well after the enlargement. If the Union encounters on-going difficulties in agreeing a joint position on the major problems within the Union, most of the energy and attention of the European leaders will be confined to internal European affairs. An inward-looking Europe would not be beneficial to Japan or to the rest of the world.

If the European Union functions well and takes the outward-looking attitude, EU-Japan relations in the future may reach still higher levels of cooperation, based on the similarity of the interest and multilateral and rule-oriented approach to the future of the world. If it does not function well, the world and Japan will not only lose one of the most important partners but also suffer the consequence of the now larger and stronger international entity straying in indecision or imposing unilaterally the result of internal difficulties on the rest of the world. Although the fear of a larger and stronger Europe becoming a "fortress Europe," as has often been cited in the earlier decades, proved largely groundless, there may still remain the fear of a stronger Europe becoming more unilaterally-oriented in relation to third countries other than the United States.

The next few years will show which course the European Union will take. Some of the matters of immediate concern to the Japanese side may be the forthcoming decision on the European Constitution and its ratification within the EU, and the approach of the EU to the multilateral negotiations on the external side. The rest of the world will have to adjust its positions in relation to developments in Europe, as a united Europe grows to be a major player in the world, both economically and politically.

CHAPTER 11

Enlarged EU and Japan Facing the Global Trade and Economic Agenda

Maria KARASINSKA-FENDLER

Jean Monnet Professor and
Director European Institute, Lódz, Poland

I. Introduction

The dynamic international political and economic environment of the Post-Cold War era is changing rapidly and continuously. The world economy has not exactly been in very good shape the past few years. The war in Iraq is still weighing heavily on the world economy. Financial markets are fickle; confidence among businesses and consumers remains subdued. We must, however, not be fooled into regarding the war in Iraq as the sole source of uncertainty or the predominant issue for the world economy. Uncertainty was around before the advent of the war, and uncertainty will linger for some time after the end of hostilities. What is more, uncertainty stemming from geopolitical strife seems to be deflecting our focus from some fundamental imbalances. Redressing these imbalances is a precondition for a necessary step to sustainable growth. There is a slow correction of the over-investment which incurred during the millennium boom. Vast spare capacity forms the backdrop for weak capital spending. The economy is bound to recover, but the recovery is not necessarily just around the corner. The IMF expected[1] the US economy to grow at the rate of 2.2% in 2003. According to this estimate, the Euro area could expect GDP growth of 1.1%. In 2002, North America and non-Japan Asia were the main contributors to world output growth, with the Euro area and Japan lagging behind significantly. Two implications merit consideration. First, the world economy is even more fragile than this titled growth performance suggests at first sight, for the growth path of the EU economy itself is

---

[1]   See http://www.whitehouse.gov/news/releases/2002/06.

189

somewhat unbalanced. Its macroeconomic imbalances deserve careful addressing. Second, the world economy depends heavily on the US taking the driver's seat. The Euro area and Japan must work on improving their ability to produce self-sustaining economic growth. The tri-polar economic and financial world can not afford to rely on one pole only. Hence, the need for closer political discussion and cooperation between global partners, like the European Union and Japan, becomes increasingly important.

The Eastern enlargement, together with the monetary union, is one of the defining issues of European integration in the 1990s and in the new millennium. The fall of the Berlin Wall in 1989 brought about, not only a change in the structure of international relations in general, but also set in motion a process of 'reunifying Europe'. This reunification process passed an important intermediary step on the way to a fully united Europe with the signing of the accession treaties by ten candidate countries in Athens on April 16, 2003. The addition of the ten new members in May 2004 will have a profound impact on the character and functioning of the EU. The decision-making system, the Union's budgetary framework, and the design of the key policies such as Common Agricultural Policy and the Structural Funds are in need of deep revision. The enlargement will also affect the EU's political cohesion and balance and its overall identity and sense of purpose. The process of the ongoing debate and negotiations on several crucial decisions will determine the precise impact of this enlargement, not only on the EU itself, but also on politics and the economy at a global level.

For Japan, the last decade marked a growing interest in Europe. The end of the Cold War and the collapse of the eastern bloc, symbolised by the demolition of the Berlin Wall, were striking developments. This increased interest was well-founded, as after 1989 the importance of EU policy *vis-à-vis* the East European countries grew considerably as the EU engaged in capacity building, supporting privatisation policies and restructuring in Eastern Europe. From an early stage, it was clear that this process was clearing the way for the eventual accession of the former eastern bloc countries. The establishment of the free trade area with the Central and Eastern European Countries (CEECs) paved the way to the facilitation of trade and the encouragement of foreign direct investment. The new member states have demonstrated that integration contributes to overcoming historic differences, animosities – even hostility.

Given the comparatively small size of the economies of the applicant countries, their accession will not change dramatically the EU's foreign economic relations. However, because of their number, their influence on the political relations with third countries will probably be substan-

190

tial. The EU has been aware of this rising diversity of interests and its potential impact on its overall institutional capacity to take and implement decisions. The Convention on the Future of Europe had the explicit task of dealing with that problem by redesigning, among other things, the institutional set-up and decision-making rules of an enlarged EU. Within this perspective, the qualitative influence of the enlargement seems to be the main operative factor.

The enlargement will influence the nature of the EU-Japan partnership. An understanding of the effects of the EU enlargement on external relations requires first an understanding of the effects of enlargement on the EU and on its new members. Through its effects on the Union, enlargement inevitably changes relations with third partners. It is clear that enlargement will not affect economic and political relationships to the same degree, nor necessarily in the same way. The economics and politics of enlargement are complex, with the shifting perceptions of 'us' and 'them' constantly changing priorities and relations with third parties. The economist's concept of a general equilibrium, or of a continuous dis-equilibrium, is perhaps a useful notion here. The enlargement can, potentially not only make the EU a stronger partner, both politically and economically, but will also engage ten new partners in more intensive cooperation with Japan.

This chapter, prepared on a basis of the paper presented during the conference, does not pretend to be an exhaustive treatment of the large topic of potential and real effects of the enlargement on EU-Japan relations. It is worth mentioning that the overall consequences of the enlargement for the shape of the world system are not discussed at any great length in the existing literature, as it is dominated by sector and country approaches and is driven by the urgency of the negotiations and of calendar concerns. Deeper research and reflection on these issues is certainly necessary. Here I would like to thank the organisers of the conference for their invitation and encouragement to take part in this particularly interesting debate. My contribution is organised within the logic of the possible qualitative changes to which the enlargement may give rise, along with their potential impact on the EU and on Japan, as key actors of the global economic system.

II. Specificity of the Ongoing Enlargement

Ever since the founding of the European Economic Community in 1958, enlargements have constituted an important feature of the EU's historical evolution and development. None of these previous enlargements was without problems or controversy. Each enlargement so far has increased the diversity of the EU in terms of economic structures and appeals to social solidarity. The upcoming round will continue this pattern. The problem of progressively enlarging the EU is how to ensure the unity of the whole while respecting the diversity of its parts. This is the paradox of European enlargement. It is clear that none of the previous enlargements have posed the same massive qualitative challenge presented by the accession of the Eastern countries. Ten adhesion countries constitute a substantial difference, compared with the much smaller number of applicants in previous enlargement rounds. The number of prospective new members, and the fact that all, except Poland, are relatively small countries, has profound implications for the structure and operation of the EU decision-making institutions. It will also lead to a more heterogeneous EU in terms of economic and political interests, as well as of historical and cultural values.

The biggest significant change regards the number of member states, which increases by 66%. Thus the EU comprises 25, instead of 15 – or 13.09% instead of 7.85% – of the 191 sovereign states (UN member states) of the world. It does not automatically follow that the enlarged EU will be more powerful. There is a question whether a bigger number of states increase the power of the EU as an international actor, in particular in international organisations. To great extent, this will depend largely on the compatibility of the EU member states' interests. Given the relatively short period of sovereignty enjoyed by most new members, many of these interests are only now being defined.

Substantial changes to the state structures in Central and Eastern Europe, massive upheaval and an equally drastic change in their foreign relations followed the collapse of communism. Some of these countries, such as Poland and Hungary (as well as Romania and Bulgaria, which will probably join the EU in the next enlargement) retained their state identity. The Soviet Union and Yugoslavia experienced disintegration and Slovenia, Latvia, Lithuania and Estonia emerged as new independent states with their own foreign, development and trade policies. The division of Czechoslovakia led to the birth of two new states: the Czech Republic and Slovakia. All of these countries quickly acceded to the World Bank, the IMF and – from 1995 – the WTO and presented their formal applications to the EU (see Table 1).

One of the key problems of the enlargement is the relatively poor economic condition of the current applicants. As a group, the 10 have a *per capita* GDP that is around one-third of the EU average[2] and about half of the average for the EU's four poorest countries. While previous enlargements also admitted countries that were far below the EU's economic level, what is different about this enlargement is the combina-

---

[2]   2002 Regular Report, at http://europa.int/comm/enlargement/report2002/index.htm.

tion of the large number of applicants and those applicants' economic condition. These two factors, taken together mean that the economic impact on the EU will be much more significant. Whereas the three-country Mediterranean enlargement of the 1980s had the effect of reducing the EU's average *per capita* GDP by 6 percent, the current enlargement to twenty-five members is projected to lower this average (for a much larger EU) by 14 percent.[3] This relative poverty of the new members has several immediate implications. Firstly, the size of the enlarged internal market of the EU increases only modestly. Secondly, the volume of the EU's exports to, and imports from third countries increases only slightly, due to the relatively weak participation of those economies in world trade. Thirdly, the new members will be entitled to profit from substantial transfers from the Structural Funds, amounting to about 4% of their GDP.

The economic status of the current applicants (see Table 2) means that substantial reform of EU policies is a necessary precondition to the enlargement. With more than 18 percent of their labour force employed in agriculture (compared to approximately 5% in the current member states of the EU), the new members would be major recipients of the CAP assistance. At the same time, expansion to 25 would more than double the EU population eligible for assistance under Objective 1 of the EU's Structural Funds. Given the resistance of current members to expanding the budget to accommodate increased spending on enlargement, it is apparent that both the CAP and the Structural Funds must be reformed. In that respect, this particular enlargement may appear to act as a catalyst to fundamental and deep reforms in the EU.

By contrast, previous enlargements had less of a budgetary and policy impact because they were smaller, involved more economically developed countries, or took place in the context of economic growth and in the absence of budgetary constraints imposed by Economic and Monetary Union.

Also different from previous enlargements is the more extensive *acquis communautaire*, which new members are required to implement. The new members will thus be joining an EU, which is much more integrated and complex than the one joined by previous applicants, making their task of adjustment more complex and the accession process more difficult. Moreover, in adopting the accumulated legal *acquis* the candidates must overcome the handicap of their 40-year heritage and limited experience of the market economy and of Western legal norms. On the other hand, EU membership is a value in itself as a huge confi-

---

[3]   A. Zielińska-Głębocka, A. Stępniak (eds.), *EU Adjustment to Eastern Enlargement. Polish and European Perspective*, Gdańsk, 2001.

dence-building measure which decreases uncertainty in wide areas of public life since membership rules – the *acquis communautaire* or the body of the EU law – are clear, well-established, have legitimacy, and are institutionally enforced.

Last but not least, another factor which differentiates the ongoing enlargement from previous ones, making it, to some extent, more problematic, is its geopolitical or security dimension. While previous enlargements occurred within the stable geopolitical context of a bipolar Europe, and within the Western half of Europe, Eastern enlargement is taking place in a less stable post-Cold War environment, and constitutes, in itself, a part of the effort to redesign Europe's political and security architecture. EU enlargement is thus necessarily linked to broader security and geopolitical issues, including NATO expansion and Western relations with Russia. It is not surprising, therefore, that security and geopolitical considerations have affected decision-making on the Eastern enlargement.

All previous enlargements have affected the basic character and identity of the EU. The Eastern enlargement will likely have an even more profound impact on the EU than any previous accessions. With the addition of the Central and Eastern European countries, the EU will become relatively poorer and more agricultural. In addition, the EU's political centre of gravity will shift eastwards, with profound implications for the Union's internal political balance. Eastern enlargement will also bring into the EU new external problems and concerns, affecting, for instance, relations with Russia. Most importantly, because of the number of new members and their specific economic and political conditions, the EU will become much larger and more heterogeneous in terms of its cultural values and political and economic interests.

III. Perception of Advantages and Disadvantages of the Enlargement

The perception of advantages and disadvantages (costs) of the European Union eastward enlargement, both in the countries concerned and in their institutions, and in the world at large, brings to bear a considerable influence on the process of accession of Central and Eastern European countries to the EU. It should also be borne in mind that the achievement of the goal of enlargement is subject to the interplay of broader world political and economic interests and forces in the international arena. The perception of costs and benefits applies simultaneously, not only to economic, political and social aspects of the inter-state or inter-governmental level, but also within individual countries and nations.

This issue, excepting the examination of interests of parties directly involved, has been otherwise subject to scant discussion and has not been adequately covered by analysis or in publications. Discussion of this issue, where it happened at all, was limited to perfunctory exchanges on the margins of a more specific discussion of the interests directly involved. It is, therefore, appropriate to attempt to review these outward perceptions as a useful input into the discussion of potential effects of the current enlargement and an examination of the broader interplay of global interests and forces that may affect the enlargement process.

The approach of the European Union countries to eastward enlargement is somewhat ambivalent. Notwithstanding the political and economic advantages resulting from the CEECs accession, as the enlargement becomes a reality, it is obvious that it will be not an easy task to absorb and digest this extension. The Amsterdam summit saw the current members in a crabby mood, unwilling to make the changes necessary to cope with a Union of 25 members. During the work of the Convention and the ongoing constitutional debate, the lack of uniformity in decision-making was also apparent.

The original rationale behind enlargement was political in nature. This should not be surprising, as politics constituted the very foundation of the creation of the European Economic Community at its outset. First of all, there was a need to accommodate Germany in a new Europe that would provide a basis for a conflict-free area. Secondly, the EEC was meant to serve as a consolidating force that might prevent the threat of Soviet expansion to the West. Thirdly, and at a later stage, the Community was viewed as an instrument establishing a third force between the two superpowers, or – especially in the French view – it was seen as means of countervailing growing US domination in world affairs. The two contemporary components of EU reform – the establishment of the economic and monetary union and the development of the two missing pillars of the European Union – are also inextricably rooted in politics. If the Community was born, as a political animal, it would be unreasonable to expect it to withdraw itself from political considerations in the process of its own enlargement.

There exist several motives that support the perception of political advantages deriving from the EU eastward enlargement, though their importance has changed with time. Just after the collapse of the Berlin Wall, it was conceivable for the EU countries to bear a bigger cost burden than would now be considered reasonable in order to secure the final collapse of the Soviet system. The most important considerations were the extension of the rule of democracy and of the market-economy system along with the concomitant spread of the zone of peace over the whole of Europe and in the world at large. At the same time, the EU became a dominant actor on the continent and an anchor of stability in this area.

Enlargement was considered also as a tool of stabilisation of the eastern flank of the Union, of particular importance in view of the unpredictability of future developments in the former Soviet Union.[4] Thus, the signing of the Europe Agreements was seen as a means by which Europe's borders might be determined by a combination of strategic, economic, and political considerations rather than by criteria of European identity. Political aspects of enlargement stem also from a moral unease in the West that followed the establishment of the post-war Yalta geopolitical system. Thus, enlargement was viewed, to some extent, as compensation for the betrayal of the East at Yalta.

In the light of these political considerations, EU membership for the CEECs would symbolise the definite end to the division of Europe and the final re-inclusion of the Eastern European states into the European 'family'. This was, likewise, assumed to be a constituent part of the process of the elimination of bi-polarity that had characterised international economic relations in the past. At the same time, however, obliteration of bi-polarity brought to the fore discords among Western partners that in the past had been camouflaged by the need to present a common strategy against the Soviet threat.

There are also some disadvantages perceived in the EU. The perception of potential upheavals in the socio-economic situation in the applicant countries may cause the EU governments to be more apprehensive about future enlargements. Enlargement is also seen as an instrument that would assist in making transformation irreversible. Commitment to the EU disciplines will signify a 'point of no return' in the process of transition to a market-based economy.

On the other hand, eastward expansion of the European Union is considered to be helpful for the enhancement of the Union's role in global politics and economics. The latter is also very important, as political gains without economic benefits would render – in the eyes of EU countries – eastward enlargement devoid of any real advantages. While political arguments might be the initial stimulus for integration, mutual economic benefits of integration must exist if long-term political support for integration is to be achieved.

However, the economic outcome of the eastward enlargement is, at present, examined above all from the point of view of the cost of any such enlargement. Some obvious direct and indirect benefits of

---

[4]   See H. Kissinger, *Diplomacy*, New York, 1994.

enlargement are admitted, such as increased export and investment opportunities, improvements in competitive position due to the supply of cheaper production inputs and economies of scale. Nevertheless, certain economists question the overall positive balance for the EU incumbents from gaining access to a larger market, if the potential dangers to output and jobs which a reciprocal opening of the EU markets to CEECs exports would entail, are taken into account.[5] Some point to the still negligible share in EU countries' exports to the East. However, CEECs play a much greater role in the growth of these exports and they may constitute a disproportionate boom for the EU's economies, especially in periods of economic slump, as was the case in 1995-96. Another important and positive economic consequence of eastward enlargement is that the ensuing increase in economic potential is very important of itself and conditions the EU's relations with other major economic powers, like the US and Japan, and in international trade and financial institutions.

In appraising the performance of the EU on global trade and security issues one can come only to one conclusion: when the EU speaks with one voice, it ceases to be just a market and becomes an actor of world influence.

At the micro level, some industrial sectors and individual plants perceive enlargement, and more precisely, more liberal access for CEEC producers to the EU markets, as a threat to their position or even existence. However, the experience in the period of trade liberalisation under the Europe Agreements does not support such apprehensions; growth and trade did not vindicate initial pessimism in this respect as the Agreements were implemented without major structural disturbances.

It is frequently stressed that some potential positive, economic and social aspects of enlargement are underestimated. On the one hand, the relatively high growth rates in applicant countries may beneficially affect economic dynamics in the European Union. On the other, cultural vitality and the energy of young, dynamic nations of Central and Eastern Europe are thought to be in a position to assist in invigorating the EU member states' mature and, therefore, more inert, societies.

The approach of EU countries to enlargement is by no means uniform. Deep divergences of interest split Union member states in their vision of both advantages and disadvantages of CEECs accession and of the scope, geographical pattern and timing of this process. One of the most discussed issues is the question of internal reforms and their inter-

---

[5] Bauer P., "East-West Economic Cooperation. Interests Involved. Institutional Possibilities and Economic Rationale," *Intereconomics*, Vol. 30, No. 6, Nov.-Dec. 1995.

relationship with the enlargement. Some people express the view that the enlargement might induce the timely adoption of the already-overdue but indispensable reforms of the institutions, of the agricultural policy and of the structural funds, which would lead to an improvement in the EU's competitiveness. It is felt that the enlargement may push to the fore with even greater force the issue of a Europe of "variable geometry" which might have an adverse impact, not only upon the acceding countries, but also on the existing member states.

Even greater conflicts are emerge in the area of competition for resources redistributed through the EU's budget. These conflicts have been given an added intensity by the decision to cap the budget at the level of 1.27% of the Union's GDP. Not only is there competition between the incumbent beneficiaries of these funds and the new Union members; there is also competition between the existing member states which stand to lose the right to tap these resources and other existing member states. Conflicts are also emerging between the net providers to the EU budget, who insist on reduction of their budgetary contributions, and the net beneficiaries. Parallel rivalries may emerge in competition for the EIB loans and foreign direct investment flows.

The interests of EU countries with respect to enlargement are also geographically diverse, prompting controversies among them. First of all, there is a concern about footing the political bill of differentiating newcomers into the first and the next waves of accession. Next, there exist differences in support for individual groups of countries, or individual countries, as they strive for Union membership.

Germany puts enlargement high on the agenda as a major instrument in the effort to stabilise democracy in neighbouring countries but also due to its trade interests as their biggest economic partner. It is also thought that the EU's eastward enlargement may add to Germany's weight in the Union, notably by tipping the balance in the German – French tandem in favour of Germany. France perceives any such enlargement as adverse to its interests for the same reason. France looks at the enlargement process also from the point of view of securing the interests of its Mediterranean allies which are closer to its concerns. Thus, it gives priority in the further enlargement to Romania, lying as it does, within its historical sphere of influence. Italy and Austria strongly supported Slovenia for the same motives.

Britain was pleased with the notion of general and broad enlargement as a way of reducing the chances of closer integration and of diluting the decision-making process in the Union. Scandinavian countries were primarily interested in accepting the Baltic States into the European Union. Former colonial powers like France and – to lesser extent – Italy and Belgium are concerned that the accession should not adversely affect the interests of their still-dependent territories or the well-being of their former colonies (mainly the ACP countries).

Greece, Italy, Portugal and Span fear that enlargement's long-term effect will be to tilt the centre of gravity of the Union away from the South.

The differentiation of interests does not only draw dividing lines between countries, but also transverse society and political life within individual EU states. It also affects the regional approach to enlargement, as certain southern regions of individual EU states are concerned at the prospect of being 'marginalised' by the process of Eastern enlargement.[6]

There exists, likewise, an old controversy between the deepening and the broadening of the European Union. As a result, in case of difficulties in driving through internal reforms, the EU may slow down the integrative effort, while concentrating on the technical implementation of the *acquis communautaire*. On the other hand, the smooth deepening of the EU could increase the functional domain of the EU's authority, while enlargement appears to be a strong incentive and catalyst for this process being achieved, without the loss of integration momentum.

In summary, it may be said that the positive approach to eastward enlargement is more pronounced in the political world. In the field of economics, costs are perceived to feature prominently. In other words, geopolitical considerations constitute the engine driving enlargement, but the economic and financial considerations constitute the brake. Some economists even think that many benefits of accession, in particular those connected with reorientation of trade flows, have already been captured. They posit that the expectations that have been created exceed the economic advantages that will accrue from accession.

IV. Potential Effects of the Enlargement

The accessible scientific writings on the potential impact of the EU's enlargement are rich in research reports that follow two main streams of thinking. The first looks for the justified – on the basis of numerous economic and econometric models – visible trade and growth effects of the economic integration within the enlarged area. The second, led both by EU members and candidates countries, refers to the notion of the cost-benefit analysis, with the aim of identifying potential losers and

---

[6] See Mantaneu J., "L'arc sud-européen pour ne pas être marginalisé," *Le Monde*, 2 August, 1999.

winners in the enlargement process. Both approaches present us with interesting conclusions.

A. The effects of enlargement on economic growth may derive from demand and supply effects, as it will imply the incorporation of economies with different levels of development and different economic structures.

Overall, total GDP of all new members is small in comparison to the EU (about 5% of EU-15 GDP, or 19% in Purchasing Power Parities).[7] This is comparable to the effects of the accession of Greece, Portugal and Spain during the 1980s. As most of the new members are small states (except for Poland), the increase in the population is rather modest. The EU, before enlargement, has a population of 383 million. The enlargement will add 76 million to this figure, an increase of 19.8%, thereby placing the EU in third position in the world ranking by population (after China and India). Its share of world population moves from 6% (before enlargement) to 7.2% after.[8] Although the enlarged EU will potentially represent a huge market of 459 million consumers, one should not forget that economic advantages of the larger population may only come on-stream over a long period of time as the populations of the CEECs are relatively poor. The enlargement contributes relatively little to the total GDP of the EU, which will increase from €9,580 billion to about €9,950 billion, an increase of less than 4%.

According to a recent Commission study,[9] enlargement could increase the GDP of new members by between 1.3-2% a year for the next ten years. The candidate countries in their numerous national research studies present figures even more optimistic than these. The extra stimulation of the catching-up process that candidates are expected to experience due to their accession will progressively increase their share in the EU GDP. However, one should not forget that this process may take a generation or even more to achieve. Given the small size of the acceding economies, the growth effects for the current member states is expected to be of marginal impact, with Germany and Austria the greatest beneficiaries.

---

[7]   A. R. Lejour, R. A. Mooij and R. Nahuis, *EU Enlargement: Economic Implications for Countries and Industries*, CESifo Working Paper Series, No. 585, CPB Netherlands Bureau for Economic Policy Analysis, September 2003.

[8]   J.-J. Boillot, *L'Union européenne élargie, un défi économique pour tous*, La Documentation Française, 2003.

[9]   European Commission, *The Economic Impact of Enlargement*, June 2001, available on the Commission website: http://europa.eu.int/comm/economy_finance/publications/enlargement_papers/enlargementpapers04_en.htm.

The overall positive influence on EU growth is estimated as to be modest in the short/medium term at cumulatively 0.7% EU GDP. It is worth mentioning that no negative effects are foreseen for any of the current member states. As a consequence, the net demand growth effect of enlargement on total EU trade with the rest of the world in the short-run is expected to be minimal. In the medium-to-long term, growth and trade effects could be more significant, not only due to higher growth and demand in the new member states but also due to stronger supply side effects, along with the restructuring of industries in both new and current member states.

B. Enlargement effects on trade are well-advanced and will continue progressively both inside and outside the EU.

The enlargement will not bring radical changes in the world trade figures, as the share of the new members in the world trade remains rather modest (see Table 3). Although the EU's position as the world's biggest exporter seems to be reinforced with the enlargement, those changes are not expected to be more than marginal, as the volume of trade of the new members is comparatively small and a large part of it is already in place between them and the present EU, thus translating into intra-EU trade after accession. There will be a certain move for formal statistical reasons, which will show a decrease in external EU trade (after the absorption of the external countries of the EU to the intra-EU classification).

Since the 1990s, the candidate countries' foreign trade with developing countries has changed in the course of the transition. This entailed a massive reorientation of Eastern European foreign trade away from the Eastern bloc to the West, and particularly to the EU. It is worth mentioning that the prospect of EU membership has already influenced the trade and development policy of the candidate countries and will continue to have a major impact on these policy fields once membership becomes a reality. At the same time, it can be assumed that the new members will in future participate in the shaping of the relevant EU policies.

Nonetheless there has been nothing short of a massive reorientation of the CEECs' trade with the EU in the last decade. Member states gained a 60-70% trade share for most candidate countries. This has not been a simple redirection of trade. It has been estimated[10] that at most 20% of exports were 'diverted' former COMECON traded merchandises. Export growth has come, either in products that were not exported

---

[10]   Natolin European Centre in Warsaw in its research project: *Costs and Benefits of Poland's Membership in the European Union (text in Polish available at www. natolinsbm.com.pl).*

at all to former COMECOM markets, or in the upgrading of existing items. The modernisation needs of the CEECs' economies create a lasting incentive to the increased and continued demand for industrial and high-tech products. Moreover, the open market incentives – that came after decades of 'economy of shortage' – stimulated a dramatic increase in consumer demand for imported goods. As a consequence, the imports figures grew up dramatically over the last decade and the surplus of imports will probably continue to be a characteristic of the new members' economies.

The share of the present EU in the candidate countries' exports ranges from 48.7% in the case of Malta to 76.2% in the case of Hungary. The EU's share regarding imports from the applicant countries lies between 49.7% for Lithuania and 68.6% for Slovenia. A rough estimate based on the data of 2002 shows an increase of the EU's share in world exports from 18.4% to 19.3% and a rise of its weight as an importer from 18.2% to 20.2%.[11]

At the same time the nature of mutual trade has clearly been changing from inter-industry towards intra-industry and intra-firm trade in the last decade. This process is expected to speed up through the increased certainty and competitive pressure of the full membership.

As concerns general trade liberalisation issues, the enlargement will decrease the overall level of tariff protection of the EU. The current average tariff in the EU, all products taken together and trade-weighted, is about 4% while the average tariff in the acceding countries is about 9%.[12] For example, the current duty in the Czech Republic for cars and trucks is 7.1%, which will decrease to 4.6% on May 1st 2004.

Japan's main trading partner (see Table 6) in the acceding countries is Hungary, which accounts for 50% of Japan's total trade with the ten countries. Hungary's average tariff (on all products) is 11.7% (see Table 4), almost twice as high as the EU's tariffs (6.3%). After the accession, Hungary's tariff protection will be cut in half. This applies to an even greater extent in the case of Poland, Japan's second largest trading partner among the future members (representing 20% of Japan's total trade with the 10 countries). Its external tariff protection will be reduced by 60% upon accession. This is the equivalent of passing from the current 15.1% to the EU's level of 6.3% on all products. Tariff protection will rise in the cases of Estonia and Latvia, which account for 0.01 and 0.03% of Japan's total external trade. As a result, the negative

---

[11]   2002 *Regular Report*, at http://europa.eu.int/comm/enlargement/report2002/index. htm.

[12]   See http://www.europa.eu.int/comm/enlargement/negotiations/chapters/chap1/index. htm.

impact on Japan should be extremely limited. Losses of €22 million have been forecast.[13] However, it is important to remember that after the enlargement, the total trade with Estonia and Latvia will amount to about €115 billion.

Since liberalisation has already occurred to a large extent and the level and structure of trade between the EU and the candidate countries is already close to the state one would expect according to gravitation models, further major diversions of trade are unlikely. Thanks to membership of the WTO, no further significant changes are to be anticipated in EU trade policy. However, accession will end certain special rights for countries in transition. In future rounds of negotiations, some of the new EU members (e.g. Estonia) may advocate a less protectionist policy, whilst others might tend to call for greater protection – depending on the pressure to adapt and on the underlying position on economic policy. The candidates could, with some plausibility, insist that trade facilitation should be granted only to genuinely poor partners in the Third World (i.e. countries that are poorer than the candidates).

The enlargement may provide an incentive for other countries to create alliances and/or expand trade and seek market access, with each other and/or with the EU. Theoretically and *a priori*, it is not clear which effect will dominate and therefore it is possible that other trade partners will suffer from trade and investment diversion toward an enlarged EU. In a limited number of cases tariffs will increase. In such cases, World Trade Organisation rules apply, whereby if a WTO member finds its interests have been damaged by enlargement, it can present claims to the WTO for adequate compensation. It is worth noting that the historical evidence solidly and clearly points to trade investment creation rather than diversion, with growth effects outweighing static trade diversion effects.

C. Accession brings concurrent pressures for economic and policy reform for both existing and new member states, which will have repercussions for the enlarged Union's external relations.

The extension of the Single Market will foster greater competition, increased investment (see Table 5) and economies of scale for the existing and new members. The accession of new members, while increasing divergence in the EU, can be a source of supply restructuring for competitive advantage. In a situation of direct competition among similar products on EU markets, the new members might have the 'home' advantage, with geographical proximity and as part of the EU. At the same time, overall competitiveness of EU industries could in-

---

[13] *Proces i skutki dostosowań do zagranicznej polityki ekonomicznej Unii Europejskie (2002)*, Warsaw, IKC.

crease as result of industrial restructuring. This restructuring process is well-advanced yet not only in the acceding countries but also to some extent in the existing members' industries. Numerous EU industries had already advanced restructuring in advance of the formal extension. Industries such as cars, machinery, textiles, consumer electronics, food processing etc. have been working to create international production networks through trade and investment in mostly low and medium value added products in candidate countries. This will subsequently impact on trade and investment flows with the US, Japan and other OECD trade partners.

There is a question concerning how rapidly new members should or would be able to accede to full monetary union. On the whole, the authorities in the acceding countries favour rapid entry, in the belief that the gains in macroeconomic credibility and associated reductions in transaction costs more than offset the loss of flexibility implicit in fixing the exchange rate. Opponents, however, fear that too rapid a move to monetary union will be a step too far for countries that have already having to deal with the twin challenges of continuing the transition to the market economy and entering the single market. The relatively favourable impact to date of the EMU on the cohesion countries and the contrast with the sluggish performance of Germany, France and the other 'core' countries, suggest that the impact of monetary union may have been more positive that some expected for the supposedly more vulnerable economies, and this would augur well for the new members.

Successive enlargements have seen far-reaching changes in some of the principal economic and social policy dossiers of the EU and in the institutional machinery for policy delivery. These changes have re-flected a combination of changing demands on policy, an element of 'learning-by-doing' and – in some cases – greater resort to partnership between tiers of government in policy delivery, and expectations of accountability in the evaluation of policy. As the new members are progressively integrated into the EU, economic, financial and social policies will face a variety of challenges that will add to the complexity of policy formulation and implementation. Difficult choices will have to be made in key areas of EU competence, such as the speed and extent of enlargement of the Euro area, the modalities of policy coordination, the aims and character of cohesion policy, and regulatory developments (including the environmental protection). In parallel, the Lisbon Agenda will continue to be a stimulus to a transformation of economic perform-ance and the recasting of the European social model. The future financ-ing of the EU, with a new Financial Perspective, needs to be agreed in 2005 for the period from 2007 onwards and will also be an important policy development.

Negotiations of previous 'financial perspectives' have always been fraught. Although the inter-institutional agreement took much of the heat out of the disputes between the European Parliament and other institutions, disputes between member states about the financing, structure of spending and net contributions to the EU budget have continued to affect successive agreements. Widening is expected to polarise these disputes still further because more member states will become net contributors, yet the number of smaller countries will also increase. In parallel, increasingly tough questions are being posed about the content of the EU budget and its biggest expenditures (Common Agricultural Policy).

All these internal debates are of great importance for the future position of the EU in the world economy and its relationships with other actors at the international arena. In the light of concurrent trends in the macroeconomic performance of the EU the competitive position of the European economy will depend largely on achieving the aims set by the Lisbon process and on the dynamics of the 'absorption' of the enlargement. 'Lisbon' encompasses not just the priority of raising growth and the quest to shift the economy in the direction of knowledge-intensive industries, but also recasting the welfare state. Sustainable development has also become an aim. Although the broad aims of Lisbon attract widespread support, problems are visible in the specific objectives – especially in clarifying the circumstances in which there is a European added value in the design and implementation of policy. More tellingly, the lack of instruments and of effective means of assuring compliance with the strategy by member states cast doubt on its usefulness.

The need for economic policy coordination, has grown as economies have become more integrated. Coordination can be seen as a device for achieving common policy, without transferring competence to the EU. However, the complexity of policy coordination – both horizontally, in a particular policy domain, and vertically, between policy domains – has grown and will become greater still in a wider Union.

V. Conclusions

Enlargement will increase the weight, power and prestige of the EU in international affairs. The EU of 15 is already economically large with a 32% share in the world GDP, and represents the largest trading group with about 25% share in world trade (excluding intra-EU trade). In the short run, however, the main effects of enlargement will be on population and the number of member states it represents, rather than its economic weight. Therefore, the short run effect will mostly be felt through the outcomes of obtained terms of trade and market access. In the longer run, the EU's economic clout will grow through higher growth, demand and supply effects. These effects depend very much on the EU's ability to reform. A plethora of good ideas are on a table and most of them have already been applied to a certain degree. It is not that we do not have enough innovators in Europe – on the contrary, it is quite difficult enough to keep track with the tons of ink spent on reform suggestions. There is a dearth of related decision-making. In this respect the enlargement can contribute positively to the whole European construction while bringing immediate and strong pressure to bear to take important decisions.

Even with the positive economic supply and demand effects for the existing and new members, it is fair to say that the main advantages of the current enlargement will not be so much economic, but more in creating an expanding zone of stability and security in Europe. EU membership is a huge confidence-building measure. It confers credibility on the member country through the acceptance of clear and enforceable mutual restraint. It is therefore a public good for economic actors and investors. Membership decreases uncertainty in wide areas of public life since membership rules are clear, well-established, legitimate, and are institutionally enforced. With the enlargement a significant number of democratised countries will join the European area of peace, the Single Market and the competitive economic structure. This qualitative change on the world map constitutes the most important characteristic of the Eastern enlargement of the European Union and brings an important added element to all actors on the international stage. Given European history, it is hard to overestimate the benefits of such a project, both, within Europe, for surrounding areas, and by implication, for the rest of the world.

Enlargement will strengthen the weight and negotiating power of the Union in international organisations, provided that Union is able to speak and act in a coherent manner. This will tend to attract, even more than in the past, a careful scrutiny of EU actions by its trade partners. The Union will need to reflect on the implications of enlargement on its positions in the WTO and on its role and representation in organisations such as the United Nations and International Financial Institutions.

Table 1. CEECs' Membership
in International Organisations

Country	World Trade Organisation	International Monetary Fund	*World Bank*	Organisation of Economic Cooperation and Development
Czech Republic	1995	1993	1993	1995
Estonia	1999	1992	1992	
Hungary	1995	1982	1992	1996
Latvia	1999	1992	1992	
Lithuania	2000	1992	1992	
Poland	1995	1986	1989	1996
Slovakia	1995	1993	1993	2000
Slovenia	1995	1993	1993	

Source: Ministry of Foreign Affairs, Poland

Table 2. Central and Eastern European Countries:
Basic Indicators

Country	INDICATORS					
	Population (thousand)	GDP (€ bn)	GDP *per capita* (€)	GDP growth (2002)	Exports in % of GDP	Inflation rate
Cyprus	762	10.2	15,100	4.1	47	2.8
Czech Republic	10,283	63.3	6,200	3.3	71	1.4
Estonia	1,364	6.2	4,500	5.0	91	3.6
Hungary	10,188	58.0	5,700	3.7	61	5.2
Latvia	2,355	8.5	3,600	7.7	45	2.0
Lithuania	3,478	13.4	3,800	6.0	50	0.4
Malta	393	4.0	10,300	-0.8	88	2.2
Poland	38,638	196.7	5,100	1.1	28	1.9
Slovak Republic	5,397	22.8	4,200	3.3	73	3.3
Slovenia	1,992	20.9	10,500	3.0	60	7.5

Source: On the basis of: Audio-visual Library, DG Enlargement, European Commission

Table 3. Exports and Imports Share of World Trade (%)

Country	Exports share	Imports share
EU	18.4	18.2
Cyprus		
Czech Republic	0.7	0.7
Estonia	0.1	0.1
Hungary	0.6	0.7
Latvia		
Lithuania		
Malta		
Poland	0.8	1.0
Slovakia	0.3	0.3
Slovenia	0.2	0.2
Japan		

Source: http://www.wto.org/english/res_e/statis_e/its2002_leading

Table 4. Tariffs (%) of the Candidate Countries Compared with the EU's External Tariff

Country	Average	Farm products	Fish products	Industrial products
EU	6.3	16.2	12.4	3.6
Czech Republic	6.1	13.4	0.1	4.5
Estonia	3.2	14.9	3.0	0.0
Hungary	11.7	30.9	14.8	7.0
Latvia	4.2	13	7.9	1.7
Lithuania	5.3	15	3.8	2.4
Poland	15.1	33.8	18.5	9.9
Slovakia	6.1	13.2	0.1	4.4
Slovenia	8.9	8.9	6.7	8.0

Source: European Commission, Progress Report 2002

Table 5. FDI Flows between the Candidate Countries and the EU (€ m)

Country	Outflows to 1996	2000	Inflows from 1996	2000
Total Extra-EU	46,992	326,983	32,422	150,903
Czech Republic	1,308	2,018	-21	53
Estonia	62	183	-1	6
Hungary	1,162	-1,104	41	149
Latvia	21	153	5	10
Lithuania	57	456	2	6
Poland	2,428	9,206	-15	-7
Slovakia	212	1,312	4	10
Slovenia	64	39	-8	102

Source: European Commission: European Union Foreign Direct Investment Yearbook 2001, Luxembourg 2002

Table 6. New Member Countries' Bilateral Relations with Japan

Country	Export to Japan (volume)	Export (products)	Import from Japan (volume)	Import (products)	Japanese inward investment
Cyprus	461 m ¥	Clothing, frozen fish, fruits	42,945 m ¥	Automobiles, vessels, trucks, air conditioners	11.2 bn ¥
Czech Republic	100 m $	Hops and malt, glass and glassware, ferro-alloys and alumnae ingots, chemical products, microbreweries and machinery equipment	350 m $	Mainly passenger cars and other automobiles, consumer electronics, advanced technologies	10.5 bn ¥
Estonia	12.7m €	Wood and articles of wood and furniture (48.5% of the total exports to Japan), machinery, foot wear, food products and animal products	194,8 m €	Electronic equipment, machinery, vehicles and transport equipment, optical an photographic equipment	2.9 m $
Hungary	299 m $	Chemical products, equipment and machinery	649 m $	Machinery, processed chemical products and food	62.8 bn ¥
Latvia	1,820 m $	Processed goods, fibres, metals, chemical products	3,120 m $	Machine tools, electronic machinery, minerals, chemicals, metal and fibres	Not available
Lithuania	12.5 m $	Milk powder, timber products, furniture, optical, measuring, medical and surgical equipment, glassware and chemical products	102.3 m $	Means of transport and equipment, machinery and mechanical appliances, plastics and optical, measuring, medical and surgical equipment	164,8 m $
Malta	1,074 m ¥	Oil, switch plug and fish	13,461 m ¥	Integrated circuits, automobiles and trucks	1,453 m $
Poland	74 m $	Chemical products, animal products and materials	150 m $	Electrical and electronic products, machinery, automobiles	564 m $
Slovak Republic	2 bn $	Machinery and electric appliances	2.6 bn $	Chemical products and glasswork	1,075 m ¥
Slovenia	2.7 bn ¥	Food and textile	10.7 bn ¥	Machinery, cars and chemicals	228 m ¥

Source: Table prepared on the basis of the data provided by Embassies of Candidate Countries in Warsaw

CHAPTER 12

Regulating "Atypical Work" in the EU and in Japan

Naoko Hɪʀoʙᴇ

*PhD Candidate, Institute of European Studies,
Université libre de Bruxelles, Belgium*

I. Introduction

This chapter aims at analysing the regulation of "atypical work" i.e. short-term and fixed-term contract work in the European Union (EU) and comparing it to the corresponding Japanese regulatory situation.

In any comparative analysis of social issues, it is true that the nation-state is the most appropriate unit of analysis. However, concerning the regulation of the labour market, the EU has become the principal polity for the member states (Walby, 2003). Therefore, it is worth comparing the EU and Japan concerning the regulation of atypical work.

Considering policy development in the EU, I will focus on part-time work and fixed-term work.

The EU regulation of atypical work was adopted in the form of directives in the 1990s by the Social Dialogue decision-making procedure. By the introduction of the European Monetary Union, member states were no longer able to resolve the problem of the labour market by the budgetary means at the national level. This is why the member states have become aware of the necessity to work together on social issues at the European level. On the other hand, it had been difficult to introduce a common European social policy, due to the nationally diverse nature of the matter, not to mention the historical and cultural background peculiar to each of the member states. Another reason for the difficulties in adopting an EU common social policy could be found in the way decisions were made by the Community. In most areas of social policy the Council is required to adopt decisions unanimously. This led to many European initiatives being blocked and the regulation of atypical work was no exception in this regard.

Through the Social Protocol of the Maastricht Treaty, a new decision-making procedure, namely the Social Dialogue method, was introduced, and was subsequently incorporated into the Amsterdam Treaty. It is a procedure based on negotiation and agreement between European Management and Labour organisations. In 1996, the first directive was adopted by the Social Dialogue method. Following that, the directive on part-time work and the directive on fixed-term work were adopted in 1997 and in 1999. These two directives have the purpose of protecting workers employed under atypical employment contracts.

Another approach to protecting atypical workers is that of indirect regulation by the EU gender policy. The EU gender policy was developed under the Community method by means of directives. At the first glance, these directives have no direct bearing on the regulation of atypical work. However, if we look at the surveillance phase of the EU method, there is evidence of the development of politics on atypical work. Based on the fact that more women are engaged in atypical work, the Court of Justice gave its opinion that discrimination against part-time workers can be considered as the indirect discrimination against women, which is in violation of the EC Treaty and ensuing directives. The main aims of these EC regulations are the prohibition of discrimination against part-time and fixed-term workers and their protection.

In Japan, the protection of part-time and fixed-term contract workers against the discriminatory treatment is also the objective of regulations; it was in 1993 that the Part-Time Work Law was introduced, thereby prohibiting certain discriminatory policies against part-time workers. Also important in this regard is the Labour Standard Law of 1954, amended in 1997, which concerns the protection of the fixed-term contract workers.

However, the way in which the workers are protected by Japanese regulations is different from that of Europeans. One of the reasons for the difference could be the political motivation which led to the introduction in each polity. Therefore, the background to the introduction of regulations must also be analysed globally.

In the following chapter, firstly the background of the EU regulatory regime concerning atypical work will be examined. It will be followed by a description of provisions concerning atypical work and the EU gender policy. In the third section, I will explain the situation in Japan. Some comparative remarks will be given in the last section.

II. EU Regulations Concerning Atypical Work

A. *The Background of EU Employment Policy*

The Origin of the Social Field

In 1957, the Treaty of Rome established the European Economic Community. The Treaty states as its purpose not only the establishment of the common market, but also the improvement of the standard of living. However, of the 248 articles of included in the text of the Treaty, most are devoted to the aim of a common market, while the number of articles devoted to social policy is very limited.

The improvement of the standard of living is seen as an achievement resulting from the integration of the common market. This was based on the idea that social policy, which has a redistributive function, should be under the competence of the member states (Collins, 1975). During the drafting of the Treaty, although the member states agreed with a certain coordination of politics to improve the standard of living, they disagreed with the coordination of social costs. France was the only country which insisted on the necessity of political coordination in terms of the social cost in order to guarantee fair competition in the common market.

Finally, the chapter on social provisions in the Treaty consisted from following five articles. Among these, the Article 118 stipulated the collaboration between member states in matters related to employment, labour legislation and working conditions. No article on social costs was inserted in the Treaty, the Article 119 stipulated that men and women should receive equal pay for work of equal value. Also, the Article 101, which stipulated the approximation of laws in case of distortion of the fair competitiveness in the common market, could be applied to the matter of social costs.

Nevertheless, despite the existence in the Treaty of the article on social policy, there has been a very little development in the social field, compared with the equivalent in the field of economics. Equally, atypical work was not the subject of the European discussion until the beginning of the 1990s.

New Debate Concerning Employment

In the early 1990s, Europe faced a difficult social problem; the unemployment rate reached as high as 10 percent. This was a source of high social costs. In 1993, the Commission published the White Paper on Growth, Competitiveness and Employment, which examined employment at the European level for the first time in the history of the EU. In the White paper, four things are identified as key aspects of the

problem: high unemployment and the low employment rate, the necessity of organising working hours and the difficulties faced by particular
groups. In order to change this situation, it proposed actions in six
fields: labour cost, flexibility of work, taxation and incentives, Small
and Medium Sized Companies (SMEs), raising the stock of human
capital and the targeting of specific groups.

Flexibility of work was encouraged with the aim of increasing employment rates and for that purpose the Commission recommended
reducing the number of hours worked per week and establishing a legal
framework for the protection of part-time workers.

Also, flexibility of work was encouraged with an eye to reducing labour costs, as this flexibility would stimulate job creation. Reductions in
the statutory charges on the flexible working arrangements were also
proposed.

Based on the White Paper, the Essen European Council in 1994
agreed on five key objectives to be pursued by the member states. These
included the development of human resources through vocational
training, the promotion of productive investments through moderate
wage policies, the improvement of the efficiency of labour market
institutions, the identification of new sources of jobs through local
initiatives, and the promotion of access to the world of work for some
specific target groups such as young people, long-term unemployed
people and women.

In 1997 a new heading on employment was inserted in the Amsterdam Treaty. It stipulates that the commitment to achieve a high level of
employment is one of the key objectives of the EU, emphasising that
employment is an issue of "common concern" of all member states. This
led to the launch of the European Employment Strategy (EES). The EES
follows the decision-making procedure of the Open Method of Coordination (OMC),[1] and guidelines are drawn up at the European level.

---

[1] The Procedure is as follows: each year the European Council considers the employment situation and adopts conclusions on the basis of a joint annual report provided
by the Council and the Commission. On the basis of this conclusion, the Council
draws up guidelines, acting by a qualified majority on a proposal from the Commission. Along with the guidelines, member states draw up a national action plan which
sets out the measures to be taken in the following year. They should provide the
Council and the Commission with an annual report on the principal measures taken
to implement its employment policy in the light of the guidelines. Based on these
reports, the Council carries out an examination of the implementation of the employment policies of the member states in the light of the guidelines for employment.
Recommendation can be made to the member states if necessary. Based on the result
of this study, the Council and the Commission make a joint annual report to the
European Council on the employment situation and on the implementation of guidelines for employment.

There are four main pillars to the EES: employability, entrepreneurship, adaptability and equality. Atypical work comes under the pillar of the adaptability, which means increasing the adaptability of companies and workers by introducing new work organisation, including atypical work.

The adaptability pillar calls for the modernisation of work organisation and for the related adaptation of the regulatory framework, while maintaining, or creating, a reasonable balance between flexibility and security.

In short, the origin of the EU policy on atypical work related strongly to the problem of unemployment; atypical work is considered as a means to reduce unemployment.

Gender Policy and Atypical Work

As it is predominantly women who find themselves doing part-time and fixed-term work, even if gender policy itself does not directly concern atypical work, there is a strong relationship between the gender policy and atypical work.

The origin of the gender policy[2] was the adoption of Article 119, which stipulates equal payment between men and women. At the time of the negotiation of the Rome treaty, France was the only country which had introduced the principle of the equal payment between men and women. Fearing the effects of economic integration France insisted on the necessity of stating the equal pay principle in the Rome Treaty (Pillinger, 1992). In the beginning it was decided to insert that clause under the title of the competition policy. However, under the pressures from the labour unions which wished to have a solid chapter on social provisions, the social affairs, it was finally placed under the title of the Social Policy (Hoskyns, 1996).

At this stage, Article 119 did not concern equality between men and women in general, as it was for the purpose of ensuring the fair competition in the common market.

The first step of the gender policy was the social action programme of 1974. It followed the declaration of the Paris European Summit which required the promotion of the social policy at the EC level. In the social action programme, gender policy is categorised as a measure for the promotion of employment and the improvement of the working conditions. As opposed to Article 119, which concerns only equality of

---

[2]   The word "gender policy" was not used until the 1990s. Previously, terms such as "policy on equality between men and women" or "equal policy" were used. However, in the interests of textual coherence, I call policy concerning equality between men and women "gender policy".

payment, the social action programme of 1974 sought to achieve equality in the employment relations in general.

Based on this action programme, the directive on the implementation of the principle of equal treatment for men and women as regards access to employment, vocational training and promotion, and working conditions (76/207/EEC) was adopted in 1976, together with the directive on equal payment[3] in 1975. At this time, because of the economic crisis, no other measures in the social field were adopted. Despite such a climate, three directives for the gender policy could be adopted for three reasons (Hoskyns, 1996; Pillinger, 1992); firstly, women became more present in the labour market than before, and the member states shared the opinion that they should take certain measures to resolve the unjust inequality of the women's situation. Secondly, after the feminism movement in 1960s, dealing with a matter of concern to women seemed to have political merit for governments. Thirdly, in order to take part in the International Women's Year Conference in Mexico in 1975, it was considered preferable to take certain measures of gender policy at the EC level.

In 1982, the first action programme on gender policy was adopted at the Council,[4] followed by the second action programme in 1985. Despite the ambitious proposal by the Commission, the resolution by the Council was watered down, and only two directives were adopted during the 1980s. One is the directive on the principle of equal treatment for men and women in occupational social security schemes (86/378/ EEC).[5] Another directive was on the application of the principle of equal treatment between men and women engaged in an activity, including agriculture, in a self-employed capacity, and on the protection of self-employed women during pregnancy and motherhood (86/613/EEC).

The most remarkable directive adopted in 1990s was the directive on the burden of proof in cases of discrimination based on sex (97/80/EC). In cases of indirect sexual discrimination of workers by enterprises, it is

---

[3]   Council Directive 75/117/EEC of 10 February 1975 on the approximation of the laws of the member states relating to the application of the principle of equal pay for men and women.

[4]   The Council adopted the action programme as a resolution, non-binding political declaration. Even though the provisions of the resolution are not binding, they play an important role in indicating the future development of the Community policy.

[5]   Because of the diversity of social security provision at the national level, national social security schemes were excluded from the scope of the Equal Payment Directive. The Directive dealt with the benefits paid from the professional social security schemes, which are the payments or the supplements to the national social security scheme.

the responsibility of enterprises to prove their innocence, not the responsibility of workers to prove the discrimination. This directive results from the series of judgements at the Court of Justice, which will be explained in more detail presently.

B. Regulating Atypical Work in the EU

Some Attempts and Failures in the Introduction of Directives

It was in 1981 that the Commission submitted the first proposal for a directive on voluntary part-time work which was rejected by the Council. The second attempt was in 1990, when the Commission submitted three proposals on atypical work: first two directives concerning the working conditions of part-time workers and fixed-term workers, and the third directive concerning the safety and health of temporary workers at work. The first two directives, which were based on the Treaty article on market competition, required a unanimous decision, whereas the third, based on the article, concerning safety and health at work required a decision by a qualified majority. As a result, the first two proposals were rejected or left on the table, while the third was adopted.

From this fact, one can say that the political advancement of the issue of atypical work was restricted by the mode of the EC decision-making procedure. The social field was under the competence of the member states, and if not, the competence of the Community was restricted by the unanimous decision in the Council, which was required for the adoption of the directive.

By the Treaties of Maastricht and Amsterdam, higher priority and stronger power were given to action at the European level in the social field. The social policy is no longer just a result of the integration of the European common market, but it has become the objective of the Community and the member states. The treaties state that the promotion of employment and the improvement of living and working condition are valid objectives of themselves.

At the level of the decision-making procedure, some changes have been made, and co-decision procedure was introduced in order to avoid the excessive use of the veto. However, the policy of atypical work, neither the social policy as global, did not advanced in the framework of the Community method.

Adoption of Directives by the Social Dialogue Method

In the end of the 1990s, two directives concerning atypical work were adopted by the decision-making procedure of the Social Dialogue, which was first introduced in the Social Protocol of the Maastricht Treaty, and subsequently included in the Amsterdam Treaty.

The Social Dialogue method is linked to the Community method; before submitting proposals in the social policy field, the Commission should consult social partners on the possible direction of Community action. Where a decision is made to take Community action, the contents of the envisaged proposal are also examined. Social partners forward an opinion or, where appropriate, a recommendation to the Commission. When consulted, social partners may inform the Commission of their wish to join the negotiations. When they conclude an agreement, it can be implemented either in accordance with the procedures and practices specific to the social partners and the member states or, in matters covered by Article 137 of the Treaty, at the joint request of the signatory parties, it can be implemented by a Council decision on a proposal from the Commission. The Council shall act by qualified majority, except where the agreement in question contains one or more provisions relating to one of the areas for which unanimity is required pursuant to Article 137(2). In such a case, it shall act unanimously.

Two directives concerning atypical work have been adopted using this decision-making procedure.

The first is the directive concerning the framework agreement on part-time work in 1997 (97/81/EC). Its purpose is a) to provide for the removal of discrimination against part-time workers and to improve the quality of part-time work; b) to facilitate workers' exercising their choice to switch to part-time work on a voluntary basis and thus, to contribute to the flexible organisation of working time in a manner which takes into account the needs of employers and workers.

Regarding the first purpose, the directive states that part-time workers shall not be treated in a less favourable manner than comparable full-time workers solely because of their working hours unless different treatment is justified on objective grounds. Regarding the second purpose, member states and social partners are invited to identify and review obstacles which limit the opportunities for part-time work. Concerning the protection of workers, a worker's refusal to transfer between full-time and part-time work should not itself constitute a valid reason for termination of employment, without prejudice to termination for other reasons such as arise from the operational requirements of the company.

The second directive was adopted in 1999, based on the framework agreement on the fixed-term work (1999/70/EC). It stated the recognition of social partners that the fixed-term work is the general form of employment relationship. It also clearly stated the need to develop more employment-friendly social security systems by "developing social protection systems capable of adapting to new patterns of work and providing appropriate protection to those engaged in such work," as declared at the Dublin European Council in 1996.

The purpose of the framework agreement on fixed-term work is to improve the quality of fixed-term work by ensuring the application of the principle of non-discrimination and to establish a framework to prevent abuse arising from the use of successive fixed-term employment contracts or relationships.

Regarding the first purpose, fixed-term workers should not be treated less favourably than the permanent workers. Concerning the second purpose, the member states and social partners at national level are required to introduce the measures concerning renewal of fixed-term contracts.

In spite of the failure to introduce directives by the Community method, the Social Dialogue yielded two directives. This is largely due to the strong legitimacy that the framework agreement by the social partners confers (Henni, 2001). It is difficult for member states to ignore decisions made by social negotiation. Therefore, the Council is less inclined to reject a proposal that has emerged from the Social Dialogue method than from the Community channel.

It should be noted that it is only the domain which falls under the competence of the EC can be implemented by directive. If it does not fall under the competence, it should be implemented by the social partners themselves. Yet, the effective implementation by social partners at national level is doubtful, because of the lack of coherence in the European organisations. On the labours organisation side, there are many pessimist views at the leadership and the coherence of the European Trade Unions Confederation (ETUC) (Marks and McAdam, 1996; Streek and Schmitter 1991; Streek, 1996). On the management organisation side, there is a lack of willingness to establish industrial relations at the European level (Streek, 1996).

European Employment Strategy (EES)

In 1994 at the Essen European Council were defined five domains of the measures which should be taken in the area of employment. Following this, at the Dublin European Council in 1996 the necessity of developing social protection systems capable of adapting to new patterns of work and providing appropriate protection to those engaged in such work was acknowledged. In the field of employment, OMC is applied to the European Employment Strategy (EES) adopted at the Luxembourg Extraordinary European Council in 1997.

EES guidelines define four pillars: employability, entrepreneurship, adaptability and equality. Atypical work is classed the pillar of adaptability, which means the adaptability of companies and workers by introducing new work organisation.

The adaptability pillar calls for the modernisation of work organisation and for the related adaptation of the regulatory framework, while maintaining, or creating, a reasonable balance between flexibility and security.

The social partners are invited to negotiate to modernise the organisation of work, including flexible working arrangements, with the aim of making enterprises productive and competitive and achieving the required balance between flexibility and security. Member states are asked to examine the possibility of incorporating in their laws more adaptable types of contract, taking into account the fact that forms of employment are increasingly diverse. Those working under contracts of this kind should, at the same time, enjoy adequate security and higher occupational status, compatible with the needs of business. They are also invited to examine the obstacles, in particular tax obstacles, to investment in human resources and possibly provide for tax or other incentives for the development of in-house training.

Resume of the Policy on Atypical Work

Policy in the field of atypical work has continued to develop during the 1990s. The roots of its development can be traced to the problem of unemployment and promoting atypical work was seen as a tool for its resolution. That is not to say that atypical work did not exist when the discussions at EU level started in the mid-1990s. In the 1980s most countries of the EC faced an employment crisis which led many of them to embark on policies of deregulation of the labour market, resulted in the increase of atypical employment; for example, in the period from 1985 to 1995, flexible employment in the EU increased by 15% (Social Affairs Series, 2000).

Rather, the development should be understood in the context of the European economic integration process;

> While the pace of European integration had accelerated in various fields, the Union did not have robust enough tools nor coherent strategies to deal with macroeconomic shocks, nor did it have very effective responses to prevent and tackle persistent unemployment levels, which would in turn develop into long term unemployment and other structural problems in the labour markets. The structural problems were not only the result of technological pessimism, jobless growth, fear of globalisation, or third world competition. There had also been "home-made" policy mistakes. The problems led to a

process of renewed interest in finding European solutions through greater coordination and convergence of policies.[6]

In short, the EU policy initiative concerning atypical work was a part of the drive for flexibility of work which aimed at resolving the employment problem. This reflects the political necessity to take a European initiative in the field of employment.

Another reason of the development of the policy on atypical work is the introduction of the Social Dialogue method. The framework agreement by social partners has a strong political legitimacy and the Council has a difficulty to reject the proposition of adopting a directive based on it. In its background, the change of political power in member states is not negligible; at the end of 1990s social democratic parties came into power in thirteen countries among fifteen member states.

C. Regulating the Atypical Work by the Gender Policy

The Function of the Court of Justice

As regards atypical work, the gender policy was developed in a significant manner by an important judgement of the European Court of Justice (ECJ).

The ECJ ensures that in the interpretation and application of the Treaty the law is observed. It also has a function of oversight of the secondary law of the Treaty, the category which includes EU directives.

Besides the Community law, there are three other types of law which the ECJ takes into account. First is international law. Where Community law is deemed to have developed from international law, the ECJ may refer to international law in its judgement (Nugent, 1994). The second is the general legal principles. These are the general norms which, although not in the form of codified statute law, are nonetheless accorded a status equal to that of the written law. Not to be confused with the natural law or the moral law, it should involve a principle which is concretely applicable to the judgement. For example, human rights are considered to be a general principal of law at the ECJ (Yamane, 1996). The third is the case law. Sometimes the interpretation of the Treaty and its secondary laws lead to the legislation of new secondary laws, which shows the semi-legislative role of the Court of Justice (Ootani, 1982). In addition, it is also important to mention that the European Court of Justice is bound by its own precedents.

There are several important functions of the ECJ, but the most important in the gender policy context is that of the preliminary ruling

---

[6]   http://europa.eu.int/comm/employment_social/employment_strategy/origins_en.htm.

mechanism. When it is related to the EC law, the supreme court of the member states may ask for a preliminary ruling on a point of law from the ECJ.

Indirect Sexual Discrimination and the Atypical Work

The role of the ECJ in the gender policy has become very important as a result of the judgement of the case Defrenne II in 1976 (Case 43/75).

The first step of the equality politics was in 1976, when the ECJ ruled that the Article 119 has a direct effect on the judgement of the Defrenne II case. The Belgian Supreme Court asked the ECJ to give a ruling concerning the direct effect of Article 119 and the possibility of its direct application. The ECJ has admitted both the direct effect and the direct application of Article 119. By that, Article 119 has become directly applicable to the individual, which means that unequal payment of men and women for work of equal value is prohibited.

With the direct effect and the direct application of Article 119, together with the Equal Treatment Directive of 1976, the ECJ has given several rulings that the different treatment and payment to part-time workers can be considered as indirect sexual discrimination. It was based on the fact that 80% of part-time workers (Commission, 1992) are female.

In 1986, in the preliminary ruling given for the case Bilka (Case 170/84), the ECJ stated that excluding part-timer workers from professional pension schemes is to be considered as unequal payment between men and women, which is an infringement of Article 119. Even it does not exclude female workers, as workers concerned are mostly women, it could be considered as indirect sexual discrimination. This being the case, the onus of proof of non-discrimination lies with the enterprise. Equally, in the case of Rinner-Kühn (Case 171/88) and of Ruzius-Wilbrink (Case 102/88) in 1989, the ECJ ruled that different treatment of part-time workers in social benefit can be considered as indirect sexual discrimination unless proving of non-discrimination by the country concerned.

Based on these rulings, the draft directive on the burden of proof was submitted by the Commission. Although it was blocked by the Council, it was firstly incorporated in the Article 6 of Equal Treatment Directive (Pillingler, 1992).[7] This is evidence of the semi-legislative role of the ECJ, and the progress of the policy on atypical work through gender policy.

---

[7] The directive on burden of proof was eventually adopted in 1997 by the Social Dialogue method.

Resume of the Gender Policy and Atypical Work

By focusing only on the legislation phase of the Community method, there is no observable progress in the domain of atypical work. However, when we look at the surveillance phase of the Community method, there is a certain progress through the application of gender policy. Based on the fact that most part-time workers are women, the ECJ opened the door to implement policies of equality for part-time workers by applying the gender policy. It is based on the principle of the equality of men and women; itself considered a basic human right, and thus a "general principal of law". Based on this principle, together with the strict application of the Article 119 and directives, the principle of the equality was given greater importance than the discrimination of the part-timer workers.

It should be noted that the motivation of its development is unrelated to the unemployment crisis. Strictly applying legal reasoning, its aim is resolving the sexual discrimination based on the fact that more women are engaged in atypical work.

III. Regulating Atypical Work in Japan

A. Regulating "Part-Time" Work

The Background to Regulation

It was in 1993 that the Law Concerning the Improvement of Employment Management, etc. of Part-Time Workers (hereafter the Part-Time Worker Law) was adopted. However, the beginning of the discussion concerning the "part-time" work goes back to the 1980s.

The problem of the part-time worker in Japan is strongly related to terms used in related discussions.

In its original meaning, part-time work meant work with shorter working time than the full-time work. However, in general usage, the Japanese term *pâto*, derived from the English work part-time, does not only mean short-time work but also work carried out by housewives working full-time but called under the name of *pâto*, part-time. (Wakisaka, 1997).[8] Another definition says that if an employee is neither working full-time nor on a permanent contract, she or he may be considered a part-time worker. (Working group on part-time workers, 2002). Therefore, the problem of "part-time" workers in Japan means

---

[8] Students working part-time or young people working on the fixed-contract are called *arubaito*.

also the problem of fixed-term workers as well. The term "atypical worker" could equally be applied to workers in these situations.

In the beginning of 1980s about 20% of *pâto* were working full-time (Shûkan Rôdo News, 24 November 1986). Around 75% of companies paid lower salaries and fringe benefits to *pâto* than to regular workers. Often there is no written contract laying down the working conditions of atypical workers in Japan. Therefore, provisions to protect part-time and fixed-term workers were required.

During the 1980s there are some attempts by the trade unions and opposition parties to introduce a Part-Time Worker Law, but because of the strong opposition by employers' organisations, no new regulations were adopted. In 1984 the Ministry of Labour drew up guidelines concerning part-time work. These required companies to issue an employment contract stating working conditions, to limit the working hours of part-time workers to less than full-time workers, to follow the Labour Standard Law concerning paid leave of part-time workers working more than 4 days per week and to give notice of non-renewal of contract at least 30 days in advance to part-time workers who had more than one year's service.

These regulations were not adopted until 1993, when the power balance between the ruling party and opposition parties changed.

Unlike the European case, the rigidity of the labour market was not the major motive of the introduction of regulations; for many companies, flexible workforce was already available by using *pâto*s and *arubaito*s. Besides of these external flexible workforce, the internal workforce was also flexible; on the condition that the companies guarantee their employment, employees accept replacement and transfer without any problem, which was not the case in Europe.[9]

Therefore, the only motive of Japanese regulations are to introduce the working conditions and rights for atypical workers to protect them from abusive uses.

Law and Guidelines Concerning the "Part-Time" Work

The Part-Time Work Law of 1993 seeks "to promote the effective utilisation of part-time workers' abilities and to improve their welfare" (Article 1). It concerns working conditions, education and training, and welfare in the company. Employers are encouraged to take necessary measures not just "to promote effective utilisation of part-time workers'

---

[9] The nenko system, based on the lifetime employment and the seniority-plus-merit, was in this background. Another important background is the strong gender role in the Japanese labour market; and the sexual segregation between masculine permanent workers and feminine temporary or part-time workers was the norm.

abilities in an effective manner" but also to "maintain the balance with regular workers by securing proper working conditions" (Article 3).

Whereas the Part-Time Work Law does not refer to the fixed-term contracts, the Part-Time Work Guideline of 1993 states that the worker should be notified of his or her employer's decision not to renew the contract. Also, the guideline states that employers are encouraged to achieve the equal payment between part-time and regular workers.

Those who work longer than 35 hours are not covered by the Part-time Worker Law, but as a fixed-term contract worker they are covered by the Labour Standard Law, amended in 2003. The length of contract should be less than three years, with some exceptions.[10] There is no limit of number of times a contract may be renewed. In order to avoid problems when contracts are concluded and renewed, the Labour Standard Law requires the Ministry of Health, Labour and Welfare (hereafter Ministry of Labour) to set guidelines which employers must follow. According to these guidelines, the employer should clearly propose a renewal of contract at the conclusion of the fixed term or give thirty days notice before the contract term expires. Non-renewal of a contract must be accompanied by a stated reason, justifying the decision.

In 1997 the working group on part-time work issued its report, by referring to the problem of equal pay for equal work between regular workers and part-time/fixed-term contract workers. It was in 1994 that the ILO has adopted the Convention on part-time work, which Japan has not yet ratified.

There is no existing regulations concerning the "equal pay for equal work," but in the judgement of the case *Maruko Alarm* in 1996, the District Court of Nagano Prefecture ruled that the salary of the fixed-term contract female workers should not be less than 80% of that of full-term female workers when they are engaged in the same work under the same conditions. In this case, the complainants were fixed-term contract workers who had worked several years for the company, on renewable two-month contracts. The longest period of service among the group was 27 years.

In its judgement the Court concluded that the principle of equal pay for equal work is legally applicable norm, as there is no positive law which stipulates it. However, the Court also concluded that if the difference of the payment to the fixed-term contract worker should not be excessive, otherwise it can be considered as against the public orders and morals. In other words, paying 20% less salary to short-term contract workers than their long-term contract colleagues is justified.

---

[10] Length of contract can be inferior to five years, in case of engagement of professional skilled workers and senior workers over 60 years old.

B. Gender Policy for Atypical Work?

Japan is not exceptional in having more women than men working under atypical contracts. In 2001, nearly 70% of non-regular workers were women. As seen above, EU gender policy dealt with the subject of atypical work by applying the principle of indirect discrimination. However, this has not happened in Japan. There is neither statute law nor case law to support such a concept of indirect discrimination in Japan. Furthermore, even the application of the concept of direct discrimination is far from well-established.

It was in 1986 that the Equal Employment Opportunity Law (EEOL), amended in 1997 was introduced. The purposes of the EEOL are "to promote equal opportunity and treatment between men and women in employment" and "to foster measures for, among others, the promotion of securing the health of women workers with respect to employment during pregnancy and after childbirth" (Article 1). It prohibits discrimination concerning recruitment and hiring, assignment, promotion, training, allocation of fringe benefits, retirement and dismissal on the basis of gender.

Despite its stated purpose of prohibiting sexual discrimination, EEOL only required employers to make voluntary 'endeavours' to treat women equally in recruitment, hiring, assignment and promotion and contains no punitive measures for firms violating the agreements on vocational training, fringe benefits, retirement age, resignation and dismissal (Bishop, 2002). The law was amended in 1998 and introduced the sanction that if a firm consistently violates prohibitions, the Ministry of Labour can publicise this fact.

Regarding payment, Article 4 of the Labour Standard Law prohibits discrimination against women.

In short, there is no evidence of the development of protecting or promoting atypical work through the gender policy and even direct discrimination is still not penalised in the statute law. It should be noted that Japan did not experience the feminist movement – a force for great change in so many countries – during the 1970s and 1980s. Even there were some active feminists it did not come to the huge social movement.

C. For the New Regulation of Part-Time and Fixed-Term Work

The research group on part-time work in 2002 pointed to some of the changes which occurred during the past decades. It pointed out that increasingly part-time workers are taking on the same responsibilities as regular workers, even though they are paid on average only 80% of a regular worker's salary. Also, only 40% of part-time workers work under non-fixed term contracts. Companies reduce number of regular workers and continue to increase number of part-time or fixed-term contract workers. The research group pointed out two problems which are caused from this situation. Firstly, young people have difficulties in finding regular work, resulting in high rates of unwilling part-timer workers or of unemployment among the young generation. Secondly, the only choice offered is between being "a regular worker with secured employment without free time" and being "an atypical worker with free time without secured employment". These are options that no longer suit people who have grown used to the diversity of life-styles and life choices that one sees in modern society. The result of this is that the rigidity of working style of regular workers has become a subject for discussion. This is due to that fact that the Japanese employment model has collapsed under the long economic depression.

Trade Unions are also actively proposing the introduction of new regulations. The Japanese Trade Union Confederation (JTUC), the national centre of Japanese Trade Unions, is proposing a new regulation concerning part-time and fixed-term workers. Under these proposals for both part-time and fixed-term contract workers, not only the discriminatory treatment of working condition and payment would be prohibited, but also employees would be obliged to pay social charges for these workers. Concerning the fixed-term workers, it proposes to limit the renewal of the fixed-term contract to once.

The JTUC also proposes the establishment of the Labour Contract Law, in order to avoid social conflict. It proposes that the in-company reshuffle of workers with relocation cannot be conducted without consent of the worker concerned. This means limiting internal flexibility which may lead to a change in the nature of external flexibility as well.

IV. Conclusion

The protection of atypical form of work is one of the main concerns in the developed countries. However, we have seen that protection can vary depending on the jurisdiction.

Both the EU and Japan introduced regulations concerning atypical work whose purposes were the protection of workers. However, the definition of discrimination is different and as a result, the way of protection is different as well. As mentioned above, it is due to the difference of the motivation in drawing up the regulation; whereas the protection of atypical work was a tool for producing a more flexible labour market in the EU, Japanese regulations are not concerned with the rigidity of working practices relating to regular workers. This could be a reason why the employers' organisation accepted to discuss and reach the agreement at the European level, while Japanese employers' organisation persistently obstructs the introduction of the new regulations concerning atypical work. This is strongly related to the difference of internal flexibility which is higher in Japan than in the EU.

The difference can also be understood from the perspective of legitimacy. Concerning the nature of the law-making process itself, Japan as a nation-state has already established its legitimacy of its legislative process, whereas the EU is still on the way to developing it. The employment issue was a tool for strengthening its legitimacy, as was the issue of regulating atypical work. Related to this, the social partners at the EU level played a role by forcing the Council to adopt directives. Though it was not the case in Japan, the adoption of the Part-Time Worker Law in 1993 is strongly related to the fragmentation of the ruling party.

The last but not the least difference is the different relation of gender policy to that of atypical work. The EU situation shows that the crosspoint of these two policies is the concept of the indirect discrimination. In the Japanese case, the prohibition of indirect discrimination of atypical workers by gender policy was not observed. To begin with, the prohibition of direct sexual discrimination has not yet been established in statute or case law.

By observing the development in each jurisdiction, it is very doubtful that the protection of atypical work will be further developed in the near future. In the case of the EU, further protection of atypical workers may be adverse to the original motivation of regulations to make the labour market flexible; furthermore, the actual discussion tend to claim the weakening of the social *acquis* to strengthen the competitiveness In the Japanese case, even if the Japanese model has started to erode in some companies, this does not lead to the approximation of status of typical and atypical worker by strengthening the protection of atypical workers; as long as economic depression continues external flexibility will be essential to companies. It seems that the protection of atypical work cannot advance much, facing the global competitiveness.

References

Bishop, B. (2002), "*Risutora* and Women in the Japanese Labour Force," in Gills, D. S. and Piper, N. (eds.), *Women and Work in Globalising Asia*, Routledge, London

Collins, D. (1975), *The European Communities: The Social Policy of the First Phase*, Martin Robertson

The Commission (1992), *The Position of Women on the Labour Market: Trends and Development in the Twelve Member States of the European Community 1983-1990*

The Commission (1993), *White Paper on Growth, Competitiveness and Employment*

Goetschy, J. (2001), "The European Employment Strategy from Amsterdam to Stockholm: Has It Reached Its Cruising Speed Yet?," in *Industrial Relations Journal 32(5)*

Henni, A. (2001), *Le dialogue social européen: Enjeux, structures, résultats*, CRISP, No. 1741

Hoskyns, C. (1996), *Integrating Gender*, Verso, London

Marks, G. and McAdam, D. (1996), "Social Movements and the Changing Structure of Political Opportunity in the European Union," in Marks, G., Scharpf, G., Schmitter, P. and Streek, W. (eds.), *Governance in the European Union*, Sage, London

Nugent, N. *et al.* (1994), *The Government and Politics of the European Union*, Palgrave/Macmillan, Basingstoke

Social Affairs Series (2000), *Atypical Work in the EU*, Directorate General for Research of the European Parliament

Streek, W. and Schmitter, P. (1991), "From National Corporatism to Transnational Pluralism: Organized Interests in the Single European Market," *Politics & Society*, Vol. 19, No. 2

Streek, W. (1996), "Neo-Voluntarism: A New European Social Policy Regime?" in Marks, G., Scharpf, G., Schmitter, P. and Streek, W., *Governance in the European Union*, Sage, London

Otani, Y. (1982), *Gaisetsu EC Hou: Atrashii Yôroppa no Houchitsjo no Keisei (The General Guide to the EC Law: Development of the New European Legal Order)*, Yuhikaku, Tokyo

Pillinger, J. (1992), *Feminising the Market: Women's Pay and Employment in the European Community*, Macmillan, Basingstoke

Yamane, Y. (1996), *EC/EU how: oushuurengou no kiseki (The EC/EU Law: the trajectory of the EU)*, Yushindo, Tokyo

Wakisaka, A. (1997), "Women at work," in Sako, M. and Sato, H. (eds.), *Japanese Labour and Management in Transition: Diversity, Flexibility and Participation*, Routledge, London

Walby, S. (2003), "Policy Developments for Workplace Gender Equity in a Global Era: The Importance of the EU in the UK," *Review of Policy Research 20(3)*

Working group on part-time workers (2002).

Websites

The European Union (http://europa.eu.int)

Japan Personnel management & safety information center (http://www.campus.ne.jp/~labor/)

The Japanese Trade Unions Confederation (http://www.jtuc-rengo.or.jp/new/index.html)

The Japanese Institute for Labour policy and Training (http://www.jil.go.jp)

The Ministry of Health, Labour and Welfare of Japan (http://www.mhlw.go.jp)

CHAPTER 13

Promoting Global Governance, the G8, and the UN

Possibilities and Limits of EU-Japan Cooperation

Reimund SEIDELMANN

Professor at the Institute of Political Science, Justus-Liebig-Universität Giessen, Germany, and at the Institut d'études européennes, Université libre de Bruxelles, Belgium

I. A Need for Global Governance

Although the general need for global governance is widely accepted in most political and academic circles throughout the world, it might be good to reflect on its origin, its necessity, and its limitations before one can deal with the specific role of the G8 and the UN within such a global governance. Focussing on the G8 reflects not only the fact that it is constituted of the most powerful nations but also that the G8 is an example of multilateral harmonisation of nation-states interests. Focussing on the UN allows us to evaluate the most important and oldest international organisation established after the end of the Second World War and involves the debate about UN reforms which aim improve global governance.

Global governance implies that the international system needs political control in order to provide optimal services in the three basic political goods: economic well-being, security, and collective self-determination. Such a need for global governance results from the following structural developments:

1. Nation-states, which still dominate the international stage, are unable and unwilling to provide adequate political governance because of

their very nature. As sovereign actors[1] their international activities are dictated by national interests and values, maximisation of these interests following zero-sum-game calculations, and the use of military or economic force in order to project power, influence, and specific interests toward their regional and global environment.

2. Globalisation of problems such as proliferation of weapons, spillover of economic and financial crises, environmental threats, and political instability, as well as global power projection and unilateral control by particularly powerful nation-states have set up traditional competences of nation-states to adequately manage and solve such problems and threats.

3. Alliances, regional and issue-oriented organisations and regimes, or multilateral cooperation of nation-states reflect such limits but follow a strategy to preserve sovereignty as much as possible or to limit coordination and harmonisation of national interests to the absolutely necessary minimum. Mechanisms such as power balance, senior-junior axes, colonial or quasi-colonial dependencies follow similar concepts – they are specific variations of an international system or its subsystem, in which the nation-state tries to keep its monopoly despite its dysfunctional or anachronistic character.

4. The emergence of globally influential non-state actors, supranational actors, and international organisations has further complicated constructive international consensus-building and problem-solving. Examples like the Asian financial crisis, the problems in re-building a democratic Iraq, and the inadequate control of global emissions demonstrate far-reaching deficits in terms of common prevention, control, and solution of global problems, if one defines common control as joint actions of the different types and categories of involved and relevant global actors.

While these four developments support a negative argumentation – i.e. making the point that global governance is necessary because traditional system management is inadequate – the need for global governance can be supported by positive argumentation as well by drawing on idealistic thinking. In this respect, one can underline the following points:

5. Basic values of modern civic society such as freedom, equality, and solidarity are not, per se, exclusively above nation-states and regions but can be pursued only on a universal or global scale. The logic that underpins these values implies a commitment to bring them into op-

---

[1] For a more detailed evaluation of sovereignty see Seidelmann, R., "Souveränität" in A. Boeckh (ed.), *Lexikon der Politik Vol. 6 Internationale Beziehungen*, München, Beck, 1994, pp. 493-495.

eration them as political concepts, not only on an individual and intra-national collective level, but on a regional and global level as
well. Thus, demands for self-determination, for example, apply for
all levels of political organisation from the individual to the global.
To limit their validity to intra-national scopes might result from specific political circumstances and constellations but are not legitimate
in conceptual terms. In brief, such values are not only valid for the
individual human being but for nation-states as well and this validity
translates into global governance based on the universalisation of
such basic values.[2]

6. In addition to this general basic-value-approach global governance is
   often regarded as a necessary complement to multilateral cooperation and regionalisation.[3] Looking at the patterns and dynamics of
   power in the international system leads to the conclusion that global
   governance is needed to defend legitimate economic, political, and
   security rights of societies and their nation-states against illegitimate
   domination. Like the introduction of the concept of sovereignty as a
   defence mechanism against oppression, the call for fair and better
   global governance can be understood as a defence against the projection of global military power, globalisation as economic penetration
   and exploitation, and political discrimination against nation-states
   with limited economic, military, and political strength.

7. Parallel, and often related to the idea of universal values,[4] is the
   concept of the international system as an international community –
   i.e. as a global society with common values and interests. This is not
   new. The Roman concept of citizenship, Bartolomé de Las Casas's

---

[2] This is not the place to deal in detail with the controversies about universal values
and norms. It is, however, interesting to note that the dispute about Asian values, as
opposed to Western values is more of a political nature. A closer look at Asian state
philosophy – such as Confucius – reveals surprising similarities and analogies
between Asian and European thinking on good governance. See, for example,
H. Roetz, *Die chinesische Ethik der Achsenzeit. Eine Rekonstruktion unter dem
Aspekt des Duchbruchs zum postkonventionellen Denken*, Frankfurt, Suhrkamp,
1992, and X. Gu (ed.), *Europe and Asia. Mutual Perceptions and Expectations on
the Way to a New Partnership in the Twenty-First Century*, Baden-Baden, Nomos,
2002.

[3] For a detailed discussion of regionalisation and regionalism see, for example,
M. Telò (ed.), *European Union and New Regionalism. Regional Actors and Global
Governance in a Post-hegemonic Era*, Aldershot, Ashgate, 2001 and R. Seidelmann,
"Internationalism, Regionalism and the Nation State" in R. Cuperus, J. Kandel (eds.),
Transformation in Progress. European Social Democracy, Wiardi Beckman
Stichting, Amsterdam, 1998, pp. 229-240.

[4] Expressed for example in the UN Charter and its convention on human rights.

demand that Christianity give Indians equal rights,[5] and Immanuel Kant's blueprint for eternal peace[6] are important points of reference. Utopian ideas of a world state are traditional elements in state philosophy and political thinking.[7] All of them define the international system, not as an accumulation of societies plagued by a security dilemma or structural malevolence, but as on order based on common basic values and harmonised interests. Similar thinking can be found in the international labour movement of the 19th century, in the many peace- and Third-World-movements of today, and in modern international law.

This means that the idea of global governance can be supported both by a rational evaluation of existing forms of government, as well as an idealistic projection of universal values onto a global community.[8] It is understood as a necessary global complement to existing multilevel governance structures,[9] which interrelate, harmonise, and globalise interests and norms in a vertical, as well as horizontal direction in order to solve global problems and to establish a global order based on common values plus common interests and their global implementation.

II. Transforming the International System

The next step after defining global governance as a basic necessity is to reflect on the possibilities and limitations of introducing, widening, and deepening global governance in the present international system. This is less a sort of feasibility study than an analysis of the structural obstacles and potential dynamics of support for such a transformation of the international system in order to evaluate the possibilities and limitations of existing strategies.

---

[5] See de Las Casas, B., "Tractatus de thesauris in regnis del Peru – Tratado de las doce dudas (1566)," reprinted in A. Maler (ed.), *Fray Bartolomé de Las Casas an Philipp II*, Wiesbaden, Harrassowith, 1992.

[6] See Seidelmann, R., "Kants 'Ewiger Friede' und die Neuordnung des europäischen Sicherheitssystems," in K. Dicke, K.-M. Kodalle (eds.), *Republik und Bürgerrecht. Kantische Anregungen zur Theorie politischer Ordnung nach dem Ende des Ost-West-Konflikts*, Weimar/Köln/Wien, Böhlau, 1998, pp. 133-180.

[7] See, for example, R. Seidelmann, "The Search for a New Global Order: Rehabilitating the Idea of the Global State" in D. Bourantonis, M. Evriviades (eds.), *A United Nations for the Twenty-First Century*, Dordrecht, Kluwer Law International, 1996, pp. 41-63.

[8] It has to be underlined that this argumentation assumes that a realistic and idealistic approach towards the idea of a better global order are not exclusive but complement each other.

[9] Multilevel governance means coordinated policies from and between the local, the regional, the nation-state, the regional (for example, the EU), and the global level.

Here – and in contrast to political simplification of international politics – international relations are understood as constituted

- first by policies in three dimensions or issue-areas – i.e. the political, economic, and military dimension;
- second by three structural dynamics – i.e. globalisation, regionalisation, and nationalisation;[10] and
- third by power strategies of economic and military strong nation-states.

The following graph is an attempt to classify existing efforts of global governance according to this approach:

	Political Dimension	Economic Dimension	Military Dimension
Globalisation	Selective, limited, and weak global governance	Strong and dominant trend	Marginal, selective, and limited global governance
Regionalisation	Limited efforts in the Asia-Pacific region but major efforts and dynamics in Europe	Strong and dominant trend	Weak and limited efforts of regional governance with the exception of Europe
Nationalisation	Strong and dominant trend	Selective but mainly marginal	US-monopoly as strong and dominant trend

The major consequences of such a view of the international system in evaluating the potential for global governance are the following:

1. Globalisation is but one of three dynamics, but not the dominant force at work; it provokes, as well as competes with, regionalisation and nationalisation.[11] Thus, functionalistic strategies, which are based on the assumption that continued globalisation would quasi-automatically lead to more global governance, neglect the negative impact of regionalisation and nationalisation *vis-à-vis* more global governance. Both have to be regarded not only as strategies to control globalisation through nation-states or regional bodies but as well as strategies of defence against global control or global governance.

2. Globalisation and regionalisation have something in common, which is fundamentally opposed by nationalisation: the will of nation-states to permanently harmonise, supranationalise, or even integrate

---

[10] The term 'nationalisation' includes re-nationalisation of foreign policies.

[11] Nation-states often participate in all three dynamics or combine unilateralism, multilateralism, regional integration, and engagement in international organisations. It is less the mix of these approaches but the priorities, which count.

their policies. While Asia-Pacific regional cooperation and EU-integration, for example, can thus be regarded as learning processes for global governance, nationalisation – and in particular US unilateralism – constitutes a dynamic fundamentally working against multi-, supra-, and superlaterisation. Furthermore, even the most advanced regionalisation plus interregionalism might promote the idea to use global governance to control relations between the regions. Thus, the interrelation between globalisation and regionalisation and its impact on global governance are of a different and more constructive type than the interrelation between globalisation and regionalisation on the one side and nationalisation on the other.

3. Introducing power analysis into this line of thinking means again to paying special attention to the US because of its absolute and relative power, its leadership approach towards international politics, and its domination of the international agenda. Therefore, US unilateralism based, on a firm and long-term monopoly of global military power projection capabilities as well as on strong economic-financial potentials[12] and related influence and leverage, becomes a major challenge to global governance, if one applies a concept of global governance as common governance and not as global governance through projection of US interests in global control and norms for behaviour in international affairs. Following and reinforcing the dynamic of nationalisation of international relations, the search for such a global governance translates into the search for strategies to overcome nationalisation in general, and US unilateralism, in particular. However, giving the existing US traditions in internationalist and value-oriented thinking,[13] existing multilateral political efforts and their institutionalisation,[14] and the challenge of a decline in relative power *vis-à-vis* both EU-Europe and Japan, this means developing strategies to gradually replace US

---

[12] Both the influence of the Japanese economic and financial power as well as the creation of the European Monetary Union – and as a consequence a bipolar, and eventually, a tripolar international monetary system – have eroded, limited, and ended US hegemony in financial-monetary global affairs. However, the experiences with economic-financial crises such as the Asian, and the recent Latin American upheaval, as well as the experiences particularly in the IMF, with US policies, underline that this bipolar or tripolar power structure is still asymmetric. Having lost its monopoly, the US has kept its dominance.

[13] Such thinking was, for example, an essential part of President Wilson's international engagement, and President Carter's approach to human rights, etc.

[14] Regional organisations with strong US engagement such as NAFTA and NATO must be regarded both as instruments of US leadership policies but also of institutionalised inroads into established learning processes towards multilaterlism and common-interest-definition within US governments and elites.

strategies of unilateral leadership through multilateral common-interest-policies and revitalise US engagement and support of common global governance.

Thus, if one agrees with the notion that effective common global governance demands a gradual reform or transformation of patterns, modes, and structures of nation-states' international behaviour, one can look at existing reform strategies. There are basically five such strategies, which are politically relevant:

1. Legalisation, i.e. control and change through the introduction of global soft laws, legal standards, and legal institutions such as international courts;

2. Institutionalisation, i.e. better global governance through widening and deepening the legitimacy, competence, and power of the UN;

3. harmonisation, i.e. better global governance through international cooperation and collective learning processes such as taking place in the G8;

4. issue-oriented globalisation, i.e. better global governance through common global policies on specific issues, such as the reconstruction and democratisation of Iraq after the end of the Hussein-regime; and

5. public movements, i.e. promoting political will and capacity for better global governance through public awareness and its political mobilisation.

These strategies do not exclude, but rather, complement each other because of their particular strengths and weaknesses. A systematic analysis of building political orders shows that the creation and stabilisation of orders is a matter for institutions, secured modalities of behaviour, cohesion through successful management of political substance and common-interest-building, and public acceptance and legitimacy. Political experience – in particular that of EU regional integration and the establishment of a supranational order within Europe – has shown that the right combination of all the five strategies produces reinforcement between the individual strategies and produces a more cohesive, sustainable, and acceptable grand strategy for transforming the international system.

An overall concept of a new global order involves strategies for reform of the international system through better global governance to a specific model of the order which one wants to implement. A gradual approach, however, which does not specify the new order in all its details, has not only the advantages of easy adaptation to change but also the advantage of broader coalition-building. Transformation strategies which seek not sudden and comprehensive structural, institutional and behavioral change in all dimensions and for all global actors, allow the building of coalitions around specific issues such in the case of Iraq (as mentioned above) and dimensions such as the economic-financial one and between actors, which prefer enhanced multilateralism and supranationalism. Positive coalition-building such as this can be complemented by the negative mechanism of the external federator – i.e. a unilateral, dominant, and national-interest-oriented US.

III. G8 and the UN

As has been shown, both the G8 and the UN represent different categories of actors but not all actors; their multilateral and international approach are important but are not the only approaches to international affairs. Although important, their relevance for global control is limited because of internal factors and external constellations:

Despite its relevance and political potential, the G8 faces major limits from the inside because of its membership: it represents only the economically and militarily strong but not the weaker powers; its lack of institutionalisation, legalisation, and international acceptance limits its impact from the very beginning; its exclusion of military and hard security matters limits its role to only political-economic issues, and the effectiveness of its decision-making is endangered both by the lack of common-interest-building as well as the principles of consensus and unlimited sovereignty. In addition, the G8 has no institutional, substantial, or power monopoly. It competes with a number of networks, regimes, organisations and unilateral policies and legitimises itself through success in terms of defining, harmonising, and implementing common solutions to problems of the global system, both between G8 members and outside the group.

Owing to its history, its formal legitimisation, and its broader membership, the UN has much greater potential for global control and governance than the G8. However, it faces major obstacles in realising such a role in an efficient and successful way. Different than the case of the G8 but similar in principle, the UN structure as an international organisation is dominated by sovereign nation-states and without its own instruments for real power projection, it faces significant internal structural deficits when it comes to effective common global control. In addition – and again similar to the G8 and the international system in general – the UN faces the problem of how to deal with a dominant, leadership-oriented, and unilaterally-minded US, which defines itself as a better global governor that the UN.

If one takes such limitations not as proof positive of the impossibility of the task but as a starting point for a gradualistic strategy of establishing, securing, and improving global control, one faces three challenges: first, to improve willingness and capability of both organisations to upgrade their global control; second, to find a constructive interrelation between the G8 and the UN and other potential alliance partners for better global governance; and third, to develop and implement strategies to integrate the US into such thinking and to ensure US support for related measures and policies.

IV. EU's and Japan's Role in G8 and the UN for the Promotion of Better Multilateral Cooperation and Global Governance

Assuming that the EU's selective globalisation, as well as Japan's growing engagement with global affairs will not only continue but are based on the idea of improving global control and common governance, both as a matter of a cost-effective pursuit of their interests as well as of a continued pursuit of a better international order, one can now look at the possibilities and limitations of both actors in the pursuit of better global governance.

Introducing the term "better" global governance implies three specific elements of global governance:

1. A model-oriented component: global governance as common governance, i.e. as governance based common decision-making and common interests, or the replacement of zero-sum through surplus-policies;[15]

2. A rationality-oriented component: global governance as the management and solution of global problems within, between, and above the political, economic, and military dimension of global affairs, which are based on cost-risk-benefit rationality, which follows a global and not a national calculation; and

3. A norm-oriented component: global governance as the projection of democratic values, procedures, and institutions towards the international level[16] to establish a civic global community of societies with

---

[15] This is not only a theoretical model but a concrete political experience of European integration, where supranationalisation meant not only overall net advantages for national interest calculation but as well the production of overall common surplus. Similar ideas, for example, of a North-South economic growth community have been proposed for many years. An early example is the report of the Brandt North-South Commission.

[16] For a detailed discussion of this understanding of democracy see Seidelmann, R. "Democracy-Building in the European Union. Conditions, Problems, and Options," in M. Telò (ed.), *Démocratie et Construction Européenne*, Bruxelles, Editions de l'Université de Bruxelles, 1995, pp. 73-89.

an optimal mix of self-determination and responsibility for global common goods.

As discussed above, multilateralism is a necessary condition for better global governance: it serves both as a learning process for harmonising interests, views, and behaviour, as well as for understanding the limits of traditional sovereignty. Given the civic character of both the EU and Japan, their traditional soft-power-approach,[17] and their considerable engagement in multilateral and international efforts for better governance on the one hand and their significant economic-financial power on the other, both the EU and Japan in general and EU-Japanese cooperation in particular carry a special responsibility for the promotion of a concept of global governance such as this.

The idea of a special responsibility[18] can be supported by the following arguments:

1. Besides the US, the EU and Japan are the most powerful actors in the G8 and the UN; in addition their political, economic, and security interests are increasingly globalised.[19] This means that a special engagement for better global governance is legitimised by their interests as well as possible because of their potential.

2. Their civic credentials as soft powers, which avoid unnecessary use of military means and seek partnerships based on mutual economic advantages provide them with the credibility and concrete experiences to promote better global governance. Thus, EU-Japanese special engagement would significantly improve acceptability and effectiveness of better global governance.

3. The EU and Japan have both a long tradition of partnership or special relations with the US and both share important global interests with the US – such as economic-financial stability and open trade. This means that influencing US behaviour or strengthening US multilaterism and internationalism is more possible than for other actors, in particular because it carries the notion of a broad win-win-cooperation between them and the US, which other actors cannot match.

4. Pursuing a doctrine of special responsibility in an effective manner would finally change the present pattern of global agenda-setting. US dominance would be replaced by a more balanced and joint

---

[17] For a detailed discussion of such concepts see Czempiel, E.-O., *Kluge Macht. Außenpolitik für das 21. Jahrhundert*, München, Beck, 1999.

[18] It has to be underlined that the doctrine of special responsibility differs significantly from the US doctrine of leadership.

[19] See, for example, energy imports, global shipping lines and financial-monetary global interdependence.

definition of priorities, which would reflect the existing multipolar structure of the international system and secure better management of global affairs.

This political concept with its specific two-fold objectives – i.e. promoting both global governance in general and integrating the US into such a political line – is a redefinition of trilateralism. But in contrast to the old idea of trilateralism as a sort of enlightened senior-junior-partnership, in which the US acts as the senior and dependent Europe and Japan play the role of a junior, this concept is based on an approach, in which all three act as equal partners. Equality does not mean to match US power capacities in all three dimensions – and in particular in the military one. It means becoming both better and more responsible partners for managing and solving global problems. Therefore, the doctrine of the EU and Japan becoming not only a better partner for the US but joining their forces to promote better global governance reflects not only the changes in the international economic power pattern but appeals to long-term US interests in burden-sharing plus continued shared new trilateral control.

Before discussion the obstacles on the way to more multilateralism and globalism one has to clarify once again the character of globalism to avoid conceptual misunderstandings or political misperception:

Global government has to be understood as the necessary and legitimate extension of multilevel governance. It does not substitute but complements the subnational, the national, and the regional levels of governance. Thus, even in the most effective global governance model the nation-state continues to exist and to have a substantial role in government.[20] However, global governance means both a constructive participation of the regional supra- or superstate and/or the nation-state in global governance as well as the political will to subscribe to the idea of limited and globally controlled sovereignty.

The promotion of global governance by actors or coalitions of special responsibility has to be based on the notion of broadest global constructive consensus both within leading nation-states, such as those cooperating in the G8. This includes active support from the US. Experience has shown that such a consensus can be reached by creating win-

---

[20]   Here, the European experience with integration might be worth considering. Against all initial anxieties about the disappearance of national identity, national interests, and national political cultures, the EU-integration process relied on and reconfirmed the constructive diversity of national member states and their specific characteristics.

win-package deals disproportionate economic-financial commitment of the promoters of such ideas,[21] and a supportive international public.

As in all major structural reform strategies the search for more and better global governance is more acceptable if it is issue-oriented – i.e. concentrates on specific important issues of global concern, focussed on task efficiency – i.e. defines institutions, procedures, and policies not as a means in itself but only as instruments to solve problems – and starts with jobs which can be solved successfully in a relatively short period of time, thereby creating acceptability and legitimacy for the whole project.

Finally and *vis-à-vis* the multiple complexities of and the many political sensitivities within the international community, gradualistic strategies promise more success than "Big Bang" or "UN institutional reform alone"[22] strategies. In reference to the above mentioned understanding of the international system as a multidimensional and multidynamic system, an optimal gradualistic strategy would begin with overcoming nationalisation through stepwise strengthening multilateralism – such as in G8 – in order to continue with introducing more globalism through an improved UN. It would focus on feasible jobs first in the economic, and then in the political domains and subsequently widen the agenda to military and security issues from relatively consensual ones such as non-proliferation and peace-keeping, to the establishment of regionally and globally secured peace-in-security-regimes.

To integrate the US as a constructive partner in a revised concept of trilateralism, associative strategies could be supplemented with limited and selected dissociative tactics in issues like the implementation of the Kyoto Protocol, the new International Court, and restraints on nuclear military capabilities and the related nuclear strategies. However, two experiences of successful international learning processes have to be applied: first, that in such a mix of positive and negative incentives the positive ones should always have priority and second, that US political

---

[21] It has to be remembered that Germany's promotion of EU-integration was linked to Germany's continued and signficantly disproportionately generous financial support of the EU. However, there is a general understanding that the economic and political advantages of German EU membership have more than compensated for the financial burdens incurred. For details, see Seidelmann, R., "Kontinuität, Rückbesinnung und Anpassung. Die deutsche Europapolitik der 90-er Jahre," in M. Medick-Krakau (ed.), *Außenpolitischer Wandel in theoretischer und vergleichender Perspektive: Die USA und die Bundesrepublik Deutschland*, Baden-Baden, Nomos, 1999, pp. 203-225. Again, this underlines the political importance of strategies of establishing net-advantages for nation-states in order to change their behaviour.

[22] There is no doubt that the promotion of more and better global governance is not possible without major structural changes, management improvements, and revitalisation of the UN system, which goes far beyond existing efforts.

elites are neither monolithic nor unable to adapt when it comes to international cooperation.[23]

However, a strategy of EU-Japanese cooperation, both to promote better and common global governance, as well as to support or educate the US to participate constructively in – or at least to tolerate – such policies will meet threefold resistance:

- The first type of resistance will come from the inside. Both the EU's interrelation between national and supranational interests and Japan's mix of national interest projection, participation in Asian-Pacific regionalisation, general multilateralism such as through G8, and internationalism, such as in the UN are result of a balance of different interests, of a specific internal power con-stellation, and of the specific limits national organised societies set against too much internationalisation. Rapid and/or significant strengthening of global governance – even under the condition of a major EU and Japanese influence – would threaten such pro-files and balances and threaten traditional national sensitivities against too much of a loss of formal sovereignty. Gradualism, package-deal methods, and focussing on global issues, which promise to be solved quickly and with convincing advantages, can assist in such changes of mode and priorities in foreign poli-cies.

- The second type of resistance will come from those forces in the international system which are neither interested in improved global governance nor in closer trilateral cooperation. Malevolent governments such as in Iraq under Hussein, in the present North Korea, or in Cuba under Castro can continue only under condi-tions of insufficient global control or open conflicts between the major powers.[24] Short-sighted exploiters of environmental "liber-alism" or players, which support a lack of effective environ-mental global governance, are not interested either in US support for international regimes for the protection of the environment or in effective political global control. And political elites, like some in Africa, that violate international democratic norms and

---

[23] Recent examples can be found in the fundamental changes between the first and the second Reagan administration *vis-à-vis* East-West policies.

[24] A good example is the first Yugoslavian War – i.e. the Bosnia-Herzegovina conflict. Lack of cohesion in the Western alliance, differences and even political conflicts for that matter between strategies of EU member states, the EU, NATO, and OSCE, and an ambivalent US position towards continued engagement in Europe allowed – and even provoked – the malevolent behaviour of the parties responsible for militarising the conflict. Recent successes in the management of the North Korean conflict demonstrate the positive role of multilateral and, in particular, regional cooperation.

constitute a threat to world peace, are equally dismissive of the norm-oriented limitation of traditional national sovereignty and of US policies, which give priority to pacification and democratisation, against tactical coalition-building with non-democratic governments. They will not only try to postpone, limit, or block relevant EU and Japanese initiatives but will do their best to avoid a closer cooperation between the EU and Japan. This is because of its specific political effects in the above mentioned global problems as well as the basic change in the international power structure both between the EU, Japan, and the US as well as between the nation state and multilateral and in particular international organisations of national or even supranational character that such a change would entail. While in the past – and in particular during decolonisation, the dissolution of the Warsaw Pact, and the emergence of new nation-states after the implosion of the USSR – sovereignty was an important concept in defending, re-assuring, and stabilising national self-determination. Sovereignty, with its doctrine of non-intervention in domestic affairs are today still used to prevent the application of international standards and norms, both in domestic and foreign policies of malevolent nation-states.

– The third type of resistance will come from within the US. While EU member states and Japan have a positive post-World War II experience in limited sovereignty, binding multilateralism, and – for the EU – transfer of selected sovereignty towards supranational bodies, both the US elites as well as the US public do not have such positive experiences of de-nationalisation. The exploitation of perceptions of a hostile environment such as those created by the East-West conflict, rogue states, or international terrorism coupled with perceptions of incompetent and unwilling alliance partners not to mention of an incompetent and ineffective UN have produced a negative image of supra-, super-, and internationalism within the US. A second dynamic – that of domestic US power formation, which refers to unilateralism, military strength, and US leadership as a legitimate and necessary historical mission, leads to the same negative image of internationalism in all its forms. A recent example is the second war against Iraq. In addition to this nationalised pattern of foreign policy and its broad public support within the US political elites, the US rightly understand such a combination of better global governance combined with better EU-Japanese cooperation as a threat to the absolute and relative global power position of the US. Despite all the long-term advantages of a new trilateralism resulting from strong, active, and effective EU-Japanese cooperation, it is obvious that this would significantly limit or even end US unilateral global leadership and control. Having already suffered a decline in relative economic – and recently, in relative monetary – power a number of political forces in the US will resist any further reduction in general, and concerning global leadership in particular, even if this were in the long-term interests of the US. Therefore, such forces will not only struggle against multi- or re-multilateralisation and internationalisation of US policies but also against a closer EU-Japanese cooperation.[25] US and NATO policies against the establishment of a European Security and Defense Identity and the build-up even of a small EU military capability for crisis-intervention illustrate what could, and would happen in case of effective and close EU-Japanese cooperation.

Although anti-Americanism has always been an attractive tactic for political, economic, and socio-cultural populism, one has to be remember once again two important points. First – whatever criticism may be made of US policies – it is less the US than the malevolent nation-state, which creates the global problem. To blame the US for misguided action, inaction or insufficient action instead of simultaneously pointing to the source of the problem, constitutes both an analytical, as well as a political, mistake. Second – and as it has been underlined above – it would be a major political mistake to marginalise or to sidestep the US in all efforts for better global governance. US opposition would render such efforts not only ineffective but would alienate those political forces within the US which constitute important partners for these efforts. Dissociative tactics in specific issues, such as the newly-established international court to sanction crimes against human rights, the implementation of the Kyoto Protocol, or against a military solution of the problems of the Korean Peninsula may make sense and can stimulate learning processes within the US political elite if adequate political compensation for the US is provided. Dissociation from the US as a strategy would prove disastrous not only for EU and Japan but for the global community; it would significantly harm the interests of all and would prevent even limited progress towards better governance for many years to come.

Finally, one has to remind both the EU and Japan that a special responsibility for more and better globalism is not only a consequence of

---

[25] An interesting experience of just such a policy can be found in US reactions to EU-Latin American, including EU-MERCOSUR, biregionalism. The NATA, as well as the FTAA project, are directed against a growing US-Latin America-EU triangle relationship and aim to re-establish dependency from the US and US dominance in Latin America.

their own norms, their now decades-long civic traditions, and their legitimate search for a better life within and beyond their territories. It results also from their economic, political, and security interests in general and their relative global power position in particular. It must be remembered that improving global peace and security through success-ful de-militarising international politics would improve the influence of both as an economic-political powers. This would establish an accepted, legitimate, and effective common global control to deter malevolence, to prevent, manage, and solve conflicts, and to reduce the causes of military power projection. These are a necessary conditions for eco-nomic growth and social well-being in the international community in general, and in the EU and Japan in particular. Here, both the EU and Japan have a special historical responsibility and face a particular window of opportunity in today's international policies. Such a mission does not contradict, but rather complements legitimate economic and political interests in promoting better multilateral cooperation and global governance. Further, it does not threaten national identity and regionalisation but relates this to a global level of governance. It would enhance both the EU's and Japan's role and standing in the international community and could constitute a significant contribution to the idea of better common governance for a truly globalised global community.

CHAPTER 14

Global Governance, New Regionalism and Japan-EU Relations

Luk VAN LANGENHOVE
and Ana-Cristina COSTEA

*Director and Assistant to the Director
at the 'Comparative Regional Integration Studies'
programme of the United Nations University (UNU-CRIS)* [*]

This chapter analyses the impact of the 'new regionalism' development in Europe and the world on the Japan-EU relations during the last
decade. The main hypothesis is that during the last twelve years since
the signing of the 'Joint Declaration on Relations between The European Community and its member states and Japan', in July 1991,
Japan's encounter with 'new regionalism' (in the form of the EU)
opened Japan towards regional integration initiatives and paved the way
for a partnership going beyond economic issues and aiming to tackle
complex problems of global governance. In order to verify this hypothesis, EU-Japan relations will be analysed on three dimensions that can be
regarded as the essence of 'new regionalism': trade, security, and
governance of global regimes. The following sections will focus on:
i) Japan – EU as partners in trade, ii) Japan-EU as partners for
promoting peace and security, iii) Japan and EU as partners for the
implementation of global regimes. But first the concept of 'new regionalism' will be further introduced.

Regional integration and globalisation are the two phenomena challenging the existing global order based upon sovereign states at the
beginning of the 21st century. As underlined by Hettne, these two
processes "deeply affect the stability of the Westphalian state system,
thus contributing to both disorder and (possibly) a new global order."
(Hettne, 1999b:1). Today's states have lost a lot of their ability to
sovereignly organise their internal affairs and they have become one

---

[*] See www.cris.unu.edu.

amongst many different actors that shape the living environment of their citizens and the way the world order is organised. Global governance has to evolve nowadays in an international context deeply marked by the phenomenon of globalisation framed in a world-wide process of changing and evolving levels of governance between city-regions, states, macro-regions and the global level. Among those levels, the regional one seems to have acquired most of the competencies lost by the post-Westphalian modern state, in a world-wide move towards regionalism which has to be understood, among other things, as a reaction aiming to 'harness' globalisation.

Regional integration has acquired several meanings as successive waves of regionalism occurred during the last half century. After the Second World War, a first wave of regionalisation focused on trade liberalisation between neighbouring countries in order to spur inter-country transactions. This first wave emerged in Europe and was originally thought of as a tool for achieving and sustaining peace. But soon the economic motives became the dominant driving force. Not only did it became clear that a more integrated Europe could strengthen its position in the world economy, but the European integration process also proved to be quite positive for the development of the poorer countries and regions. Not surprisingly then, the European example – and especially its focus on economic integration – became a pattern copied all over the world. But, due to lack of success, many of those regional integration schemes died out in the late 1960s and early 1970s. Even in Europe itself, the integration process proceeded only slowly until the mid-1980s, when it was revived with the Single European Act. The renewed European integration project became an inspiration for a second renewed wave of integration projects all over the world. This current second wave of regionalism is different from the first one, as it is increasingly no longer about trade only, but presents itself as a "multidimensional form of integration which includes economic, political, social and cultural aspects and thus goes far beyond the goal of creating region-based free trade regimes or security alliances. Rather, the political ambition of establishing regional coherence and identity seems to be of primary importance." (Hettne, 1999a:xvi)

The *new regionalism* is a multi-faceted phenomenon, which touches a much wider range of policies than the 'old' trade-based regionalism, and aims to promote certain "world values" such as security, development, ecological sustainability with greater success than globalism (Hettne, 1999). Accordingly, the role of regionalism in global governance has become much more complex. New Regionalism fulfils nowadays at least eight important functions which could be grouped under three main headings: *trade, security* and *governance of global regimes.* (Van Langenhove, 2003:4):

- contribution to peace and security in the region;
- the creation of an appropriate enabling environment for private sector development;
- the strengthening of trade integration in the region;
- the development of strong public sector institutions and good governance;
- the reduction of social exclusion and the development of an inclusive civil society;
- the development of infrastructure programmes in support of economic growth and regional integration;
- the building of environment programmes at the regional level; and
- the strengthening of the region's interaction with other regions of the world.

The EU is the paradigm of the '*new regionalism*' *par excellence*, as it has managed to develop a model of integration that incorporates political elements in deep economic integration. Europe has built a complex multi-level governance system with a deep cooperation between states, with firm devolution of power within states and a strong supranational legal framework. The EU's evolution has gradually developed all the functions enumerated above and the European construction during the last decade, especially after the Treaty of Maastricht, has been directed towards the consolidation of the political integration, the increased interaction with other regions in the world and the affirmation of the region as a 'global actor' (Breherton and Vogler, 1999) aiming to have its say in global governance and to promote *new regionalism* worldwide.

Simultaneously, Japan has increased its role both regionally, in the ASEAN+3 framework, and globally, thorough its active promotion of sustainable development, aid policies, human rights, security and stability at UN level. Although justly considered as the regional superpower in the East Asian region, Japan's policy has not directly evolved towards building regional integration. It has nevertheless followed a path of adaptation to the new context of globalisation, increased role of regionalism and new challenges for global governance. The Japan-EU relationship during the last decade are a good example in this regard.

I. New Regionalism and Japan-EU Economic Relations

In the decades following the Second World War, the relationship between the EC/EU and Japan has been, as underlined by several authors, '*primarily economic*' (Steinert, 1985:42; Reiterer, 2003:85). That is why we will try to assess, first of all, the influence of 'new regionalism' on the Japan-EU relations in the economic field, following a threefold analysis, focusing on their interaction as partners at the bilateral, regional and global level.

Regional integration was conceived from the beginning as a tool for enabling free trade among the countries involved in this process. This was the main function of 'old regionalism', with the creation of Free Trade Areas (FTAs) inside which members removed tariffs against each other and kept their own barriers against non-members, and which could evolve in time into customs unions possessing a common external tariff against non-member countries. There has been a wide academic debate in the economic field aiming to measure the extent to which regional integration can increase free trade. At the beginning of "old regionalism," the creation of a FTA and a Customs Union (CU) were justified, in economic terms, as long as the trade creation induced by the tariff removal between member countries exceeded the trade diversion brought by the displacement of imports from low-cost third country producers to high-cost new FTA partners (Viener). The old regionalism theory was based on the concepts of trade creation and trade diversion derived from a partial equilibrium analysis of the welfare effects of tariff elimination.[1] The customs union theory can give no definitive answer as to which effect will predominate and it fails to take into account the dynamic effects of regional trade areas (RTAs) – arguably the most important in the long run.

'New regionalism' theory integrates the dynamic effects of economic integration, the interaction between trade and investment, and the role of institutional arrangements as incentives for regional integration.[2] A larger regional market provides the opportunities for economies of scale, stimulated competition and provides incentives for investment. Achieving economies of scale is very important for firms in small countries and especially in developing countries. Economies of scale may occur through product specialisation, enabling firms in two countries to specialise in particular product lines, instead of producing the full range (to rationalise production and to internationalise production). Perhaps the most important effect of a RTA is the stimulus to competition and investment, which it brings. Large firms in small countries protected by tariffs will lose their monopolistic quiet life as

---

[1]   The concept of old regionalism is built upon the seminal work of customs union theory by J. Viner (1950).

[2]   For the essentials of new regionalism theory, see R. Z. Lawrence (1996), *Regionalism, Multilateralism and Deep Integration*, Brookings Institution Press, Washington, and W. J. Ethier (2001), "Regional Regionalism," in S. Lahiri (ed.), *Regionalism and Globalization Theory and Practice*, Routledge, London.

border protection falls, forcing them to compete in the larger market. The investment stimulus will include foreign direct investment (FDI), which brings added competition.

Following successive trade liberalisation in the GATT/WTO, FDI has become much more important in the global economy, as investment flows are now growing faster than trade flows. Firms have an incentive to switch from trade to FDI when trading costs (transport costs and government regulatory barriers) are high and investment costs (including communications costs) are rapidly declining. The size of the market is another factor which encourages FDI. Experience shows that as countries converge in their factor endowments, technical efficiency and market size, there will be a move from intra-industry trade to intra-industry investment, provided that transport costs remain significant.

The development of economic integration in the European Community from the late 1950s to the 1980s has followed the path of the 'old' economic regionalism with the removal of the tariff barriers and the creation of a Customs Union. This has resulted in an increased intra-EC trade but the persistence of an important number of non-tariff barriers was still considerably affecting the economic exchanges. During this period, Japan-EC relations were quite tense and dominated by several trade conflicts. The evolution towards 'new regionalism', determined by the structural changes in the global economy of the 1990s and brought about by globalisation, has undoubtedly brought an important impetus to Japan-EU trade relations.

A. Bilateral Level

With the fall of the Berlin Wall and the creation of the Single Market at the beginning of the last decade, bilateral economic relations between the EC/EU and Japan have increased, intensified not only at the level of the cooperation of policy-makers in different political *fora*, but also at the level of the informal business community contacts, and through an increase in trade flows. The 1991 'Joint Declaration on Relations between the European Community and its member states and Japan', established a framework of dialogue and consultations on several topics, among which market access and the removal of "obstacles whether structural or other, impeding the expansion of trade and investment, on the basis of comparable opportunities". The Japan-EU Action Plan from 19 July 2001, established a long-term partnership having among its four main objectives '*The Strengthening of the Economic and Trade partnership Utilising the Dynamism of Globalisation for the Benefit of All*' in bilateral relations and in multinational *fora* including the WTO.

With the achievement of the Single Market project, the EU has consolidated its position of the 'world's largest trading entity' with a share of global imports and exports at around 20% (Breherton and Vogler, 1999:48) and has offered external partners like Japan the prospect of trading with an economic entity with a unified set of rules and standards. The Japanese traditional fear of "Fortress Europe" started gradually to wane, and trade has considerably increased during the period from 1993 to 2001, when, according to Debroux, Japan's exports to the European Union increased "by over 40% between 1993 and 2001 from 50.1 billion euro to 72.3 billion. However, the European exports to Japan almost doubled from 28.8 billion euro to 53.7 billion euro during the same period. In 2001, Japan's trade surplus with the European Union amounted to 2.4 trillion yen (about 22 billion euro), a decrease of 29.1% as compared to the year 2000 (Eurostat, 2002)." (Debroux, 2003:102)

Additionally, the expansion of European regionalism, with the current Enlargement of ten new members seems to be positively perceived by both the EU and Japan as an opportunity for increased trade. On the EU's side, the main arguments brought forward underline the opportunities for Japanese firms of targeting a larger market, with the extension of the EU set of rules and high standards to the new members, and clear prospects for Japan's benefit in areas such as manufacturing, automotive, electronics and IT (European Commission, 2003:6-7). The 12[3] Japan-EU Summit held in Athens in May 2003,[3] underlined the beneficial impact of the Enlargement on Japan-EU trade, but at the same time highlighted the complexity of this process and the necessity for consultations between the two partners. Japan's position on enlargement is therefore slightly more prudent: the EU-Japan Business Dialogue Round Table which gathered the same month in Brussels noted the potential of the EU's enlargement for growth and investment and 'stressed the importance of ensuring that the Enlargement would benefit both EU and Japan'.[4]

Another important evolution in economic relations between Japan and the EU has taken place in the field of FDI, which, as underlined above, has increased in importance with the changes of the global economy in the 1990s. During the years following the 1997 Asian financial crisis, which deeply affected the Japanese economy, the EU became the main investor in Japan, following what Labohm described as a "paradigm shift in Japan investment – it is not seen as an invasion of home turf but *inter alia* as a tool to save bankrupt Japanese compa-

---

[3]   12th EU-Japan Summit, *Joint Press Statement*, Athens, 1-2 May 2003.

[4]   EU-Japan Business Dialogue Round Table, *New Challenges for Sustaining Growth and Competitiveness: Promoting Mutual Investment and Securing Benefits from EU Enlargement. Recommendations to the Leaders of the EU and Japan*, Brussels, 27-28 May 2003.

nies and expose the Japanese companies to more competition and increase technology transfer." (Labohm, 2001:37)

Nevertheless, although Japan has opened more to European exports and FDI, its economy is still a very closed one. In this context, the Regulatory Reform Dialogue, undertaken between the EU and Japan on an annual basis since 1994, aimed to unlock some of the barriers faced by EU trade and FDI in Japan (and simultaneously to answer Japanese concerns regarding EU regulations). Starting from 1st January 2002, the EU-Japan Mutual Recognition Agreement allowed for acceptance of conformity assessment conducted in one party according to the regulations of the other in four product areas. The opening of the Japanese economy will be, without a doubt, a long-term process. While welcoming the recent positive developments in the areas of legal services, competition policy and the investment environment, the *EU Priority Proposals for Regulatory Reform in Japan*,[5] from 16 October 2003, continued to press for the further improvement of the business environment and the reduction of the burden of regulation.

B. Regional Level

The expansion of the 'new regionalism' world-wide and co-operation between Japan and the EU seem to have increased Japan's acknowledgement of the importance of regional integration for trade, although this country has been traditionally reticent about getting too closely involved in the emerging Asian regionalization trend. Very recently, the Deputy Director-General of the Economic Affairs Bureau of the Japanese Ministry of Foreign Affairs noted that Japan is currently going through a shift in its trade policy towards FTA approval, following the tide of formation of new FTAs in Asia. According to Watanabe, the Japanese proposals of FTAs with Singapore, Mexico and South Korea which have been carefully planned in the recent years stem from three main motivations:

One is that the East Asian region has become increasingly important to Japan in recent years. Some 30% of Japanese imports from other parts of Asia are exports of Japanese-affiliated firms, making them "reverse imports." Such tightening of relationships among markets constitutes an important facet of institutional integration through arrangements like FTAs.

The second impetus of the shift to a stratified trade policy is the spreading recognition among Japanese business leaders that abstaining from regional integration has drawbacks. This point is often made in reference to Mexico. The third factor is the rising expectation that FTAs can reinvigorate the

---

5   European Commission, *EU Priority Proposals for Regulatory Reform in Japan*, Brussels, 16 October 2000, http://jpn.cec.eu.int/english/eu-relations/proposals.pdf.

Japanese economy and boost its competitiveness. The experiences of the EU and NAFTA demonstrate that national economies can become more dynamic. (Watanabe, 2003:6)

The relations between ASEAN and Japan have also considerably evolved during the last five years. After the 1997 Asian crisis, Japan was the largest bilateral donor of official development assistance (ODA) for ASEAN, with $ 2.1 billion accounting for 60% of the overall DAC countries' assistance[6] for the region. In October 2003, the 9th ASEAN Summit, held in Bali, adopted the Declaration of ASEAN Concord II (Bali Concord II) establishing the goal of creating an ASEAN Community supported by three pillars, which should be put in place by 2020: the ASEAN Security Community, the ASEAN Economic Community (AEC) and the ASEAN Socio-Cultural Community. The ASEAN Economic Community aims to create a free trade area characterised by "free flow of goods, services, investment and a freer flow of capital, equitable economic development and reduced poverty,"[7] by reducing tariff and non-tariff barriers and accelerating regional integration in eleven key areas. The creation of this AEC, which was of the utmost importance, brought into discussion at the Seventh "ASEAN+3" Summit, also held in Bali, the possible creation of free trade zones with China in 2010, India in 2011 and Japan in 2012. Assuming that these negotiations come to a successful conclusion, the resulting economic community will comprise almost half of the world's population. The leaders of the governments of Japan, China and South Korea concluded a tripartite agreement on economic cooperation in this framework.

C. Global Level

The transformations of the global economy, brought about by the dual process of globalisation and the development of 'new regionalism', have increased the cooperation between Japan and EU, aiming to tackle the problems of global trade governance at the beginning of the 21st century. As underlined by Owada, the cooperation between Europe and Japan in the management of the world economy was mentioned already in Prime Minister Fukuda's speech during his visit to Brussels on 19 July 1978. At that time the aim was the fight against global recession and "at a more fundamental level, maintenance and development of an open international economic system, promotion of economic cooperation with developing countries and securing of a stable flow of

---

[6]   Source: Minister of Foreign Affairs of Japan, *ASEAN-Japan: Acting Together – Advancing Together*, www.mofa.gov.

[7]   Association of Southeast Asian Nations, *Declaration of ASEAN Concord II* (Bali Concord II), § B.1, Bali, 7 October 2003, http://www.aseansec.org/15159.htm.

raw materials and energy resources". (Owada, 2001:15) In July 1991, the 'Joint Declaration on Relations between the European Community and its member states and Japan' mentioned the aim for both parties of 'pursuing cooperation aimed at achieving a sound development of the world economy and trade, particularly in further strengthening the open multilateral trading system, by rejecting protectionism and recourse to unilateral measures and by implementing GATT and OECD principles concerning trade and investment'.[8] This priority was reiterated in the second objective of the 2001 *Action Plan for EU-Japan Cooperation* under which Japan and the EU commit themselves to reinforcing co-operation on multilateral trade and economic issues and select three main initiatives to be launched immediately: a) the strengthening of the multilateral trading system by ensuring a successful outcome of the Doha Round; b) the facilitation of the accession of existing applicants, such as China, to the WTO; and c) the "close cooperation on how best to integrate developing countries fully into the multilateral trading system, including through trade-related technical assistance for the least developed, and initiatives such as the EU's 'Everything but Arms' initiative or other improved forms of market access for less developed countries."[9]

Beyond rhetoric and declarations of intent, what have been the concrete achievements of this partnership so far? The most successful Japan-EU actions to date were in the field of promoting the accession of existing applicants to the WTO, such as China and Taiwan in December 2001. Although the EU-Japan bilateral efforts worked in favour of the adoption of the Doha Development Agenda at the November 2001 Quatar Ministerial Meeting, the two partners determination to maintain their agricultural subsidies at the Cancún Ministerial did not favour a successful outcome to the negotiations. Agriculture was the main issue discussed at Cancún in September 2003, with a strong position from the developing countries asking for the elimination of the trade-distorting practices such as domestic support, obstacles to market access and export subsidies. Faced with the persistent retention of farm subsidies by developed countries, the poor countries refused to extend the negotiations to new topics and especially the Singapore issues as proposed by EU and Japan. The Cancún failure has seriously put into question the efficiency of the WTO as an institution and the effectiveness of multilateralism as a method of negotiation in international trade.

---

[8] *Joint Declaration on Relations between The European Community and Its Member States and Japan*, 18 July 1991, Brussels, p. 2.

[9] European Union-Japan Summit, *Shaping our Common Future. An Action Plan for EU-Japan Cooperation*, Brussels, 2001, p. 14.

It is difficult for Europe and Japan to promote trade liberalisation worldwide while at the same time protecting their own agriculture industries. In the long-run, what is maybe more important is the fact that both partners have reached a common position on the negotiations, due to their constant consultation since 1998, as well as the fact that Japan's position regarding the role of regionalism in the WTO context has evolved. The question whether regional trading arrangements hinder or contribute to the good functioning of the multilateral trading system is a very interesting one. In the EU's external trade policy vision, the widening and deepening of the European regional integration is not at all incompatible with multilateralism. In Pascal Lamy's terms, EU trade policy works on two complementary levels: the *bilateral/regional* level and the *multilateral level*, through the WTO:

> regionalism and multilateralism are not mutually exclusive but complementary: regional arrangements are governed by the multilateral rules and disciplines of the WTO. How do we strike a balance between the bilateral/regional level and the multilateral level? The multilateral level, through the WTO, provides the set of rules that international trade requires and a level playing field. More importantly, this is the framework that gives the EU the best means to influence global governance and to negotiate balanced arrangements. (Lamy, 2002:1)

Although continuing to be concerned over the possible negative effects of the FTAs on the multilateral system, the Japanese position has shifted due to the arguments already presented above in favour of FTA creation, and already conceives a new division of tasks between regionalism and multilateralism in world trade:

> Future trade liberalisation within East Asia is likely to be driven forward mainly by FTAs, while trade among the world's three big regions – North America (NAFTA), Europe (the EU) and East Asia – will be governed by the MFN principle of the WTO. This may give rise to a division of roles between regionalism and multi-lateralism. The trade between the three major regions, which amounts to about one-third of total world trade, is already carried out on an MFN basis. As long as this "tri-polar trade" proceeds freely and openly, FTAs and other forms of regional integration should work to the benefit of the world economy overall. (Watanabe, 2003:6)

'New regionalism' has therefore strongly influenced the Japan-EU economic interactions at the bilateral-, regional-, and global level. But the trade/economic dimension was not the only one affected by this phenomenon.

II. New Regionalism and Japan-EU Peace and Security Cooperation

The increasing role of regional integration organisations as an instrument for peace and security in the 1990s is another characteristic feature of the 'new regionalism'. This evolution was due to the change of the definition of security in the aftermath of the Cold War. The security agenda has shifted from a bipolar confrontation to the spread of regional and local "low intensity conflicts". At the same time, the security threats are no longer linked simply to military conflicts but also to political, economical, social and even environmental concerns, expressed in the term of "societal security" coined by the Copenhagen School at the beginning of the 1990s. (Weaver, 1993; Buzan, 1993; Wiberg, 1993). This shift in the content of security has brought about a change in the nature of international action, mainly UN-led, from classical operations of peace-keeping (mainly consisting in the interposition between parties in conflict) to second-, and even third generation operations, focusing on peace building after the end of conflicts and peace enforcement. The new security agenda became "considerably less monolithic and global, and considerably more diverse, regional and local, in character than the old one." (Buzan, 1999:12)

Aware of this transformation of the security agenda, several regional initiatives have extended their functions from economy to cooperation in security-related problems. The EC is a good example in this sense, as it has followed the path towards achieving a political union and creating, with the Treaties of Maastricht and Amsterdam, a Common Foreign and Security Policy pillar which aspires to give Europe the opportunity to act as a fully-fledged 'global actor'. But this was not an easy task, even for a strong regional integration scheme like the EU. As shown by its 'low profile' in Yugoslavia and the Middle East crises, the EU was confronted with a *capabilities-expectations gap* (Hill, 1993:315; Hill, 1998a:23; Peterson, 1998:5-7) brought about by the lack of a valid military capability to support its policy goals. Following the 1998 Saint-Malo Declaration, which removed the UK veto on defence, letting 'the genie out of the bottle' (Howorth, 2000:10), the Cologne and Helsinki summits focused on the achievement of the '*headline goal*' of creating a European Rapid Reaction Force. But the emerging European security and defence policy (ESDP) is still confronted with several problems, such as the problem of resources (Howorth, 2000:47), the lack of cooperation between the European defence industries (Schmitt, 2000), the need to avoid duplication (Heisbourg, 2000:53), and, most of all, the need to clarify the relationship with NATO. Following the 2001 Gothenburg Council, given the difficulties in the build-up of military capabilities, and the widening of the concept of security, the EU also set up a

Conflict Prevention and Peace Building Capacity and, at the same time, widened the scope of such actions extending crisis management beyond military and police measures to development cooperation and conditionality of aid (Laakso, 2002).

Japan-EU cooperation in security matters has been influenced, as underlined by Drifte, by their sharing of "a more comprehensive concept of security in contrast to the US which tends to define security in a narrow military sense" (Drifte, 2003:113) as well as their striving for the maintenance of multilateralism. Although trying to build up its own military capabilities, during the 1990s the EU kept its main dimension of 'civilian power', more successful in soft security matters, while trying to promote specific values through the political conditionality elements comprised in the development cooperation and Europe agreements, as well as the spreading of its model of regional integration worldwide. Similarly, Japan's foreign policy focused on the promotion of 'human security' and the avoidance of military involvement outside its own borders.

The Japan-EU relationship has become more complex and has surpassed traditional economic relations with the Hague 1991 Joint Declaration, specifically in that period when, taking advantage of the opportunities offered by the end of the Cold War, the European Community was enacting the structural transformations mentioned above on the path towards what was to become the first example of 'new regionalism'. The Hague Joint Declaration mentioned the objective of enhancing policy consultation and policy coordination on "the international issues which might affect world peace and stability, including international security matters such as the non-proliferation of nuclear, chemical and biological weapons, the non-proliferation of missile technology and the international transfer of conventional weapons,"[10] stipulating in this regard, the creation of a multi-level system of diplomatic contacts. Ten years later, following the incentive contained in Prime Minister Kono's Paris speech in January 2000, the promotion of peace and security has become the main objective of the Japan-EU Action Plan, the new partnership between Japan and the EU. The Action Plan enumerated a wide range of issues to be addressed by both parties, such as: the strengthening of the UN system, arms control, disarmament and non-proliferation, the promotion and the protection of human rights, democracy and stability, conflict prevention and peace building, along with specific regional security issues.

---

[10] Joint Declaration on Relations between the European Community and Its Member States and Japan, The Hague, 18 July 1991.

Issues such the reform of the Security Council and the strengthening of the UN are still problematic. Concrete results of cooperation have been more visible in the field of conflict prevention and peace building, often coinciding with interventions in each other's region. Since 1999, Japan has been a solid partner of the EU in the Stability Pact for South Eastern Europe and a major donor in the Balkans, supporting the peace building and peace consolidation in this area. By its participation in the Korean Peninsula Energy Development Organisation (KEDO), and its involvement in East Timor, Cambodia, Sri Lanka, and Afghanistan, the EU has supported the process of reducing tensions in Japan's proximate neighbourhood, although its financial contribution is still meagre, compared to the US$ 1bn of Japanese aid in the Balkans. Also, in the framework of the new partnership drawn up in the Action Plan, the two partners consult each other on their diplomatic actions concerning specific topics such as Russia, China, or the Middle East peace process.

The influence of 'new regionalism' on Japan's global promotion of stability is also visible in the Japanese efforts supporting regional organisations in Africa. Through its foreign policy, Japan has tried to enhance the conflict prevention capabilities of several regional organisations in Africa, perceiving regionalism in the African context as a potential tool for peace and good governance. This strategy is visible both at supra-regional continental level, in Japan's sustained support of the New Partnership for Africa's Development (NEPAD) and the Conflict Prevention Management Mechanism of the Organisation of African Unity (OAU), and, at sub-continental level, where Japan's activities aimed to improve the human security capacity of regional organisations such as the Economic Community of Western African States (ECOWAS) and for Southern African Development Community (SADC).

The security cooperation between the EU and Japan has considerably increased during the last decade, influenced by the new security challenges and by the new foreign policy building of the EU. However, although the two partners have great potential for safeguarding peace and security globally, there are still weaknesses which seem to currently affect their capabilities and their visibility in international crises.

First, both the EU and Japan are perceived as '*civilian powers*' focusing on peace building and stabilisation, as 'payers' rather than 'players' in the international system. These are rather negative connotations associated with what was originally a positive concept developed by François Duchêne in the 1970s, who considered that 'More and more, security policies today, even for super-powers, consist in shaping the international *milieu* often in areas which at first sight have little to do with security' (Duchêne, 1972:43). The EU and Japan have acquired a certain leadership status in non-military areas or 'soft security': international trade, development aid, environmental negotiations and the promotion of regional cooperation. But this seems not to be enough to increase their efficiency and their visibility on the international scene. One solution would be to launch a more active cooperation at the stage of conflict resolution, rather than in the post-conflict peace building process (Keukeleire, 2001:181; Shinyo, 2003:8).

Presence on the ground often increases the visibility and the efficiency of the security actors. In Europe's case, the achievement of a 'package of capabilities' combining 'soft power' and 'hard power' elements could allow the EU to promote a unique vision of international affairs, in which multilateralism would prevail over unilateralism, and a specific strategy of conflict prevention, where civilian aspects prevail over the military considerations. But in this regard we are still a long way before such a package could be obtained. The EU's good results in the first Rapid Reaction Force Mission in Macedonia are a good stimulus for future action. Japan has also registered a certain shift in its strategy, by launching on 26 January, 2004, its first mission to supply humanitarian assistance in Iraq. This has nevertheless encountered a strong public opposition, as it runs counter to a strong tradition of defence-oriented security policy. Therefore, in the short-term, as underlined by Reiterer, the only realistic solution for Japan and the EU is to concentrate on continuing their political partnership by putting the accent on conflict prevention cooperation, particularly 'through know-how related to "soft power"' (Reiterer, 2003:101).

Second, the Japan-US alliance is visibly stronger than the Japan-EU one. As underlined by the Japanese Foreign Ministry policy objectives, among the country's three main security pillars, first comes firmly maintaining the Japan-US security arrangements, followed by "(2) building up Japan's defence capability on an appropriate scale; and (3) pursuing diplomatic efforts to ensure international peace and security".[11] The EU is therefore not the main priority in security cooperation. Moreover, as underlined by Shinyo: "Most of the EU countries and Japan are allies of the US and share similar security concerns. If, however, there were to be differences between the US and the EU over their security interests, or the approach to vital security issues, Japan would find it difficult to share a common strategy with the EU." (Shinyo, 2003:8)

Third, as highlighted by Keukeleire in his 2001 analysis of the EU-Japan partnership in crisis management and stabilisation, the co-

---

[11] Ministry of Foreign Affairs of Japan, *Japan's Diplomatic Bluebook 2003*, p. 120, http://www.mofa. go.jp/policy/other/bluebook/2003/chap3-a.pdf.

operation in this field is also affected by internal factors, such as organisational and bureaucratic barriers. These are especially relevant on the EU's side, where the complexities of the Common Foreign and Security Policy (CFSP) formulation make EU-Japan cooperation often "frustrating" for Japan: "One example is the issue of the reform of the UN Security Council. Discussions on this important subject have been conducted for more than 10 years, but in vain. One of the main reasons could be found in the tug-of-war among EU countries." (Shinyo, 2003:8).

Despite these obstacles, there is enough evidence that the development of 'new regionalism' in Europe has brought the Japan-EU relations to an upper level, paving the way to the creation of a partnership aiming to promote peace and security in the world. As noted by Drifte, both Europe and Japan have advantages in cooperating in the security field, and by further exploiting their common positions, they can maximise their gains:

> EU-Japan political cooperation enhances the foreign policy leverage and scope of both sides, facilitates a more global reach and enables a better response to allied burden sharing demands. However, as the Iraq case clearly shows, each side is hampered by its different domestic and external circumstances in more fully exploiting synergies deriving from cooperation. Nevertheless, the gains still warrant greater efforts to tap potential synergies. (Drifte, 2003:118)

Beyond trade and security, the role of regional integration initiatives has become increasingly important by actively contributing to the construction of global governance regimes aiming to tackle the new challenges brought by globalisation. A strong EU-Japan cooperation has also developed in the field of global environmental governance, and especially in the field of the fight against climate change.

III. New Regionalism and Japan-EU Cooperation in Global Climate Change Governance

Another important characteristic of the 'new regionalism' is that regional integration initiatives are becoming increasingly important elements for implementing global governance regimes. Their situation as an intermediary level between the national and the global has brought macro-regions, together with national, micro-regional and global levels, as necessary for the efficient implementation of global regimes. Globalisation has brought transnational flows and a number of challenges, which reach beyond the traditional functions of the states. Although there is a need to find global solutions to global problems, there is not sufficient global support for global institutions and regimes to deal with such problems, and regional initiatives could lead the way in the implementation of policies until such a consensus is reached.

The climate change regime is a good example in this regard. Since the first conference on the Environment in Stockholm in 1970, the United Nations (UN) have played a leading role in developing a global approach to environmental problems and in creating common platforms of action on environmental issues. The UN pioneered the creation of a global climate change regime in 1992, with the Rio Earth Summit, which was a catalyst for public recognition of the planetary nature of environmental problems. The Rio Summit gave birth to the Framework Convention on Climate Change (UNFCCC), which aimed to stabilise CO_2 emissions in industrialised countries at 1990 levels by the year 2000, to set up global monitoring and reporting mechanisms for keeping track of greenhouse gas emissions, and establish national programmes for reducing emissions.

The UNFCCC entered into force in 1994 and under its framework the Kyoto Protocol (KP) was developed at the COP-3 in December 1997, setting the target for the developed world to reduce its greenhouse gas emissions to 5% below 1990 levels between 2008 and 2012. Four other Conferences of the Parties to the UNFCCC have followed so far. However, the Kyoto Protocol has not yet become a global regime: it is not yet ratified globally and the 'rules of the game' for the reduction of greenhouse gases are still unclear. The collapse of the COP-6 negotiations in The Hague in November 2000 and the repudiation of the Protocol by the US administration in March 2001 could have entirely compromised the move towards a global regime tackling global warming. Nevertheless, after the US withdrawal from the negotiations the EU has been catapulted into the role of global leadership. The EU has managed to maintain the determination of the UNFCCC participants to work towards the implementation of the Kyoto Protocol. It has successfully pushed for the political commitment enshrined in the "Bonn Agreements," adopted in July 2001, and for concrete results in the following technical negotiations in Marrakech COP-7 (November 2001) and New Delhi COP-8 (October 2002).

In its internal Climate Change policy, the EU has done some very good work, going even further than the obligations of the Kyoto Protocol: the fifteen member states have shown their commitment to contribute to the global target by making a bigger cut, of 8% below the 1990 level. Through the European climate change programme (ECCP) launched in June 2000, the EU has worked towards implementing the three flexible mechanisms introduced by the Kyoto Protocol: the creation of an Internal Emissions Trading System through a '*burden-sharing*' agreement between the member states, the Joint Implementation of projects designed to cut emissions in other industrialised countries, and the Clean Development Mechanism (CDM) which aims to help financially projects in developing countries.

EU's "climate change leadership" (Gupta & Grubb, 2000) has influenced Japan's position regarding climate change. The third main objective of the 2001 Japan-EU Action Plan of "coping with global and societal changes" launched a partnership going much further than climate change, and encompassing all the relevant conventions on environmental issues adopted since the 1992 UN Conference on Environment and Development, as well as the wider topic of sustainable development. Japan ratified the Kyoto Protocol after long negotiations, on 4 June 2002, engaging to cut its emissions by 6% from the 1990 level between 2008 and 2012, even though this required important efforts and debates at national level. The Japanese government has since worked as a strong partner of the EU in promoting the efficient implementation of the Kyoto Protocol, both at global and regional level.

At global level, in order to ensure the enactment of the Kyoto Protocol, Japan is actively campaigning in order to secure Russia's ratification of the accord.[12] With the Russian ratification, the threshold of Annex I Parties, accounting for at least 55% of the total carbon dioxide emissions in 1990 would be reached and this will allow for the entry into force of the Protocol. At the regional level, the EU's efforts of implementing an efficient multi-layered environmental governance system at regional level can offer an incentive for Japan to enhance its leadership role in South-East Asia. Researchers already hope that the EU's Emissions Trading System, viewed as a model of equity between poor and rich countries, could be taken as an example and other regional burden-sharing schemes could be negotiated. According to Aidt and Greiner, Japan could play such a role together with the South-Eastern Asian countries: "Japan and South-East Asia together with Australia and the Pacific island states as well as North and Latin America could form regional blocks. This form of regional grouping has the advantage that national particularities can be taken into account more appropriately and differentiated obligations can be negotiated" (Aidt and Greiner, 2002:18).

Although the US withdrawal from the Kyoto Protocol has strongly affected the credibility of this regime, the partnership between the EU and Japan, by maintaining the international commitment and obtaining further ratifications by key players, represents an important cornerstone for a future global climate change regime.

---

[12]   The Ministry of Foreign Affairs of Japan, *Request for Russia's Early Ratification of the Kyoto Protocol*, November 2003.

Conclusion

Japan-EU relations are evolving in a rapidly changing world. This chapter has highlighted three main aspects of those relations: trade, security and global governance. Europe, with its policy of enlargement and with its move towards new regionalism (meaning that it is heading towards a common foreign, security and defence policy) is emerging as one of the poles in world politics. Japan has a long tradition of commitment to multilateral trade but, since 1999, when it concluded a bilateral free trade agreement with Singapore, it has taken its first steps towards regionalism. More recently, the ASEAN + 3 evolutions have shown that new regionalism is no longer a purely European endeavour.

We are clearly moving towards a multipolar world with, at this moment, three 'engines': US, Japan and the EU. But while the present EU-15 has a GDP of about € 8.5 billion and the GDP of the US is more than € 10.6 billion, Japan has a GDP of only € 5.6 billion (Eurostat figures for 2000). In terms of population, Japan counts 127 million people, the US, 278 million and the EU-15, 377 million. These figures show the economic and demographic importance for Japan of further engagement in regional integration. With Debroux (2003), one can pose the question to what extent Japan is economically, politically and even psychologically prepared for a far-reaching regional integration under its leadership. The evolutions briefly described in this article seem to indicate that Japan is indeed increasingly playing such a role. This opens interesting prospects for a world-order that is based upon a balance of power and upon inter-regional and intra-regional cooperation.

References

Aidt, T., Greiner, S., "Sharing the Climate Policy Burden in the EU," *HWWA Discussion Paper* 176, Hamburg Institute of International Economics, 2002.

Berkofsky, A., "Japan's New 'Assertive Foreign Policy' and US-Japan Security Relations," *EurAsia Bulletin*, Vol. 5, Nos 6&7, June-July 2001, pp. 3-7.

Bretherton, C. and Vogler, J., *The European Union as a Global Actor*, Routledge, London, 1999.

Buzan, B., "The Logic of Regional Security in the Post-Cold War World," in B. Hettne, A. Inotai and O. Sunkel (eds.), *The New Regionalism and the Future of Security and Development*, Macmillan, London, 2000, pp. 1-25.

Debroux, P., "Japan-EU Economic Relationship: The Evolving Pattern," paper presented at the International Symposium "The Creation of a New Japan-EU Relationship after the Enlargement of the EU," organised by the Institute for Research in Contemporary Political and Economic Affairs, at the Waseda University, Tokyo, 16-17 May 2003, pp. 102-110.

Drifte, R., "A European view of contemporary EU-Japan relations," paper presented at the International Symposium "The Creation of a New Japan-EU

Relationship after the Enlargement of the EU," organised by the Institute for Research in Contemporary Political and Economic Affairs, at the Waseda University, Tokyo, 16-17 May 2003, pp. 111-118.

European Commission, *Enlargement of the European Union: The Implications for Japan*, Brussels, September 2003.

Falk, R., "Regionalism and World Order After the Cold War," in B. Hettne, A. Inotai and O. Sunkel (eds.), *Globalism and the New Regionalism*, Macmillan, London, 1999, pp. 228-250.

Forsberg, T., "Japanese-Russian Relations and the Territorial Dispute from the Point of View of the EU," in T. Ueta and É. Remacle (eds.), *Japan-EU Cooperation: Ten Years after the Hague Declaration, Studia Diplomatica*, Vol. LIV, Nos 1-2, Institut royal des relations internationales, Bruxelles, 2001, pp. 203-217.

Gavin, B., and Van Langenhove, L., "Trade in a World of Regions," in G. P. Sampson and S. Woolcock (eds.), *Regionalism, Multilateralism and Economic Integration. The Recent Experience*, UNU Press, Tokyo, 2003, pp. 277-312.

Gupta, J., and Grubb, M., *Climate Change and European Leadership A Sustainable Role for Europe?*, Kluwer, The Hague, 2000.

Hettne, B., "The New Regionalism: A Prologue," in B. Hettne, A. Inotai and O. Sunkel (eds.), *Globalism and the New Regionalism*, Macmillan, London, 1999a, pp. xv-xxxi.

Hettne, B., "Globalization and the New Regionalism: The Second Great Transformation," in B. Hettne, A. Inotai and O. Sunkel (eds.), *Globalism and the New Regionalism*, Macmillan, London, 1999b, pp. 1-24.

Intarasuvan, P., "EU-Japan Business Dialogue Round Table Meets in Brussels," *EurAsia Bulletin*, Vol. 5, Nos 6&7, June-July 2001, pp. 6-9.

Joint Press Statement, *Twelfth Japan-EU Summit*, Athens, 1-2 May 2003.

Keukeleire, S. "The European Union and Japan: Partners in Global Crisis Management and Global Stabilisation?," in T. Ueta and É. Remacle (eds.), *Japan-EU Cooperation: Ten Years after the Hague Declaration, Studia Diplomatica*, Vol. LIV, Nos 1-2, Institut royal des relations internationales, Brussels, 2001, pp.159-185.

Kivimäki, T., "Regional Institution Building as a Tool in Conflict Prevention: An Overview of Empirical Generalisations," in L. Laakso (ed.), *Regional Integration for Conflict Prevention and Peace Building in Africa. Europe, SADC, and ECOWAS*, University of Helsinki, Department of Political Science, 2002, pp. 14-34.

Laakso, L. (ed.), *Regional Integration for Conflict Prevention and Peace Building in Africa. Europe, SADC, and ECOWAS*, University of Helsinki, Department of Political Science, 2002.

Laakso, L. "European Integration for Conflict Prevention and Peace-Building," in L. Laakso (ed.), *Regional Integration for Conflict Prevention and Peace Building in Africa. Europe, SADC, and ECOWAS*, University of Helsinki, Department of Political Science, 2002, pp. 34-45.

Labohm, H., "EU-Japan Cooperation in the Field of Trade: A Dash of Liberalization," in T. Ueta and É. Remacle (eds.), *Japan-EU Cooperation: Ten Years after the Hague Declaration, Studia Diplomatica,* Vol. LIV, Nos 1-2, Institut royal des relations internationales, Brussels, 2001, pp. 29-39.

Lamy, P., *Fifth EC/Candidate Countries Ministerial Conference on Trade – Opening speech,* Malta, 31 May-1 June 2002

Mathis, J., "Japan and the European Union, Resolving the WTO Regionalism Impasse," in T. Ueta and É. Remacle (eds.), *Japan-EU Cooperation: Ten Years after the Hague Declaration, Studia Diplomatica,* Vol. LIV, N°1-2, Institut royal des relations internationales, Brussels, 2001, pp. 39-59.

Mittelman, J. A., "Rethinking the 'New Regionalism' in the Context of Globalization," in B. Hettne, A. Inotai and O. Sunkel (eds.), *Globalism and the New Regionalism,* Macmillan, London, 1999, pp. 25-54.

Owada, H., "The Japan-EU Joint Declaration and Its Significance Towards the Future," in T. Ueta and É. Remacle (eds.), *Japan-EU Cooperation: Ten Years after the Hague Declaration, Studia Diplomatica,* Vol. LIV, Nos 1-2, Institut royal des relations internationales, Bruxelles, 2001, pp. 11-29.

Pettman, R., "Globalism and Regionalism: The Costs of Dichotomy," in B. Hettne, A. Inotai and O. Sunkel (eds.), *Globalism and the New Regionalism,* Macmillan, London, 1999, pp. 181-202.

Prodi, R., *The New Europe and Japan,* Speech to Keidanren at Keidanren Kaikan, SPEECH 21/2000 Tokyo, 19 July 2000.

Quigley, J., "The EU-Japan Political Relationship," *EurAsia Bulletin,* Vol. 5, Nos 6&7, June-July 2001, pp. 48-51.

Reiterer, M, "The Decade of Japan-EU Cooperation and EU-Enlargement – A New Challenge," paper presented at the International Symposium *"The Creation of a New Japan-EU Relationship after the Enlargement of the EU,"* organised by the Institute for Research in Contemporary Political and Economic Affairs, at the Waseda University, Tokyo, 16-17 May 2003, pp. 85-101.

Saito, M., "Japan's Russian Policy and CFSP of the European Union on Russia," T. Ueta and É. Remacle (eds.), *Japan-EU Cooperation: Ten Years after the Hague Declaration, Studia Diplomatica,* Vol. LIV, N°1-2, Institut royal des relations internationales, Brussels, 2001, pp. 185-203.

Shinyo, T., "EU-Japan Political-Security Cooperation," in *EurAsia Bulletin,* Vol. 7, No. 4, April 2003, pp. 7-10.

Söderbaum, F., "The Role of the Regional Factor in West Africa," in B. Hettne, A. Inotai and O. Sunkel (eds.), *The New Regionalism and the Future of Security and Development,* Macmillan, London, 2000, pp. 121-143.

Sung-Hoon, P., "East Asian Economic Integration – finding a balance between regionalism and multilateralism," EIAS Briefing Paper, European Institute for Asian Studies, Brussels, February 2002.

Telò, M., "Introduction: Globalization, New Regionalism and the Role of the European Union," in M. Telò (ed.), *European Union and New Regionalism,* Ashgate, Aldershot, 2001, pp. 1-20.

Telò, M., "Between Trade Regionalization and Deep Integration," in M. Telò (ed.), *European Union and New Regionalism,* Ashgate, Aldershot, 2001, pp. 71-96.

Telò, M., "The European Union, Regionalism and Global Governance," in T. Ueta and É. Remacle (eds.), *Japan-EU Cooperation: Ten Years after the*

Hague Declaration, Studia Diplomatica, Vol. LIV, Nos 1-2, Institut royal des relations internationales, Brussels, 2001, pp. 81-103.

Ueta, T., "Japan and the European Security Institutions," in T. Ueta and É. Remacle (eds.), *Japan-EU Cooperation: Ten Years after the Hague Declaration, Studia Diplomatica*, Vol. LIV, Nos 1-2, Institut royal des relations internationales, Brussels, 2001, pp. 131-149.

Van Ginkel, H., J. Court and L. Van Langenhove (eds.), *Integrating Africa: Perspectives on Regional Integration and Development*, United Nations University Press, Tokyo, 2003.

Van Langenhove, L., and Costea, A. C., "The Relevance of Regional Integration for Africa," Paper presented at the REGGEN 2003 Seminar "*Hegemonia e Contra-Hegemonia: Os Impasses da Globalização e os Processos de Regionalização*," 18th August 2003, Rio de Janeiro.

Van Langenhove, L., "Regional Integration and Global Governance," *UNUnexions*, August 2003, pp. 1-4.

Van Langenhove, L., and Costea, A. C., "Integrating Global and Regional Approaches to Climate Change," Paper presented at the one-day conference on "Globalism and Regionalism in Climate Policy, 25 September 2003, Montecatini.

Watanabe, Y., "FTA's and Japan's trade strategy," *EurAsia Bulletin*, Vol. 7, No. 4, April 2003, pp. 4-7.

CHAPTER 15

The Enlarged EU, Japan and the United States

Partners in a New Global Order?

Fraser CAMERON

Director of Studies at the European Policy Centre, Brussels

I. Introduction

Following the enlargement of the European Union (EU) on 1 May 2004 to 25 member states, the Union has a population of 450 million (compared to 272 million for the United States (US) and 126 million for Japan). The GDP of the EU is roughly equal to the US ($ 8,000 billion) and double that of Japan. The enlarged EU will have a new constitution, its own currency and will be playing an increasing role in global affairs.[1] At present, the EU, Japan and the US are three of the most important actors on the global stage. In the early 1990s there was much talk of the new trilateralism involving these three actors. There was perhaps more enthusiasm in Brussels and Tokyo for the trilateral concept than in Washington, yet George Bush Sr envisaged a key role for the three actors in his concept of a new World Order. The EU also saw the trilateral regime as the essential building block for wider multilateralism. In Japan it was viewed as a possible way to ease the country's strategic dependence complementing the bilateral military alliance with the US.[2] But little has been achieved in practice and few political leaders are pushing for such cooperation. Indeed Prime Minister Junichiro Koizumi

---

[1] I am grateful for comments by Axel Berkofsky on this chapter. See also F. Cameron (ed.), *The Future of Europe: Integration and Enlargement*, Routledge, London, 2004.

[2] See e.g. Hook, G. D., Gilson, J., Hughes, C. W., Dobson, H., *Japan's International Relations-Politics, Economics and Security*, Routledge, London, New York, 2001, pp. 66-67.

is committed to the maintenance and expansion of the bilateral military alliance with the US which, he argued, became all the more relevant after 9/11 and Japan's role in the US-led fight against international terrorism.[3] Despite apparent declining enthusiasm for the trilateral approach, it is nevertheless worth exploring the nature of these relations and examining what possibilities exist for cooperation in the new global agenda.

II. The Enlarged EU

After the historic events of the late 1980s and early 1990s, the fall of the Berlin Wall, the collapse of communism, and the end of Soviet domination, one of the first decisions of the countries of central and eastern Europe was to turn to the West for admission to the 'Euro-Atlantic' framework, in particular through membership of the EU and NATO. The reunification of Germany in 1990 effectively 'enlarged' the EU through the integration of the German Democratic Republic into its Western neighbour. The other former communist countries were determined to join the EU too, not only for symbolic reasons – as a return to the European family from which they had been separated in the aftermath of the war – but for basic political and economic reasons. In terms of security, they perceived EU membership as a supplement to NATO membership because of the powerful 'bonding' effect of its institutions and policies, and it would also bring economic gains through full access to the EU's market and budgetary receipts from its policies.[4]

The enlargement negotiations of 1998-2003 were thus the culmination of a historic process that brought the countries of central and eastern Europe back fully into the European political and economic sphere. Although they waited for more than a decade for membership of the EU, the time was needed for adequate preparation and the prospect of membership was instrumental in helping them to pursue reforms. The nego-

---

[3] Amongst many others see Sakamoto K., "Expanding the Scope of Japan-US Cooperation," *Japan Echo*, Vol. 30, No. 2 April 2003, pp. 17-19; Watanabe, H., "How to Be Pro-American," *Japan Echo*, Vol. 30, No. 2, April 2003, pp. 20-23; Halloran, R., "Shifting U.S. Alliances and the New Debate," *Gaiko Forum-Japanese Perspectives on Foreign Affairs Summer*, 2003, pp. 16-23; Mizukoshi, H., "Japan's Counter-Terrorism Policy," *Gaiko Forum-Japanese Perspectives on Foreign Affairs Summer*, 2003, pp. 53-63; Okamoto, Y., "Japan and the United States: The Essential Alliance," *The Washington Quarterly*, Vol. 25, No. 2, Spring 2002, pp. 59-72; Nabers, D., "Japan's Reaction to the Terrorist Attacks on Its Closest Ally," *NIASNytt, Nordic Newsletter of Asian Studies* 4/01; 8 January, 2002; Berkofsky, A., "Japanese Military Support for the U.S. Military Campaign," *RUSI Newsbrief*, December 2001, pp. 136-138

[4] Avery, G. and Cameron, F., *The Enlargement of the European Union*, Sheffield Academic Press, Sheffield, 1999.

tiations themselves, despite some frustration on the part of the applicant countries, were conducted without major setback, and concluded on time. As the EU's expansion continues, the process will not become easier, and, in retrospect, the preparation of the enlargement of 2004 will surely be seen as a considerable success.

Unlike the US and Japan, the EU is not a single nation state. It is a *sui generis* political and economic union with no clarity as to its final dimensions. The debate over widening and deepening continues. One certainty is that there will be further enlargements. There are doubts, however, on the modalities of further integration. Will the enlarged EU be able to move forward together or are we moving towards a multi-speed Europe? Another key issue is what role the enlarged EU will play on the world stage.

There are signs of a determination to increase EU influence. Partly due to the shock of the Iraq crisis, the EU agreed its first security strategy at the 2003 December European Council. The report, prepared by Javier Solana, the EU's High Representative for common foreign and security policy (CFSP), stated that the EU was not threatened by military attack from any other state or regional grouping. But security today is much more than the absence of any direct military threat. The EU's security could be threatened by instability in its immediate neighbourhood, interruption to its energy supplies, terrorist attack, the spread of Weapons of Mass Destruction (WMD) as well as a breakdown in the multilateral system that has developed since 1945. The EU's security is thus inextricably linked to developments in the global arena.

III. The United States of America

The USA is unquestionably the most important power in the world, in political, economic and, above all, in military terms. Described by former Secretary of State Madeleine Albright as "the indispensable nation," the US was a clear victor in the Cold War against Soviet communism. It is the only power which has a truly global reach and which maintains military bases in more than a hundred countries. It plays a dominant role in most international organisations despite a reluctance to embrace multilateralism. Following 9/11 the US is engaged in a global war on terrorism in which 'regime change' figures highly on the agenda. The removal of the Taliban regime in Afghanistan and Saddam Hussein in Iraq are two recent examples of US policy in operation. Now the Bush administration is talking of promoting regime change across the wider Middle East, a truly momentous task and one which arouses considerable scepticism in Europe and Japan.

271

Foreign policy has become more partisan in the past decade in the US since the dramatic changes in the 1994 Congress. The liberal internationalist wing of the Republican Party almost vanished overnight and the leaders in Congress displayed little enthusiasm for the UN or international bodies that might constrain Washington's ability to act unilaterally. President Clinton was an avowed multilateralist but he was handicapped by Republican opposition in Congress. President Bush rejected the Clinton approach and seemed to enjoy giving the message to Europe and Japan that the US was adopting a different tack.

There were hopes that after the shock of 9/11 the US approach would change. But Bush's emphasis on the 'axis of evil' and preference for military options dashed the hopes of multilateralists in Europe and Japan. The Iraq War was the biggest clash between these different policy attitudes.[5]

IV. Japan

Compared to the enlarged EU and the US, Japan is essentially a *status quo* power. Sheltered by the American nuclear umbrella for the past fifty years it became an economic giant while eschewing any global political and security pretensions, apart from its desire to gain a permanent seat on the UN Security Council.[6] It has frequently threatened to reduce its contributions (it is the second highest national contributor) if its demands are not met. In February 2004 the MFA announced Japan's intention to reduce its percentage contribution to the UN budget from 19.5% to 15% by 2006.[7] Furthermore, Japan demands that its name be removed from the UN's Charter's so-called "enemy clause." This remains a very emotional issue in Japan, which does not see why it should pay roughly a fifth of the UN budget, yet be classed as an "enemy state".

---

[5] For a view of the foreign policy debate see Gaddis, J. L., "A Grand Strategy of Transformation," *Foreign Policy*, Nov./Dec. 2002; Cameron, F., *US Foreign Policy after the Cold War*, Routledge, London, 2002; Daalder, I., and Lindsay, J. M., *America Unbound: The Bush Revolution in Foreign Policy*, Brookings, Washington, 2003.

[6] For a detailed analysis of Japan's bid for a permanent seat on the UN Security Council see e.g. Drifte, R., *Japan's Quest for Permanent Security Council Seat*, Macmillan/St. Anthony's College, London/Oxford 1999; Shinyo, T., "Security Council Reforms and Japan's Options," *Gaiko Forum – Japanese Perspectives on Foreign Affairs* November 2003, pp. 26-33; Satoh, Y., "Keep Pushing for Reform of the UN Security Council," in *Japan Echo*, Vol. 30, No. 6, Dec. 2003, pp. 35-39; also Hisane, M., "Japan Rethinks Strategy for Gaining Permanent UN Security Council Seat," *Japan Times*, 20 May 2002.

[7] See Nishiyama, George, *Japan Plans to Cut Contributions to United Nations*; Reuters, 22 January 2004.

Now Japan faces a number of difficult internal reform issues (political, economic and social) and is confronted by another potential superpower on its doorstep, China, plus a perceived threat from North Korea. Political, economic and social reforms remain largely unimplemented. Japan's banking crisis and the bad debt problem are unresolved.[8] At the same time, Tokyo has taken its first step towards international peace-keeping engagement with the sending of troops to Iraq in early 2004. This was done under heavy US pressure and would seem to indicate PM Koizumi's preference for bilateral ties, with the US in the first instance, than over any trilateral arrangements. It is worth noting that Japan had already sent troops to UN peace-keeping operations in the 1990s: first to Cambodia in 1992, then to the Golan Heights and to East Timor.[9] Dispatching troops to Iraq, however, was the first troop deployment to a country without specific UN authorisation. It was defined as a humanitarian mission, authorised by Japan's "Iraq Reconstruction Law."[10]

The bilateral US-Japan security alliance remains the cornerstone of Japan's security and defence policy (40,000 American troops stationed in Japan, of which 75% are on Okinawa). In recent years Japan has undertaken a number of initiatives (purchasing new military hardware, as well as signing up to US defence missile projects) boosting the country's capabilities to defend itself militarily.[11]

Officially, Japan is strongly committed to global (and regional) multilateralism and throughout the 1990s has been an advocate of regional and global multilateral institutions.[12] Until recently, Japan's policy-

---

[8]   See the Economist's coverage on Japan's banking crisis and Japan's economy in general; see e.g. "Bad for Koizumi, Good for Japan," *The Economist*, 13 November 2003; "Fixing Japan-Kill or Cure," *The Economist*, 25 September 2003; "A Pair of Deadbeats," *The Economist*, 18 September 2003; "The Only Way Is Up," *The Economist*, 27 February 2003; "The Non-Performing Country," *The Economist*, 14 February 2002;

[9]   See e.g. Ledgerwood, J. L., "UN Peacekeeping Missions: The Lessons from Cambodia, in Asia Pacific Issues," *Analysis from the East-West Center*, No. 11, March 1994, pp. 1-10

[10] Amongst many others see "Rebuild Iraq, Redefine Iraq," *The Economist*, 31 January 2004; Piling, D., "Japan Readies Ground Troop Dispatch to Iraq," *The Financial Times*, 7 January 2004; Funabashi, Y., "Koizumi Opens a Pandora's Box," *The Financial Times*, 7 January 2004.

[11] See e.g. Moffet, S., Fackler, "Marching on to a New Role," *The Far Eastern Economic Review (FEER)*, January 2004, pp. 18-21.

[12] See Ikenberry, J. G., Tsuchiyama, J., "Between Balance of Power and Community: The Future of Multilateral Security Cooperation in the Asia-Pacific," *International Relations of the Asia-Pacific*, Vol. 2, No. 1, 2002, pp. 69-94; Fukushima, A., *Japanese Foreign Policy: The Emerging Logic of Multilateralism*, Macmillan, London, 1999; Hook, G. D., "Japan and the ASEAN Regional Forum: Bilateralism, Multilateralism or Supplementarism?," *Japanstudien*, 10, 1998; Deutsches Institut

makers advocated the principle of "UN-centrism," a concept developed in the 1980s, as the key pillar of the country's diplomacy.[13] Japan's "UN-centrism," however, seemed to have lost its key role in the country's diplomacy after September 11 and US pressure on Tokyo to "unconditionally" support its war against global terrorism. Japan's support for the US-led war against Iraq without a UN mandate confirmed the judgement of many analysts and commentators that Japan seems prepared to support US unilateralism instead of multilateralist approaches towards international security.[14] However, in view of its economic and political multilateral commitments, it is unlikely that this approach remains sustainable for Japan.[15]

V. What Common Views?

Although there are many areas of dispute between the EU, US and Japan, it is also true that they have much more in common than divides them. The EU and US are more than close allies. The two sides of the Atlantic have common roots in the European enlightenment. They made common sacrifice of blood and treasure in defence of freedom in two world wars. The US and Europe also engaged together in the strategy and the structures largely conceived and implemented under US leader-

---

für Japanstudien, Tokyo, pp. 159-188; Hook, G. D., "The Japanese Role in the Emerging Asia-Pacific Order," in Legewie, J., Blechinger, V. (eds.), *Facing Asia-Japan's Role in the Political and Economic Dynamism of Regional Cooperation*; Monographien aus dem Deutschen Institut für Japanstudien, Tokio, Band 24, 2000, pp. 87-110.

[13] See Ueki, Y., "Japan's UN Diplomacy: Sources of Passivism and Activism," in Curtis, G. L. (ed.), *Japan's Foreign Policy after the Cold War-Coping with Change*, The East Asian Institute of Columbia University, East Gate Book, 1994, pp. 347-370.

[14] Japan "unconditionally" (as Japan's Prime Minister Junichiro Koizumi put it) supporting the US-led war against international terrorism caused significant controversy in Japan; criticism and controversy became even stronger when Prime Minister Koizumi supported the US-led war against Iraq and in December 2003 decided to dispatch Japanese military to southern Iraq to support the country's reconstruction; Japanese military started to be dispatched in January 2004 and will be providing humanitarian aid and funds for the reconstruction of infrastructure, hospitals, schools etc. in and around Samawah in southern Iraq; see e.g. "GSDF Advance Team for Iraq Gets Kanzaki's Nod," *The Japan Times*, 8 January 2004; "Kanzaki OK with Sending Advance GSDF Team to Iraq," *Kyodo News*, 7 January 2004; Faiola, A., "Iraq Mission Endorsed by Japanese Cabinet," *The Washington Post*, 10 December 2003; Piling, D., "Japan Readies Ground Troop Dispatch to Iraq," *The Financial Times*, 7 January 2004; Takahara, K., "First Troop Deployment to Conflict Area Since WWII a Foreign Policy Watershed," *The Japan Times*, 10 December 2003.

[15] See Glosserman, B., "One-sided Bilateral Relations," *The Japan Times*, 2 September 2003; Glosserman, B., "Does Irrelevancy Await Japan?," *The Japan Times*, 4 July 2003 .

ship after the Second World War: a combination of containment of the threat of communist totalitarianism, and promotion of open markets, democracy and the rule of law through global institutions such as the UN; the Bretton Woods institutions; GATT, which became the WTO; NATO; and the Conference on Security and Cooperation in Europe (CSCE, now OSCE). It is often forgotten that the OSCE (including Japan) played a crucial role in promoting mutual confidence during the Cold War and helped to establish the principle that intercession to protect human rights and other international norms could not be dismissed as illegitimate interference in the internal affairs of another state. In the 1990s Japan provided significant financial and technical assistance during and after the war on the Balkans. This support was Japan's first direct contribution to peace and security in Europe.

All this culminated in what Fukuyama called "the end of history:" the triumph of democracy, market economics and individual freedom over "total solutions," whether of communism or of national socialism – and over regimes which used those ideas to give intellectual respectability to dictatorship and brutality.

Apart from all this, the US and Europe enjoy a one and a half trillion dollar trade and investment relationship. And the two partners cooperate closely all over the globe from the Balkans to Afghanistan. If the US is the "indispensable nation," the US and Europe really do constitute an "indispensable partnership." That was underlined by the 2003 GMF poll of European and American attitudes to foreign policy which showed that most ordinary Americans and Europeans still share a strong belief in internationalism, and in many respects, a very similar world view.[16]

The EU-Japan relationship is based on the 2001 Action Plan. Over the past decade there has been a steady increase in political and economic ties. Japan has twice the FDI in Europe that it has in the US. The EU is the largest investor in Japan. But there has been some disappointment with the political relationship. The EU-Japan Action Plan remains largely unimplemented. There has been a joint EU-Japan demining project in Cambodia. However, there is certainly scope for further EU-Japan cooperation in a number of fields. Promoting global peace and security through the promotion of soft security and human security concepts is at the centre of the 2001 Action Plan[17] which de-

---

[16] Details available at www.gmfus.org.

[17] For details and background see "An Action Plan for EU-Japan Cooperation-European Union Japan Summit Brussels 2001", at http://www.mofa.go.jp/region/europe/eu/summit/action0112.html; 10th EU-Japan Summit: Joint Press Statement Brussels, 8 December 2001, at http://www.jmission-eu.be/relation/basicdoc/10 sumpre.htm; EU-Japan Cooperation Programmes: Working Together to Address the

fines the EU and Japan as "civilian powers" jointly promoting global peace and security. In light of the proposals on soft security in the Solana strategy paper, EU-Japan security cooperation is very likely to gain further importance.

VI. Difficult Relationships

In terms of the trilateral relationship, the transatlantic relationship is by far the most important. The EU-US relationship may be indispensable but it has never been straightforward. Apart from the inevitable trade disputes, there are more complicated jealousies, resentments and differences of outlook arising from separate histories and geographical situations. That is hardly surprising. The United States is still a young country that has had to fight Europe (or at least a part of Europe) for its independence. The US pays much more attention to religion than is the case in Europe or Japan. There is much more of a 'can do' spirit than in Europe or Japan. In Europe and Japan the bloody experience of centuries of war has left both profoundly uncomfortable with fervent nationalism. Both tend to prise consensus over conviction. Both are world-weary: even cynical. In contrast to the US, both mistrust science and doubt progress. Europe and Japan are more cautious and tend towards pessimism.

These points paint a certain caricature. But there are underlying differences of outlook which fuel misunderstanding and popular resentment. There has long been an ugly tendency for some in Europe and Japan to measure their political commitment by their anti-Americanism. And there has been a tendency in the US to dismiss European and Japanese consensus-seeking as wimpishness: condescension masquerading as sophistication. There is resentment, too, in the US, that Europeans and Japanese have for so long taken free shelter under the US security umbrella.

World's Challenges, Delegation of the European Commission of in Japan, at http://jpn.cec.eu.int/english/eu-relations/e3-05-0.htm.

VII. The Post 9/11 Agenda

The terrible events of 11 September 2001, and reactions to them, brought into sharp focus what unites Europe, Japan and America and what divides them. On day one, both sides of the Atlantic were united in shock and in grief. *"We are all Americans now"* proclaimed *Le Monde.* In Japan there was a similar outpouring of solidarity. Unity was reflected in common endeavour. The US, Japan and the EU engaged in close and continuous consultations on a long and substantive counter-terrorist agenda, including a legislative framework on definitions of terrorism, for example, and a European arrest warrant to replace national extradition procedures. Brussels and Tokyo have since worked closely with the US on everything from peace-keeping and reconstruction in Afghanistan to international efforts to dry up sources of terrorist funding. At the end of 2001, Japan dispatched troops and supply ships to the Indian Ocean to provide British and US warships with logistical support during the military campaign in Afghanistan. This was a controversial move domestically but sent a signal to the US that Japan was not only prepared to provide cash (recall the first Gulf War when Japan and Germany both paid 13 billion dollars and were both accused of conducting "chequebook diplomacy"), but also prepared to deploy troops abroad.[18]

Yet instead of drawing the US, Japan and Europe together, the reactions to the US war on terrorism and in particular the Iraq crisis tended to expose differences. The extent of the US trauma was not, perhaps, fully appreciated in Europe or Japan: the sense of violation felt by a people who had believed themselves to be invulnerable. The subsequent "war on terrorism" has been understood in Japan and Europe as a metaphor: a phrase to describe the myriad responses required of the civilised world to address problems that do not allow of definitive solutions, let alone of military ones. America, by contrast, has really felt itself to be at war, and it is a war that ratcheted up patriotic sentiment to unparalleled heights, and was a major issue during the 2004 presidential election campaign.

Europe and Japan felt uncomfortable with the widespread view in America that the beginning and end of any discussion of terrorism is

---

[18] For details on the deployment of Japanese military to the Indian Ocean in 2001 to provide logistical support for US and British warships see "Special Report: Japan's Support to the War on Terrorism-Recent Contributions Not Enough;" The Virtual Information Center (VIC) November 2002; for detailed information on Japan's peace-building efforts and engagement in Afghanistan in the 1990s see e.g. Miyahara, N., "Peace and Stability in Afghanistan: A Japanese View of the New Road," *Gaiko Forum-Japanese Perspectives on Foreign Affairs*, Fall 2003, pp. 45-56.

that it is irredeemably evil: inexplicable except as the work of barbarians, impervious to reason – as if any discussion of the causes of alienation and hatred was evidence of appeasement. The idea of a world divided between good and evil – between us and them – sits uncomfortably with most Japanese and Europeans.

No-one can deny that 9/11 was an outrage. The cause was unjust and the means abominable. But these issues cannot be placed beyond rational discussion. Nor can terrorism ever be eradicated from the face of the earth. Complete elimination of the threat could only be achieved in an Orwellian police state that denied individual freedom. That would negate the values for which the US, Japan and EU stand.

Different European (and by implication Japanese) and American attitudes to the war on terror are explained in Robert Kagan's essay on "Power and Weakness" as a mere reflection of different capacities to meet the threat. He takes the analogy of a man and a prowling bear. If the man is unarmed, he will decide, *faute de mieux*, that the bear constitutes a tolerable threat. If he has a gun he will arrive at a different conclusion, and shoot. That may be right. But there is a positive as well as a negative strand to Japan and Europe's lack of enthusiasm for military solutions except as a last resort.

Japan suffered terribly in the final stages of the Second World War, after inflicting terror itself across much of Asia and the Pacific. Europe also engaged in two internecine civil wars in the first half of the 20th century. The impulse for a new European architecture after the Second World War was profoundly political. The EU was never just an economic project. The founders recognised that in the modern world European nations needed to pool their sovereignty to deal with problems that extended beyond national boundaries. They sought not just reconciliation on the European continent, but partnership at a deeper level: a union that would endure because it was rooted in fundamental structures rather than in alliance or deterrence.

The question that Europe, Japan and America now face is whether this insight has wider application. Nations will always pursue what they believe to be their national interests. But what *is* that interest in the modern world? And what should be the primary purpose of foreign policy? Is it defensive: to keep bad guys down and to defend the homeland? Or is it positive: to build a system of cooperative global governance – an international community legitimised by representative institutions and by the rule of law? The suggestion might once have seemed naively altruistic: but the emergence of shared global interests means that it has become a matter of hard-headed calculation.[19]

---

[19] See F. Cameron, *The EU and Global Governance, EPC Working Paper*, No. 7, 2003.

VIII. Changing International Environment

The enlarged EU, Japan and the US have to consider their global ambitions against a rapidly changing international environment. Amongst the most significant of these changes are the following:

- a continual process of globalisation, including international terror
- the rise of China and India, with major implications for the world
- the predominance of US military power and emphasis on unilateralism
- the development of regional blocs (EU, ASEAN, Mercosur, etc.)
- the increasing number of global issues, from health to the environment
- a growing north-south divide, impacting on trade and poverty
- an increasing number of 'failed states' with security implications

The changing international environment has led to the emergence of new threats and challenges. More than a decade ago the West lost the frightening, but also reassuring certainties of the Cold War, which defined friends and enemies for a generation. The struggle to maintain and extend spheres of influence had many bad effects. The West often encouraged poor countries to spend too much on arms. It turned a blind eye to departures from democracy and good government. Above all there was Vietnam, and the appalling fall-out (including Pol Pot). But it was an era of certainty in the superiority of Western values. The transatlantic and Pacific bonds were strong and self-evident. It was a time of unparalleled economic and political success. Now many people are alienated from Western values. Traditional communities and cultures are undermined by urbanisation and modern science which constitute a threat to existing beliefs. We might describe this trend as the revolt of the alienated.

It is not easy to adapt to new ideas, new science and new influences that challenge traditional authority and received opinion. We are inclined to forget how difficult was the Reformation in Europe, and how bloody. The point is that religious fundamentalism can also find expression in political radicalism and hatred of alien, often Western – and specifically American – influences. Radicalism may be eminently justified by the brutality, greed and inefficiency of a great many governments in this world. The hatred of America is *not* justified. But nor will it be eliminated by dropping bombs on the haters.

Closely allied to the revolt of the alienated is the revolt of the dispossessed. The simple fact is that much of the world is desperately poor. More than a billion people subsist on less than a dollar a day. In 2003, the revenue of General Motors – with 340,000 employees worldwide – exceeded the combined GNP of 45 African countries with a population of about 600 million. And with modern communications and the aggressive marketing of western culture the poor are now much better informed about how the other half live. It is hardly surprising that there is widespread hostility to globalisation as a Western ramp. This is profoundly wrong. Far from generating world poverty, globalisation – if we can learn to manage it better – contains the seeds of international prosperity. But, again, bombs and coercion are not going to convince people of that.

A third modern threat is the one that we pose to our own planet, and so to ourselves. Environmental policy is no longer just a national concern. *Climate change*, for example, is everyone's business – and we need a coordinated international approach to it. That is why Japan and the EU, unlike the US, have been such strong champions of the Kyoto Treaty. It is clear that many other issues from water to fisheries management to biodiversity have to be treated at an international level because they are everyone's business.

The environment is only the most obvious example of how problems thrown up by increasing globalisation require coordinated international policy responses. Globalisation offers tremendous opportunities. But as well as the benefits of modern science, medicine and communication and the prosperity that may be derived from the engine of open trade – there is also what has been called the '*dark side of globalisation*'. We have already mentioned massive inequality. But we also have to contend with the international drugs trade, transnational crime syndicates, communicable diseases like AIDS, international terrorism, the proliferation of weapons of mass destruction, the threat of information warfare, and so on. All these problems remind us that stability and prosperity – the goal of foreign policy in each separate nation – can only be achieved if the international community can act together in pursuit of interests that transcend national boundaries.

Finally, in this catalogue of modern threats, we should include *failed states*. In the past developed countries perhaps kidded themselves that they could insulate themselves from the problems of the world. If a country collapsed into penury and civil war, that was sad for its people. We might offer them loans and assistance. We might lecture them about the benefits of open trade, good government and so on. But ultimately it was their problem if they could not dig themselves out of their hole. Today we see that we cannot wall ourselves off from the misery around us. First, there is the so-called CNN effect. It is harder to inure ourselves to starvation and genocide when we witness it in our homes. But even if we could, there is the problem that failed states become the breeding ground for terror. Once, our concern was with state-sponsored terrorism. Today we are equally concerned by terrorist-sponsored states of the kind that existed in Afghanistan. So much for the new challenges. The question is how to respond to them.

IX. Responding to the New Threats: US Choices

The question of the response to new threats is for the United States, above all, not just as the pre-eminent world power – but as the only power with truly global reach. The essential choice is between two courses. First, that the US could establish itself as the world hegemon, setting and imposing rules (but not itself bound by them) in pursuit of its own national interest. Or second, we could move towards a global system where international rules set the parameters for the legitimate pursuit of interests, but where the same laws apply to all (though the strong, of course, have more influence on their formulation and application).

The first option would, surely, be a recipe for long-term instability. Even the most benign interpretation – that the US, through the pursuit of its own interests, would be seeking global stability and prosperity – cannot avoid the problem that it would be doing so according to rules unilaterally and self-referentially conceived. The approach would be a retreat to the dubious charms of a world in which absolutely sovereign nation states seek to define and defend their own interests without reference to international rules and codes. But that is a vision that America herself did so much to dispel after the Second World War. The world is simply too small for us to fence ourselves off from one another. We are too interconnected.

The other problem with the vision of a hegemonic, imperialist America is that when the most powerful state in the world throws its weight around, unconstrained by rules or norms of legitimacy, it risks a backlash. Past empires have collapsed when others have joined forces to oppose them. It may be that the US can maintain her political, military and economic superiority in perpetuity, but history suggests that this is unlikely.

X. The Need for Cooperative Global Governance

There is only one real option – that America should be the leading participant in a system of cooperative global governance. The concept of a rule of law applying universally and equally is fundamental to the values shared by Europe, Japan and America. That is why the three powers must work together:

First, there is a need to make globalisation more inclusive. The alienated and the dispossessed are a reproach to those who live with superabundance. They will become an increasing threat, too, if there is not a better attempt to spread the benefits of progress. The EU manages some 55% of all international aid, and 66% of all grant aid. The US and Japan are the next two contributors. In the past, too much international development aid has been wasted. But the conclusion is emphatically not that we should give up. It is that we should try harder.

In particular, there must be much more attention to corruption, which is one of the most certain ways in which governments have destroyed their own economies; and one of the greatest sources of poverty and misery in the world. The EU's trade and cooperation agreements now contain clauses establishing good governance and human rights as a condition for their application. Those countries that treat their own citizens most decently are also the most likely to attract investment and to achieve growth.

The international community still has much to learn about how to encourage growth. Clearly improving access to markets is one of the most certain ways in which the developed world can help the less developed. Japan, Europe and the United States have to face up to their responsibilities here – not least when it comes to agricultural products and textiles. The US, Japan and the EU have been guilty of preaching free trade where they are most competitive, and then closing their markets, or introducing other obstructions, as soon as they find that others can match or outperform them. One wonders how long consumers in the three powers will accept such high prices for food products.

The world needs a stronger World Trade Organisation and a successful Doha Development Round, because only with stronger rules will it be possible to see fair play. One of the great ironies of recent times is that those most passionately concerned about world poverty and injustice have tended to be the most outspoken critics of the WTO. The EU, Japan and the US should work together on WTO reform with the emphasis on increased resources, granting the director general the right of initiative, and introducing some form of qualified majority voting system.

This is part of the second strand of the agenda that the US, Japan and the EU should be following. As well as making globalisation more inclusive, there is a need to strengthen the global rule-book. As mentioned earlier, the US was the progenitor of the great international institutions of the past half century. This infrastructure needs to be strengthened and given deeper democratic roots. This agenda should include UN reform (both UNSC and internal procedures), moving ahead on conflict prevention (The Responsibility to Protect report) and strengthening the Bretton Woods institutions.

It is in meeting the challenges of the new global agenda that the enlarged EU, Japan and the US can develop a strong partnership. The EU has already taken a lead in areas such as the Kyoto Protocol, the International Criminal Court (ICC), the Doha development round at the WTO and arms control. One of the key passages in the Solana document was to stress the importance of 'effective multilateralism'. Japan and the EU share this commitment to multilateralism and are both concerned at US voices emphasising the unilateralist approach. It is understandable that Japan seems able to accept different approaches for hard security. Tokyo came under strong US pressure to follow the US line on the war on terrorism. Defence Secretary, Donald Rumsfeld, made veiled threats to withdraw US troops from Japan (protecting Japan from North Korea) if Japan should fail to support the Iraq War (South Korea received a similar message).

A third strand of what is an essential common agenda for the EU, Japan and the US is the promotion of regional cooperation. Nation states are here to stay. But international relations cannot be managed by 189 independent voices. It is neither efficient nor equitable that major world issues should be addressed at international conferences in which the US and Japan each have the same number of votes as Tuvalu. Regional groupings are one obvious way to address this dilemma. Regional groupings are also valuable because the compromises required to achieve common positions tend to mute ethnic passions and hatreds, and to develop wider loyalties. The EU, as the most advanced system yet developed for pooling national sovereignty, has a particular role to play in promoting regional integration.

The EU is engaged around the world, from ASEAN and the ASEAN Regional Forum in South East Asia, to Mercosur in South America, to the Andean Pact, to the San Jose Group further north, to the new African Union, in sharing its experience and forging new inter-regional structures and relationships. It can be frustrating work – but it is important. And this is an area in which the EU can perhaps offer more than Japan or the US, which have such a strong national ethic.

A fourth strand in this common agenda should be to attempt more preventive diplomacy. Together, the US, Japan and Europe, and other developed countries devote fantastic sums of money and expend untold energy on the management of crises and on mopping up after catastrophes. But we do too little to avert them. There have been successes. The decision to send NATO troops into the Former Yugoslav Republic of Macedonia in 2002 calmed ethnic rivalries that threatened to spiral out of control. The troops gave credibility to the peace plan that the EU had helped to negotiate. In the Balkans, again, the European Union helped to draw Serbia and Montenegro closer together in 2003, as an exercise in preventive diplomacy. Japan has made a major financial contribution to the region while a continuing US presence remains vital. The US, for its part, has also played a quiet but hugely important mediating role in Sudan. And there are many other examples.

But more often, as a world community, we fail. It is difficult to spot impending calamity; and it is hard, in a democracy, to arouse sufficient parliamentary or public concern to take decisive action until a storm actually breaks. But with the benefit of hindsight, should we not have done more to help build Afghanistan more than a decade ago, after the departure of the Soviets? Should we not have done more not just to impose sanctions but to apply them effectively on Iraq through the 1990s? Should the world community not have cooperated more closely and sooner to counter the international terrorist threat? Should we not have engaged sooner to prevent the bloodshed and ethnic cleansing that accompanied the break-up of Yugoslavia or the genocide in Rwanda?

Some problems *are* foreseeable. We know that the Middle East is a powder keg, and that UN Resolutions have been flouted there with impunity over many years. Scientists have given us good notice of the problem of global warming. We have an opportunity over the coming period to help build better relations between India and Pakistan before events spiral out of control with potentially devastating consequences. We know that the international community will have to devote enormous resources to Afghanistan over a long period if we are to achieve stability there.

XI. A Credible Threat of Force: The Challenge for Europe and Japan

Neither Japan nor Europe can hope to match US defence capacity – nor would it be wise to try. If they were sharply to reduce their development assistance and their other contributions to soft security in order to devote all that money to higher defence spending – hard security – it is doubtful that the world, with more poverty and degradation as a result of that switch, would become safer.

Nevertheless, Europe and Japan need to be able to make a more credible military contribution. In early 2004 the EU was contributing to ten peace-keeping missions around the world and providing about 85% of the forces in the Balkans. But it is still insufficient. European governments, in general, went too far in reaping the so-called 'peace dividend' after the collapse of the Soviet Union. They have since made good resolutions: to develop an independent European rapid reaction force. But they have not been willing to devote the budgetary resources to make that a really credible ambition. And they have not done enough to break old patterns of national research, national policy on arms trade and production which vitiate the common effort. It is absurd, for example, that defence reviews in Europe are still conducted essentially as national exercises. The EU will not deserve to be taken seriously as international actor, and as a counterpart – if not a counterweight – to the US, if it does not make a more serious effort in the field of defence and security. The US, for its part, might do more to encourage that development. The US was a champion of European integration from the beginning, in the 1950s. But the US often complains when the EU has no common policy – and often resents it when the EU *does* get its act together, as we are increasingly beginning to do. Washington happily seek to divide and rule on issues like defence contracts or air service agreements. If the US more systematically sought to deal with the EU as a whole, and to encourage an EU single voice – for example in UN bodies and in the international financial institutions – then it would help the EU to develop its capacity to share the burden of global governance.

As mentioned above, Japan has become more active in international peace-keeping missions over the last decade and now discussions on the use of military force to defend Japanese territory have lost their taboo status, in light of North Korean missile tests. Japan has recently implemented legislation, the so-called "national emergency laws" equipping its troops with the necessary legal basis and competencies to defend the country from a military attack and guerrilla invasions (from North Korea).[20] The Prime Minister now has the *de facto* right to declare martial law in Japan.

In both Europe and Japan the realisation is growing that diplomacy will only be effective if it is backed by the credible threat of force. Luckily, most serious power in this world is in the hands of a beneficent US. But it is in the US interest that that power should be constrained by global rules and that it should be used with international agreement. If the US were to fall prey to the temptation to act alone and outside the framework of international order, even for the best of motives, it would

---

[20] Amongst many others see Yoshida R., "War-Contingency Bills a Wobbly First Step," *The Japan Times*, 22 May 2003; "Roles Defined to Protect Public in Military Attack," *The Asahi Shimbun*, 22 November 2003; "Civilian Mobilization Adopted for SDF Law," *The Asahi Shimbun*, 4 October 2003; for background information, on the so-called "National Emergency Laws" see e.g. Kamiya M., "Learning to Live with Military Power," *Japan Echo*, Vol. 30, No. 5, October 2003; Tatsumi Y., *Japan's Homeland Security: Police, or Self-Defense Forces?*, Japan Watch; Center for Strategic and International Studies (CSIS), May 2002; Hoshuyama N., "Japan's Legal Structure and National Emergencies," in Cossa, R. A. (ed.), *Restructuring the U.S.-Japan Alliance-Toward A More Equal Partnership*, Significant Issues Series, CSIS, The Center for Strategic and International Studies (CSIS), Washington, DC, 1997, pp. 139-144.

be setting off down a very dangerous path. What if its new doctrine found admirers and imitators in other parts of the world – such as India or Pakistan?

If, however, the US accepts the merits of working within the framework of the United Nations, then it is essential that the international community, for its part, should accept the corollary: that nations cannot flout UN Security Council Resolutions with impunity. In the last resort, we must be prepared to back the use of force to require compliance. This would seem to be accepted now in Japan with its decision to send troops to Iraq. It is also recognised in the Solana security strategy report.

Partly because of its own history of sharing sovereignty and constant inter-governmental negotiations, the EU has been more willing than the US and many other countries to work through multilateral institutions. The importance of this goal was emphasised in the draft constitutional treaty, which contains a number of interesting proposals aimed at strengthening the external voice of the Union. These include the new post of EU foreign minister, a stronger EU role in international organisations, an EU diplomatic service, an armaments agency, strengthened cooperation in defence and a potential single voice for the Euro Zone.

XII. Who Speaks for Europe?

At present, the EU's external representation varies between different policy areas, CFSP, trade, financial, economic, environmental and development affairs. Every six months the US Secretary of State has a new European interlocutor. It is little wonder, therefore, that Colin Powell knows the telephone number of Javier Solana better than whoever of the fifteen foreign ministers of the EU is currently holding the presidency of the Council. When it comes to military action, however, the first addresses for Washington are London, Paris and Berlin.

Although Colin Powell has Solana's telephone number, Washington may need to call one of several Commissioners dealing with aspects of external relations. Washington may also wish to speak to one of the EU's special representatives dealing with the Middle East, the Great Lakes, or Kosovo. Depending on circumstances, the EU may be represented, therefore, by Solana or the presidency alone, the presidency and the Commission, or by all three. If the US, with its lengthy history of close cooperation with the EU finds the situation baffling, other partners are even more perplexed.

The EU disposes by far the largest diplomatic network in the world. More than 40,000 officials work in the foreign ministries of the member states and the circa 1500 diplomatic missions abroad. Each member state maintains between 40 and 160 diplomatic missions while the

Commission has a network of over 120 delegations around the world. These numbers will increase significantly as a result of enlargement with ten new countries joining the Union in 2004. In comparison, the US has about one third of the human resources that the EU devotes to diplomacy and one fifth of the diplomatic missions. It is not apparent, however, that the US is less effective than the EU in pursuing its policy objectives.

The situation is further complicated because of the G7's move to G8 with Russia involved in some, but not all of the discussions. In recent years there has been mounting criticism of the G8 for its lengthy communiqués, lack of follow-through, lack of transparency and restricted membership. Given the lack of substance of G7/8 meetings, it is not surprising that there have been calls, not just from anti-globalisation protesters, to abolish the G7/8. Abolition is unlikely but the G7/8 could either be transformed into a G20 (upgrading the existing G20) or a G3 with the US, EU and Japan or East Asia as members. As in any international grouping there is often a trade off between increased size, and thus greater legitimacy, and reduced size, and allegedly greater efficiency. But after the 2003 meeting in Evian there were a chorus of calls to abolish the G8. Despite this pressure, it is unlikely that the current members will agree to change the *status quo* as it suits their vested interests.

So far, *ad hoc* solutions to external representation have prevailed for the IMF, G7 finance ministers, the Financial Stability Forum, the G20 and other groupings where issues relevant to EMU are discussed. Member states have begun to realise, however, that these *ad hoc* solutions are not the best way for the Community's voice to be heard internationally. There is also increasing pressure from emerging markets and non-European G7 countries for streamlining EU representation in bodies such as the IMF.[21]

XIII. Conclusion

Henry Kissinger has written that the challenge facing the US is "*to transform power into consensus so that the international order is based on agreement rather than reluctant acquiescence*". The US is so strong, as a nation, that some neocons are tempted to think that she has both the capacity and the duty to manage the world order on her own, unconstrained by international agreements and organisations unless they happen to suit her agenda. This is a flawed approach. Strong international institutions are more than ever necessary in our interconnected

---

[21] F. Cameron, "Who Speaks for Europe?", *Journal of Global Governance*, Oxford, Spring 2004.

world. They restrain unilateralist tendencies in others who might otherwise threaten the world order underwritten by the US. The US also gains more by working with the grain of international opinion than she loses in freedom of action by accepting external disciplines.

If America relinquishes respect and affection in favour of fear and coercion, the world will be a colder and more frightening place. It is sometimes forgotten that Kennedy's famous inaugural "*ask not what your country can do for you – ask what you can do for your country*" concluded: "*My fellow citizens of the world: ask not what America will do for you, but what together we can do for the freedom of man.*"

For both the EU and Japan, the most important relationship is with the United States. At present it would seem that the EU and Japan share similar views on global governance and how to react to the changing international environment. In contrast, the current US administration has shown little enthusiasm for the multilateral approach. But hopes of achieving real progress in global governance can only be achieved by the EU, Japan and the US working together.

INTERNATIONAL INSIGHTS

International Insights brings together studies from various and mixed disciplines to put forward new analyses of issues and developments on the world stage. This series seeks to address in an open-minded and critical manner both theoretical and empirical questions arising from the major shaping forces at work in the modern world. The series will deal with the following subjects: armed conflict and wars in the 21st century, globalisation and transnational developments, new forms of world and regional organisation, political applications of international law and the transformation of the role of the state in international relations.

International Insights is a crucible of debate concerning the key questions discussed by researchers and students of international relations. The series will publish reference texts as well as theoretical and empirical studies.

The series gratefully acknowledges the logistical support of the Réseau d'Etudes en Politique internationale (REPI) (Network of Studies in International Politics) and of the Pole Bernheim for Peace and Citizenship Studies at the Université libre de Bruxelles.

> *Series Editor*: **Éric REMACLE**, Professor of International Relations and European Studies at the Université libre de Bruxelles and Director of the Pole Bernheim for Peace and Citizenship Studies.

Editorial Board

Alyson BAILES, *Stockholm International Peace Research Institute*

Esther BARBÉ IZUEL, *Universitat Autònoma de Barcelona*

Anne DEIGHTON, *Oxford University & Geneva Centre for Security Policy*

Barbara DELCOURT, *Université libre de Bruxelles*

Yves DENÉCHÈRE, *Université d'Angers*

Véronique DIMIER, *Université libre de Bruxelles*

Klaus-Gerd GIESEN, *Universität Leipzig*

A.J.R. GROOM, *University of Kent*

Jean-Jacques ROCHE, *Université Panthéon-Assas – Paris II*

Alberta SBRAGIA, *University of Pittsburgh*

Takako UETA, *International Christian University (Tokyo)*

SERIES TITLES

N° 1 – Pierre CALAME, Benjamin DENIS & Éric REMACLE (dir.), *L'Art de la Paix. Approche transdisciplinaire*, 2004, 363 p.

No. 2 – Gustaaf GEERAERTS, Natalie PAUWELS & Éric REMACLE (eds.), *Dimensions of Peace and Security. A Reader* (provisional title) (forthcoming).

N° 3 – Yves DENÉCHÈRE (dir.), *Femmes et diplomatie. France – XXe siècle*, 2004, 200 p.

No. 4 – Takako UETA & Éric REMACLE (eds.), *Japan and Enlarged Europe. Partners in Global Governance*, 2005, 288 p.

N° 5 – Barbara DELCOURT, Denis DUEZ & Éric REMACLE (dir.), *La guerre d'Irak. Prélude d'un nouvel ordre international ?*, 2005, 259 p.